# ECONOMICS OF UNEMPLOYMENT

# ECONOMICS OF UNEMPLOYMENT

**MARY I. MARSHALLE**
**EDITOR**

Nova Science Publishers, Inc.
*New York*

**Library of Congress Cataloging-in-Publication Data**
*Available upon request.*

ISBN 1-60021-138-0

*Published by Nova Science Publishers, Inc. ✛New York*

# CONTENTS

# PREFACE

The unemployment rate is the number of unemployed workers divided by the total civilian labor force, which includes both the unemployed and those with jobs (all those willing and able to work for pay). In practice, measuring the number of unemployed workers actually seeking work is notoriously difficult. There are several different methods for measuring the number of unemployed workers. Each method has its own biases and the different systems make comparing unemployment statistics between countries, especially those with different systems, difficult. This new book brings together diverse new research on this important area of economics.

Chapter 1 argues that the form in which collective bargaining is organised might be a decisive factor in determining the performance of modern industrialised economies. The whole literature on corporatism is concerned with showing that the degree of centralisation and coordination in wage determination is a key factor in ensuring either a more or less painful adjustment to adverse economic conditions. In this sense, labour market institutions might assume one of two roles: (i) uncertainty reducers and catalysts of more flexible markets; or (ii) free-rider agents which would only be worried about appropriating product market quasi-rents. The first case seems to be more recurrent in corporatist countries where bargaining is centralised and coordinated. The second, more apparent where bargaining is decentralised and/or intermediate-centralised, is where rent-sharing seems pervasive and wage rigidity a strong possibility.

Chapter 2 identifies a broad concept of unused labour force. This concept can be related to the transitional labour market theory. It is next reviewed in the light of economic studies using a similar construct. Pro's and con's of our approach are discussed and the literature is used to assess characteristics of groups building this concept and to identify transition from these groups to (more) employment. A first assessment of the size and some of the main characteristics of such groups is made using the Dutch Labour Force Surveyof Statistics Netherlands. As far as transitions are concerned, international studies imply flows of persons from such different groups into labour will almost unavoidably have to be identified using linked longitudinal surveys among individuals. These are currently under construction at Statistics Netherlands.

Youth unemployment has almost become a natural phenomenon in most industrial countries due to global economic restructuring. To resolve the problem of youth unemployment, numerous youth training and employment programs have been developed in many industrial countries. The main purpose of these programs has been largely to enhance the youths' human capital by improving their job skills. However, the effectiveness of these programs is uncertain, particularly their ability to link unemployed youth to the labour market, the entry into which is largely dependent on social capital (*i.e.* who one knows) rather than human capital. Drawing on empirical studies, chapter 3 will conceptually examine how the collective tradition within Chinese culture may prove a rich source of social capital for young people hoping to mount a successful job search. This chapter will also offer some practical and research recommendations for the social work profession in rethinking the roles of culture and social capitals in resolving youth unemployment issues in a Chinese context.

Chapter 4 analyzes factors affecting the duration of registered unemployment and the likelihood of individual transition from unemployment. The results help to evaluate the process of population adaptation to the government system of employment assistance in Russia and the effects of this system on the relative chances of employment for various socio-demographic groups. The empirical modeling is done using transition data analysis. The results indicate significant effect of rules and regulations on incentives to find a job for unemployed individuals inquiring for the state assistance.

In chapter 5, the authors analyze the effects of unemployment benefits on unemployment. Following Harris and Todaro (Harris, J. R. and Todaro, M. P., *American Economic Review* 60, 126-142, 1970) and Harberger (Harberger, A. C., *Journal of Political Economy* 70, 215-240, 1962), they consider an economy which consists of two sectors – the corporate sector and the non-corporate sector – and two factors of production, labor and capital, while the corporate wage is indexed to the general price level. Since the corporate wage is assumed not to be market clearing, there is unemployment in equilibrium. The unemployment is thus exclusively a feature of the corporate sector.

The authors elaborate Miyagiwa's (Miyagiwa, K., *Journal of Public Economics* 37, 103-112, 1988) work in several respects. First, they deal with unemployment benefits indexed to the competitive wage rate. Second, they explicitly consider the government budget constraint in which case unemployment benefits are financed by the corporate income tax. Third, they focus on an issue of balanced-budget incidence analysis.

The authors derive a counter-intuitive result that unemployment benefits, instead of increasing unemployment, may well decrease unemployment, while they establish Walras' law and the zeroth order homogeneity of the system and also ensure the local stability of the system. This counter-intuitive result regarding the effects of unemployment benefits involves inelasticity in either of the following situations: wages with respect to the 'manufacturing' price or production with respect to factor prices. For instance, as shown by Rao (reprinted in Agarwala, A. N. and Singh, S. P., *The economics of underdevelopment*, New York, Oxford University Press, 1958), Keynesian ideas would not work in India because of the high agricultural component of GNP and the inelasticity of the developing countries (LDCs) supply. These points should take them back to the original debate on the applicability of Keynesian ideas. Their considerations are thus of some intuitive appeal from the real world point of view. This contributes to an older debate on unemployment policy.

The Brazilian unemployment insurance (UI) system is the largest in Latin America, serving an average of 300,000 to 400,000 beneficiaries each month. According to Law No. 7998 from 1990 the objective of the Brazilian unemployment system is to: (1) provide temporary financial assistance to a worker dismissed without just cause and (2) assist workers in their search for a new job. Concerning the provision of financial assistance to the worker, the law is silent on whether UI benefits are aimed at smoothing consumption or are primarily intended to prevent unemployed workers from falling into poverty.

In chapter 6, the authors look not only at unemployment rates, but analyze the determinants of the probability of becoming unemployed, as well as unemployment duration. Separating these two factors is crucial for analyzing the existing UI system. They show that informal sector employees who have neither access to unemployment insurance nor FGTS are most likely to become unemployed in Brazil. Furthermore, the conditional probability of becoming unemployed is highest for minimum wage earners.

While formal sector workers are less likely to become unemployed than informal wage earners ceteris paribus, they are more likely to remain unemployed once they have lost their job. Unemployment duration among formal sector workers is higher for those who received FGTS before becoming unemployed. This may hint at the fact that only the "rich" can afford a longer unemployment duration. However, this kind of statement should be treated with care. Formal sector workers may just face a longer unemployment duration as they are more selective when accepting a new job.

The authors provide evidence on this fact by estimating a competing risk model, which allows to consider not only unemployment duration, but also exit states. Independent of the exit state, formal sector workers are less likely to leave unemployment than informal wage earners. However, this difference turns out to be insignificant when they consider exit to the formal sector.

Among formal sector workers, FGTS (and hence UI) recipients are less likely to exit unemployment. This proves to be independent of the exit state. Thus, at least in terms of the employment sector, the unemployment insurance system seems to fail in its objective to assist workers in their search for new employment. Whether this also holds in terms of wages remains a question to be answered.

The chapter is organized as follows. Section II describes the Brazilian unemployment insurance system and the FGTS. Section III discusses the data used in this analysis and provides some descriptive statistics. Section IV analyzes the evolution of unemployment rates. Estimates of the probability of becoming unemployed and unemployment duration conditional on worker specific characteristics are provided in Section V. Section VI discusses policy implications and concludes.

Chapter 7 provides an overview of the status of employee wages and benefits, including retiree benefits, when an employer files in bankruptcy, and the amendments made to the U.S. Bankruptcy Code by the Bankruptcy Abuse Prevention and Consumer Protection Act. Private pensions, regulated by the Employee Retirement Income Security Act, are generally protected, although defined benefit pension plan payments may be substantially reduced. Health and life insurance benefits, which are not required by federal law, are vulnerable to an employer's bankruptcy-driven modification or termination. This report examines those provisions in the U.S. Bankruptcy Code which govern the priority of employee wage and benefit claims, including severance payments; procedures for a chapter 11 debtor to modify benefits under a collective bargaining agreement; and procedures for a chapter 11 debtor to modify retiree life and health insurance benefits. It examines the role of employees on creditor committees and procedures in bankruptcy that facilitate lawsuits that may be directed at an employer/debtor. Finally, it considers the treatment accorded some aspects of managerial compensation, such as retention bonuses.

Non-voluntary unemployment is a risk outside the control of the individual. By selecting certain occupations the individual knows that he or she may be exposed to a higher risk of unemployment than in other occupations, e.g. workers in the construction and building industry are exposed to unemployment due to the weather to a higher degree than employees in the IT industry.

Unemployment insurance benefit schemes are not the only relevant ones in this context. Many countries have unemployment assistance schemes as follow-on schemes to insurance benefits, other countries have social assistance schemes to fulfil this role. These schemes will also be studied in chapter 8, but they are not the only ones.

In most West European countries there are hundreds of thousands (many millions in the large countries) outside the labour force even if they are in the 'working ages'. Some persons are long term ill or disabled, other persons have retired early. Illness and disability are usually caused by health problems and cannot be directly compared with unemployment. Never the less, financial incentives to apply for these schemes as well as to stay in them will be studied. Several countries, e.g. the Netherlands who has particularly many disability pensioners, have tightened the access criteria, reduced benefits and introduced more frequent control to ensure continued eligibility for benefits. Other countries, e.g. Denmark, have turned the medical criteria 'up side down', the focus is now on what the disabled can do, not on how disabled in general terms he or she is. The potential gains from avoiding people to enter these schemes 'incorrectly' are very substantial.

Future ageing problems and early retirement from the labour market is a bad mixture. Early retirement is very popular in many countries and there are several roads leading to this situation, in some countries also via public schemes, which almost guide to early retirement. Early retirement may be interpreted as a kind of voluntary unemployment. The incentives to join and to stay in such schemes will be studied.

The debate about the impact of the introduction of a minimum wage into the economy, or even of changes in the level of the minimum wage on employment, wages, and poverty is the subject of a separate chapter in the literature on labor markets. In the case of Brazil, this debate dates back to the 1970s, when a controversy arose as to whether or not changes in the minimum wage could affect all wages in the economy [e.g., Souza and Baltar (1979)]. Now this debate has been revived, in terms not only of the possible impact of the minimum wage on other wages, but also of its effects on the levels of employment, informal labor, and poverty in this country. The debate becomes more relevant when discussions are held regarding possible future trends in the minimum wage policy in Brazil as a result of its impact on government accounts, and the feasibility of adopting a system that combines regional minimum wages with a national wage floor.

In chapter 9, the authors review the literature on the impact of the minimum wage on the Brazilian labor market. First, they will examine the key results pertaining to the employment-effect of the minimum wage in Brazil, and contrast the results that were based on data at the family level and at the individual level. Similarly, they will analyze the main results with respect to the impact on other wages and on poverty levels. Since in Brazil there is a direct connection between the minimum wage and the benefits paid by the social security system, they will also present an analysis of the impact of changes in the minimum wage on the government accounts. Lastly, they undertake a critical analysis of some options for the minimum wage policy in Brazil..

In: Economics of Unemployment
Editor: Mary I. Marshalle, pp. 1-16

*Chapter 1*

# DO LABOR MARKET INSTITUTIONS AFFECT MACROECONOMIC PERFORMANCE?

*Francisco G. Carneiro[1], Amit Dar and Indermit S. Gill*
The World Bank
Washington, DC 20433, United States

## ABSTRACT

The paper argues that the form in which collective bargaining is organised might be a decisive factor in determining the performance of modern industrialised economies. The whole literature on corporatism is concerned with showing that the degree of centralisation and coordination in wage determination is a key factor in ensuring either a more or less painful adjustment to adverse economic conditions. In this sense, labour market institutions might assume one of two roles: (i) uncertainty reducers and catalysts of more flexible markets; or (ii) free-rider agents which would only be worried about appropriating product market quasi-rents. The first case seems to be more recurrent in corporatist countries where bargaining is centralised and coordinated. The second, more apparent where bargaining is decentralised and/or intermediate-centralised, is where rent-sharing seems pervasive and wage rigidity a strong possibility.

**Keywords**: Corporatism; unionism; bargaining models.
**JEL Classification:** J5, J50, J64

## 1. INTRODUCTION

The worldwide macroeconomic crisis triggered by the 1973 oil shock provoked different reactions amongst the industrialised nations. In overall terms, the 1970s were characterised by low rates of economic growth and high inflation in all countries, but there were marked differences in terms of unemployment experiences. In the case of the European Community, while most of the economies experienced relatively high and increasing average unemployment rates for most of the period between 1973 and 1990, a group of countries of the so-called European Free Trade Area (EFTA) survived the crisis with relatively low and stable average unemployment rates. In three distinct phases of the crisis, the inter-shock period (1974-79), the period of climax (1980-85), and the post-stagflationary period (1986-90), average unemployment rates in the main industrialised countries of the European Community (Belgium, Denmark, France, Germany, Ireland, Italy, Netherlands, Spain and UK) reached 5.2%, 10.1% and 10.4%, respectively, compared to average rates of 2.0%, 2.9% and 3.0%, respectively, for the countries of the EFTA group (which contains the countries which are usually classified as strongly corporatist: Austria, Finland, Norway, Sweden and Switzerland).[2] Thus, with the observation that the diversity of economic performance varied with the degree of institutionalisation of the different countries, economists have become increasingly aware of the importance of particular institutional set ups in affecting macroeconomic performance.

In the specific case of wage determination, it has been now widely suggested that wage moderation is usually associated with a more coordinated bargaining structure, or what has been termed corporatist arrangements. On the other extreme, however, strong wage demands have been usually associated with a lack of coordination and synchronisation in the wage bargaining. In the first case, favourable demand shocks in the economy would tend to be converted into more jobs while a negative shock would tend to be accommodated with little employment cost. In the second case, however, it might well be that wages will tend to be rigid downwards and employment scarce, as the most powerful and organised sectors tend to bid up their wages in the event of a positive demand shock in detriment to the rest of the economy.

The discussion on the role of institutions and wage bargaining structures in determining wage moderation cannot be dissociated from the debate on labour market flexibility. In the competitive model of the labour market, for example, wages are dictated by the balance of supply and demand in the whole market. Hicks's Theory of Wages (1932) was the starting point for this argument, but even Hicks himself became sceptical about the overall applicability of the competitive model, as he made clear in the preface to Hicks (1963). It has been a long debate whether wages are to be thought of as fixed by non-competitive pressures. A common argument that is usually mentioned against the competitive theory of the labour market refers to the fact that in most cases wages are determined by collective bargaining and also that other non-competitive factors might be important (e.g., in efficiency wage theories).

The purpose of this paper is to review the recent literature on the effects of different collective bargaining arrangements on economic performance. The paper is organised as follows. Section 2 reviews the literature on the role of institutions in affecting economic performance referring particularly to the debate on corporatism. We stress the point that despite the existence of a variety of notions of corporatism in the political science literature, the concept which has been extensively used by economists associates corporatist arrangements to the degree of centralisation and the level of coordination of collective wage bargaining: the more centralised and coordinated wage bargaining, the more corporatist the country. Next, section 3 presents some recent empirical evidence to assess the actual impact of different collective bargaining arrangements on economic performance. Although most of the evidence comes from OECD

---

[1] Correspondence Address: The World Bank, 1818 H Street, NW, 20433, USA. Email: *fcarneiro@wordbank.org*
[2] The chronology of the crisis is as in Henley and Tsakalotos (1995) and the figures for European unemployment are compiled from their Table 9.1, p. 177.

countries, there are a few studies for the case of developing countries. Finally, section 4 summarises the main results reviewed and points future research to test hypotheses that postulate complementarities between collective bargaining institutions and the economic environment in which bargaining takes place, rather than focusing on the effect of individual institutions alone.

## 2. INSTITUTIONS, CORPORATISM AND ECONOMIC PERFORMANCE

This section reviews some of the literature on the institutional determinants of economic performance referring particularly to the debate on corporatism. Along with many authors, we stress the point that labour market institutions can affect economic performance by altering the flexibility of real wages (e.g., Crouch, 1985; Freeman, 1988; Calmfors and Driffill, 1988; Henley and Tsakalotos, 1991, 1992, and 1995; Calmfors, 1993; Cubitt, 1994; and for surveys Layard et al., 1991; Pekkarinen et al., 1992; Henley and Tsakalotos, 1993; Amadeo, 1994; Flanagan, 1999, *inter alia*).

The 1980s were marked by a widespread interest in the macroeconomic consequences of various wage-bargaining systems. During the 1970s and the 1980s, the labour market performance of the advanced economies exhibited sharp cross-country divergences. Employment increased in the USA, Australia and Japan, but stagnated in many Western European countries (Freeman, 1988). During all this period, the liberal challenge to the post-war economic consensus was that deregulated markets were essential to promote efficiency and improve economic performance (Henley and Tsakalotos, 1993).

The diversity of economic experiences of the OECD countries, however, has been attributed to differences in institutional arrangements prevailing in each economy. In line with this, it has been claimed that centralised wage bargaining is conducive to real wage restraint and low unemployment (early empirical references include Bruno and Sachs, 1985; Bean, Layard and Nickell, 1986; McCallum, 1986; and Newell and Symons, 1987). Subsequent research suggested that both very decentralised and very centralised wage bargaining systems seemed to be consistent with good macroeconomic performance (Calmfors and Driffill, 1988). However, more recent research (Aidt and Tzannatos, 2001) seems to suggest that there is no real support for the "hump" hypothesis – semi-coordinated bargaining does not necessarily lead to worse outcomes as compared to highly coordinated and decentralized bargaining.

## 2.1. The Importance of Institutions

Within the traditional neoclassical theoretical framework, institutions are invariably seen as rigidities that restrict the free operation of markets. As argued by Henley and Tsakalotos (1995), the nature of the neoclassical world, assumed in the economic modelling of Walras, Marshall and Edgeworth, suggests that atomistic individuals interact socially only through the market mechanism. As the auctioneer of the Walrasian economy is supposed to organise the trade of all commodities, individuals do not combine in a social production process and will meet only briefly to buy and sell in the market place (Rowthorn, 1980). Such a framework, based on axioms of rationality and sustained by the logic of individual choice, inspired very little attention on the role of institutions in purely orthodox economic analysis. Early contributions on this area, therefore, are mainly found in the work of political economists and sociologists (e.g., Goldthorpe, 1984).

As we are not concerned with the arbitration between institutionalists and non-institutionalists, what follows will just briefly review some of the main arguments that can be put together to assess the role of institutions in the economy. Henley and Tsakalotos (1993, 1995) argue that institutions can influence the market outcome basically by reducing the uncertainty involved in market exchanges. In the Walrasian economy, one of the basic assumptions is that of perfect and costless information which warrants the nonexistence of transaction costs and therefore the efficiency of competitive equilibrium. In the real world, however, we know that market transactions take place in a web of institutions which include the state, employers' and employees' organisations and regulatory bodies. In this particular scenario, therefore, institutions make market transactions possible by providing easy access to information, reducing uncertainty and also the possibility of conflict.

The problem of uncertainty is closely related with the notion of transaction costs. These can be broadly associated with for example the process of gathering information about potential trading partners, enforcing contracts, and supervising property rights. Henley and Tsakalotos (1995) point out that the existence of such transaction costs will force agents into long-term commitments and relational contracts with the objective of reducing the "uncertainty involved in spot exchanges which so often lead to conservative, or risk-averse, economic decision making" (op. cit., p. 183). In this sense, Hodgson (1988) argues that in contrast to the neoclassical view, a more efficient operation of markets is made possible because of the existence of certain imperfections (institutions) and not in spite of them.

It is also possible to illustrate the role of institutions regarding the issue of uncertainty by referring to game theory (see Taylor, 1976; Lange, 1984; Henley and Tsakalotos, 1993)[3]. Authors who have used this analytical tool very often intended to examine the logic of decision-making, or collective action, under conditions of uncertainty. The classical example used in the context of collective action is the prisoners' dilemma[4]. The main message from this game is that a non-cooperative behaviour may be sub-optimal, because despite the possible gains from cooperation there are strong incentives to cheat. We can think of the prisoners' dilemma with an example on wage determination, assuming a system in which wages are set centrally by a single annual binding contract for all workers, but in which there are possibilities for wage drift in excess of the wage norm at the plant level[5].

The game can be thought of as being played between a group of workers and all other workers. When the wage rule is announced, the group of workers has two strategies: (i) cooperation, by accepting the regulated wage; or (ii) defection, or free-riding, by going for the best wage it can obtain at the time. The payoffs from these strategies are such that each group will receive a higher payoff if he chooses to defect, no matter what the other group chooses; the strategy which calls for defection is said to dominate that of cooperation for each group player. If both groups choose their dominant strategies, they may receive a payoff which is lower than under cooperation. Thus every player would prefer the outcome of cooperation to the outcome of defection, but as they do not communicate and do not know what the other player will choose,

---

[3]Hodgson (1988) discusses some of the limitations associated with the use of game theory.

[4]For a formal analysis involving the prisoners' dilemma, see Taylor (1976), and for a general exposition and critical evaluation Henley and Tsakalotos (1993).

[5]It is implicit here the assumption that there is scope for collective bargaining in the wage setting.

there is a strong incentive to cheat (defect). In this example, therefore, any group would prefer to free-ride while all others cooperate resulting in all players defecting and no wage regulation will be achieved.

One condition to allow for cooperation would be the existence of binding pre-commitments. That is not the case in the prisoners' dilemma because it is assumed that the players do not communicate. The importance of institutions in this context can be seen if they act as providers of information. By doing this they would be not only reducing uncertainty concerning the intentions of other agents, but actually expanding the opportunity sets available to all agents (Henley and Tsakalotos, 1993, p. 33).

Another characteristic of capitalist economies raised in the political science literature is the existence of conflict and instability (Sawyer, 1989). In the theoretical framework of Walras, market outcomes are efficient and any social conflict or opposition are considered irrational. However, economic agents who do not consider market outcomes as fair will try to reverse them most invariably by organising against the market (Goldthorpe, 1987). One way of doing that involves the collective action of individuals to form an institutional body that will actually work to impose an alternative outcome which is not the result of the operation of the market. In this sense, we can now consider the role of corporatist arrangements which have been widely recognised as responsible for affecting economic performance in many market economies.

## 2.2. Corporatism and Economic Performance

The seminal contribution on the debate concerning the ability of organised groups to affect economic performance is attributed to Olson (1965, 1982). His view is that the final effect of the action of interest groups in a society is mostly negative. Olson is particularly worried about the fact that interest groups tend to act in detriment to the rest of the society by appropriating to themselves any improvement in efficiency that their collective action might have generated. Also he argues that special-interest coalitions tend to take decisions more slowly than firms or individuals because they must use some sort of consensual bargaining. They are also more concerned with fixing prices rather than accepting a market-liberal outcome in most situations being, therefore, responsible for sticky or inflexible prices and wages in sectors where special-interest groups are important (Olson, 1982, p. 57). The accumulation of these groups may ultimately increase the complexity of regulation, the role of the government, reducing allocative efficiency and therefore the rate of economic growth (op. cit., pp. 65-73). His preferred solution, therefore, seems to be a reduction in the capacity of economic interests to organise at all.

Crouch (1985) argues that Olson's perception leads to a paradox. In Olson's view, once economic interests have become organised, they will be less likely to act in line with the idea of allocative efficiency. This is so because they will be acting as if they were a single agent which, in the context of a market-liberal economy, believes its own actions are irrelevant to interfere in the operation of the market. The Organised groups will not take any decision considering any common interests since they have no concern for general political questions. But as the level of organisation increases these special-interest groups may broaden their interests and become more politicised, aggregated and centralised (op. cit., p. 108). These encompassing organisations may then include concerns about economic growth amongst other interests that they might also have (e.g. regarding the politics of income distribution). Considering the case of trade unions, Crouch suggests that the more centrally united is organised labour, the more are its actions compatible with the stability of the market economy (op. cit., p. 139)[6].

The term corporatism has often been used to represent collective interests. In this sense, corporatism can be viewed as a non-pluralist system of group representation. For some authors, corporatism has been introduced from above by elites, acting through the state, to help them pursue a variety of goals, including the co-optation of labour to win its political support (Collier and Collier, 1979). In this context, the notion of corporatism could be represented by an interplay between inducements and constraints. Constraints are seen as producing compliance by application, or threat of application of negative sanctions while inducements, by contrast, involve the application of mechanisms of co-optation leading to social control (op. cit., p. 976). This is what political scientists call "state corporatism" as the corporatised groups are created and kept as auxiliary and dependent organs of the state.

Another vein of this debate has related the notion of corporatism to systems of pluralist interest representation in advanced industrial societies in which corporative patterns of state-group relations are autonomous and have penetrative power - the so-called "societal corporatism" (Schmitter, 1974). Lehmbruch (1984) introduces yet another concept of corporatism which he calls "sectoral corporatism" - a corporatist representation of interests that is limited to specific sectors of the economy (op. cit., p. 62).

But the core notion of corporatism which seems to attract a broader consensus is associated with the idea of wage restraint and political responsibility. Along these lines, authors such as Panitch (1980), Soskice (1983), Cameron (1984), Newell and Symons (1987) *inter alia* seem to agree on a general view that there exists a monotonic relationship between the development and consolidation of corporatist institutions and better economic performance (translated in terms of greater wage restraint and lower unemployment). In line with this general view, corporatism has been widely proxied by a high degree of centralisation and coordination of collective bargaining leading many to suggest that corporatist arrangements may help wage bargainers to become aware of the possible macroeconomic implications of collective bargaining.

Empirical support for such monotonic relationship between corporatism and real wage moderation was provided by econometric studies which typically estimated wage and/or price equations in such way that allowed the effects of corporatism to be assessed (e.g., Bruno and Sachs, 1985; McCallum, 1986; Bean, Layard and Nickell, 1986; and Newell and Symons, 1987). Most of these studies are evaluated critically by Calmfors and Driffill (1988) who questioned the validity of these results. Calmfors and Driffill were basically concerned with the vagueness of this concept of corporatism, which made it unclear what the results were capturing, and with the lack of a firm theoretical basis to support the econometric analysis.

By investigating if, among the several characteristics which make up corporatism, centralisation was empirically relevant, Calmfors and Driffill were able to suggest that the claimed monotonic relationship between centralisation and economic performance was not always true. By using rank correlations of unemployment and the degree of bargaining centralisation they found that economies with either highly decentralised or highly centralised labour markets tend to enjoy better economic performance than those at an intermediate stage (see also Freeman, 1988)[7]. Rather than confirming the absolute superiority of corporatism, their

---

[6]See also Bruno and Sachs (1985); Bean, Layard and Nickell (1986) and Newell and Symons (1987).

[7]Freeman argues for care on this issue as centralised corporatist labour markets are primarily found in small countries while decentralised markets characterise larger economies. In this context, any policy recommendation should not

results implied the existence of a hump-shaped relationship between unemployment and bargaining centralisation.

The rationale for this divergent performance is in terms of the differing ability of the bargaining structures to mimic the textbook competitive outcome. In the polar case of decentralisation, negotiations between workers and firms are the ultimate determinants of wages; the fact that agents are too small in this context to interfere in the operation of the market means that wage restraint holds because competitive pressures put a cap on price and wage increases. In the other extreme of centralised, economy-wide bargaining, the idea is that corporatist arrangements may serve to increase the awareness of wage setters to the macroeconomic consequences of their actions. As affirmed earlier, in periods of adverse shocks, corporatist institutions may thus contribute to reduce uncertainty regarding the deleterious consequences of possible distributional conflict and facilitate a relatively painless adjustment process.[8]

In the case of the intermediate group, where bargaining takes place mostly at the industry level, the explanation for the poorer performance relatively to the two polar cases is usually associated to the existence of poorly coordinated monopolistic power in the labour market that constrains the successful operation of either competitive market forces or corporatist coordination. In this context, trade unions' bargaining power may be quite strong since rapid labour turnover is restricted by high training costs. Insider bargaining power is also high meaning that workers perceive that by pressing for higher wages the firm's product price may increase without however affecting the aggregate price level and therefore their real take home pay. As bargaining is at the industry level, an individual firm will not achieve a competitive advantage over the others and, assuming that industry demand is relatively inelastic, all the firms believe that the overall employment consequences will be irrelevant. In opposition then to the corporatist case, in the intermediate case, agents are not able to visualise the economy-wide effect of their actions and, once each industry has concluded a separate wage agreement, the aggregate consequences tend to be significant, with price increases spilling over across sectors. Overall, therefore, the situation of intemediate collective bargaining with strong trade unions may be quite conducive to poor employment and inflation performance, with rent-sharing being a pervasive characteristic.

Amadeo (1994) argues that intermediate economies can be grouped into two distinct categories: (a) the Hybrid I case, which is made up of those with collective bargaining at the industry level but with a high degree of synchronisation (coordination) of wage adjustments (e.g. Japan); and (b) the Hybrid II case of those with industry-wide bargaining but with a low degree of synchronisation (coordination) of wage adjustments (e.g. Belgium and France). Along with others (cf. Soskice, 1990) he is thus challenging the Calmfors and Driffill ranking of corporatist economies as those authors rank Japan as one of the most decentralised economies. The main criticism on the Calmfors and Driffill ranking, therefore, rests on the excessive emphasis given to the centralisation dimension of corporatism and the lack of importance attributed to the issue of coordination.

A new strand in the literature focuses on how corporatism interacts with other policy and institutions in labour and output markets. In a number of recent papers, these interactions are

---

concentrate only on a particular set of institutions which work better but rather try to identify specific policies which can succeed in particular environments (op. cit., p. 80).

[8]Freeman (1988) and Rowthorn (1992) show that wage dispersion also tends to be lower in corporatist economies as opposed to economies with a decentralised labour market.

found to be powerful tools to explain economic performance. In particular, in countries with an intermediate degree of corporatism, the costs of some regulations (e.g., high taxes on labour use or employment protection legislation) are not transferred to wages and lead to lower equilibrium levels of employment and higher unemployment. Daveri and Tabellini (2000), for example, suggest that the heavy tax burden on labour use tend to raise unemployment and reduce growth especially in countries with an intermediate degree of corporatism. In the same vein, Elmeskov, Martin and Scarpetta (1998), have also found that employment protection legislation strongly affects unemployment in countries with this type of collective bargaining. Moreover, Scarpetta et al. (2002) have found that productivity growth at the industry level is also negatively affected by employment protection legislation in countries with an intermediate degree of corporatism.

## 2.3. Wage Drift under Corporatism

There is also some evidence regarding the existence of considerable wage drift in corporatist economies. It has been argued that wage moderation at the central level may be offset to a substantial degree at the local level if agents perceive that the centrally determined wage is too low (see e.g. Holmlund and Skedinger, 1990, for the case of Sweden, and other country studies in Calmfors, 1990). According to Jackman (1990) this has led to a more critical view on the general belief that centralisation of collective bargaining is conducive to wage moderation. The main points raised by the critics of the corporatist system are that a high degree of centralisation of wage bargaining gives trade unions excessive power, and may also erode economic efficiency and competitiveness. It may also lead to an excessive public sector, as the government is forced to provide more jobs because of the decline of private sector employment (Jackman, 1990).

Estimates by Flanagan (1990) suggest that wage drift in the Nordic countries since the 1970s has accounted for at least 30% and in some cases as much as 70% of the total growth of hourly earnings. Pissarides and Moghadam (1990), however, present evidence showing that the level of wage settlements in different sectors is remarkably uniform, suggesting that wage drift cannot be particularly responsive to local or sectoral factors, as it is mostly the case in decentralised economies. In fact, Holden (1990a, 1990b), Holmlund and Skedinger (1990), Calmfors and Forslund (1990) and Forslund (1994) present econometric evidence indicative that wage drift in the Nordic countries is significantly limited by the conditions of the outside labour market; that is, outside wages, the rate of unemployment, and active labour market policies are significant determinants of wage drift. Rather than distancing corporatist economies from the competitive world, these results seem to corroborate the fact that the occurrence of wage drift in the Nordic countries can be viewed as an adjustment of the centrally negotiated wage to supply and demand conditions ensuring thus that the final outcome approximates that of a competitive market (Jackman, 1990)[9].

---

[9]Jackman also argues that centralisation of collective bargaining might be the key factor in explaining the success of Nordic countries relatively to the rest of Europe in terms of low unemployment rates. The differences in unemployment rates amongst the corporatist economies, however, may be attributed to different approaches to payments of unemployment benefits and special employment measures (op. cit., p. 316).

## 3. THE EMPIRICAL EVIDENCE

In this section, we review studies that aim at capturing the macroeconomic impact of the institutional framework of collective bargaining. While there are differences in bargaining institutions across sectors and changes do take place in the long-term within a given economy, the institutional framework is, by and large, unchanged in the short- and medium run. To investigate the impact of collective bargaining on macroeconomic performance, it is, therefore, necessary to take a comparative approach and look at cross-country evidence. Though there is scattered evidence from developing countries, most of the studies reviewed focus on the group of OECD countries.

Union density and bargaining coverage have been related to a variety of economic performance indicators in several studies, especially for OECD countries. From a theoretical standpoint, the impact of union density on economic performance is not very clear. In countries with high union density, unions are more likely to succeed in pushing wages up, leading to less employment, more unemployment and inflation. However, the argument can also be made that as unions engage in productivity-enhancing activities at the firm level, they may have a positive impact on economic performance.

Most of the empirical papers that have investigated the relationship between union density and economic performance have found that union density per se (i.e., for a given bargaining coverage and for a given level of bargaining coordination) appears to have little or no impact on comparative labor market performance, as measured by the unemployment rate, inflation, the employment rate, real earnings growth, the level of compensation, labor supply, adjustment speed to wage shocks, real wage rigidity, labor and total factor productivity (e.g., Bean et al., 1986; Freeman, 1988; Scarpetta, 1996; and OECD, 1997).

There is, however, one significant exception to the general result that the association between union density and economic performance is weak: union density compresses the wage distribution and reduces earnings inequality. Freeman (1988) shows that wage dispersion tends to be lower in corporatist economies as opposed to economies with a decentralized labor market. There are, however, exceptions to this finding also. Arbache and Carneiro (1999) show that this is exactly the opposite in the case of Brazil, where collective bargaining is believed to be intermediate-centralized. For the case of New Zealand, Maloney and Savage (1996) have shown that the decentralization of collective bargaining was accompanied by increasing pay dispersion.

The evidence for developing countries, however, appears quite different from that described so far. Rama (1995), and Fields and Wan (1989), for example, present evidence for Latin America, the Caribbean, and South East Asia that suggests that union density has a negative impact on output and employment growth. Rama (1997) argues that the difference between the impact of union density in developing and OECD countries is caused by differences in the general economic and political environment. Hence, if unions operate in an environment of generally ill designed labor and product market regulation in which rent-seeking is a profitable business, it is no wonder that the correlation between union density and economic performance is negative. Likewise, if unions operate in the context of an unstable political environment, the incentive to "invest" in real wage restraint in exchange for expected future returns is low and union militancy comes at no surprise.

Carneiro (1998, 1999) and Carneiro and Henley (1998) provide evidence of this sort of behavior for the case of Brazil. According to the authors, by the end of the 1970s, inflation was growing rapidly in Brazil and this provoked the upsurge of strike activities in the most organized sectors of the economy. The re-emergence of political democracy in the 1980s combined with labor dissatisfaction with the State wage policy led to the development of a new unionism. Unions have slowly increased their role in the wage determination process and have experienced an enhancement in their bargaining ability at both the regional and industrial levels. With union density estimated to be over 30 percent, what has emerged is an intermediate level of collective bargaining. In the late 1980s and early 1990s, control of inflation became much more problematic in Brazil and a consequence of the generally unsuccessful counter-inflationary policy shocks was an increased defensiveness on the part of labor unions, keen to protect real wage levels in the face of deflationary shocks. This contributed to the breakdown in coordination and synchronization of wage determination, and the development of a structure for collective bargaining much more akin to that prevailing in western Europe.[10]

The case of India is discussed in Besley and Burgess (2004) which investigates whether the industrial relations environment in Indian states affects the pattern of manufacturing growth. The authors have found that the states that have adopted employment protection legislation experienced lowered output, employment, investment, and productivity in the formal manufacturing sector. By contrast, output in the informal manufacturing sector increased. Greater regulation in a pro-worker direction was also associated with increases in urban poverty, which led the authors to conclude that attempts to redress the balance of power between capital and labour can end up hurting the poor.

A strong conclusion in favour of a reduction in the degree of corporatism in the labour market is advocated by Feldmann (2003). The author investigates the link between labour market regulations and labour market performance, based on evidence gathered from surveys among senior management business executives. His analysis suggests that employment protection legislation is a major cause of unemployment and that a move towards more flexibilization in the labour market should be encouraged. Scarpetta et al. (2002) using firm-level data for ten OECD countries and industry-level data for a broader set of countries, together with a set of indicators of regulation and institutional settings in product and labour markets arrive at similar conclusions. In addition, Padovano and Galli (2003) investigated whether corporatist wage setting and policy making institutions negatively affect the slope of the growth path of the economy. The authors considered whether corporatism increases the transaction costs involved in the policy decision making process. Their empirical results revealed a negative partial correlation between corporatism and growth.

As regards bargaining coverage, the evidence seems to suggest that, after controlling for union density and bargaining coordination, countries with high bargaining coverage (such as Austria, France and Finland), ceteris paribus, experience higher unemployment rates, lower employment rates, and more inflation than countries with low bargaining coverage (such as USA, Japan and Canada). The evidence presented by Henley and Tsakalotos (1993), Appelbaum and Schettkat (1996), Siebert (1997), Nickell (1997), and OECD (1997) indicate that the performance of highly centralized or "corporatist" economies, such as Sweden and Austria, have in the past been superior to those of the European Community, and that institutional rigidities, high coverage rates, and generous benefits and protection have adverse impacts on employment. Additionally, Nickell and Layard (1997) point that high bargaining coverage appears to increase the supply of labor but that it has no effect on labor and total factor productivity. Finally, high

---

[10] Guasch (1999) provide similar evidence for the case of Argentina.

bargaining coverage is associated with higher real earnings growth and a reduction in earnings inequality.

These findings suggest that an increase in coverage at a given level of union density has a greater impact than an increase in density at a given level of coverage (at least in OECD countries). One explanation of this result is that in those parts of the economy to which bargaining results are extended, only the monopoly effect of unions is present. The economic effects of the wage mark-up is, therefore, not compensated by worker/management cooperation or other institutional factors that could lead to productivity gains. On average, bargaining coverage can, therefore, affect unemployment, employment and inflation adversely, while the impact of unionization per se can be less significant. However, there is little evidence available on this issue from developing countries.

There are some studies that have already attempted to summarize the empirical results about the relationship between bargaining coordination and economic performance. Aidt and Tzannatos (2001) and Flanagan (1999), for example, have focused on two hypotheses: (a) Coordinated collective bargaining leads to better economic outcomes compared to semi-coordinated collective bargaining which, in turn, performs better than uncoordinated collective bargaining; and (b) The hump hypothesis - Semi-coordinated collective bargaining leads to worse economic outcomes than both coordinated and uncoordinated collective bargaining.

According to their findings: (i) countries with coordinated collective bargaining systems tend, ceteris paribus, to have lower unemployment rates than other countries;[11] and (ii) countries with a high level of bargaining coordination tend to have a more compressed wage distribution. This seems to be the most robust result. It can be attributed to a number of causes, including egalitarian bargaining; a reflection of the fact that centralized bargaining reduces the scope for firm- and/or industry-specific factors to enter the wage bargaining; or a reflection of a concern for social insurance. Aidt and Tzannatos have also explicitly tested for the hump hypothesis by surveying a large number of studies which look at this issue. They find that evidence in favor of the hump hypothesis is weak.

# 4. CONCLUSION

The role of labour market institutions in modern economic societies has deserved a great deal of attention lately. The degree of centralisation of collective bargaining and the mechanisms by which organised labour (unionised or not) has affected economic performance are two examples of recurrent issues in recent literature. This paper has reviewed the most important theoretical contributions in these areas and its main conclusions are as follows. Firstly, institutions can play an important role in the operation of the markets. The evidence collected has shown that where collective bargaining is centralised and coordinated, economic performance is, in general, better. It has been argued that in countries where bargaining is centralised and highly coordinated labour markets operate much more like a competitive market with agents accepting falls in their real incomes in exchange for a longer commitment with full employment. This is so because the existence of corporatist arrangements actually help to guarantee the efficient

---

[11] Studies that use composite measures of unemployment (such as Okun's index, which controls for inflation, and the open economy index, which controls for current account deficits) show the same tendency (e.g., Layard et al., 1991).

operation of markets by reducing uncertainty and increasing agents' awareness of the likely macroeconomic implications of their actions.

Second, the political science literature posits that a different mechanism operates in countries where bargaining takes place at the plant level and is therefore decentralised. The influential work of Calmfors and Driffill (1988) has proposed that in extremely decentralised economies market forces tend to put a cap on excessive wage demands and that the capacity of adjustment to a shock tends to be similar to that of a corporatist economy. The result is that in both highly centralised and highly decentralised economies real wages would tend to be flexible and employment higher. By contrast, in countries where bargaining takes place at the industry level, agents are bound by neither corporatist commitments nor market forces and as a consequence real wage rigidity and rent-sharing activities tend to be pervasive. It has also been claimed that the extreme case of centralisation would entail a fairer wage structure than in the other two cases of decentralisation and intermediate-centralisation. That is, in centralised economies wage dispersion would tend be lower than in the other two situations.

Third, more recent evidence for OECD countries points to union density having little or no impact on indicators of comparative labor market performance – other than wage distribution. Increased bargaining coverage, on the other hand, seem to affect unemployment and employment adversely. However in developing countries, evidence suggests a negative relationship between union density and employment growth – it is possible that these results could be more due to the environment that unions operate within rather than what unions do.

With respect to bargaining coordination, highly coordinated collective bargaining systems tend, ceteris paribus, to have lower unemployment rates and more compressed wage distribution. Most of the evidence from OECD countries seems to show that countries with a high or low level of coordination are associated with low persistence in unemployment, while those with semi-coordinated systems have higher persistence (hysteresis). Evidence for the case of Brazil, for example, give evidence of insider-induced hysteresis (e.g., due to union membership). These results seem to show that unions may be more interested in protecting the incumbent workforce rather than supporting the interests of the unemployed.

Finally, and in a broader sense, the impact of collective bargaining on various aspects of economic performance depends on the economic and political environment in which collective bargaining takes place – this is especially true in developing countries where it appears that the environment that unions operate in may play a more significant role in determining economic outcomes than what unions, per se, do. Future testable formulations of the corporatist hypothesis should postulate complementarities between collective bargaining institutions and the economic environment in which bargaining takes place, rather than the past focus on the effect of individual institutions. Research that follows this guidance may also elucidate the apparent changing relationship between collective bargaining institutions and economic outcomes, given the growing importance of international trade and nonunion work in most industrial economies.

# REFERENCES

Aidt, T. and Z. Tzannatos (2001), *Core Labor Standards and the Freedom of Association: Economic Aspects.* Working Paper. The World Bank.

Amadeo, E.J. (1994), *Institutions, Unemployment and Inflation*, Aldershot: Edward Elgar.

Appelbaum, E. and R. Schettkat (1996), The Importance of Wage-Bargaining Institutions for Employment Performance, in: G. Shmid, J. O'Reilly, and K. Schömann (eds.), *International Handbook of Labour Market Policy and Evaluation*, Chelteham: Edward Elgar.

Arbache, J. and F.G. Carnciro (1999), Unions and Interindustry Wage Differentials. *World Developmen,* 27, pp. 1875-83.

Bean, C. , P. Layard and S. Nickell (1986), The Rise in Unemployment: a Multi-Country Study. *Economica* 53, pp. 1-22.

Besley, T. and R. Burgess (2004), Can Labor Regulation Hinder Economic Performance? Evidence from India, *Quarterly Journal of Economics*, 119, No. 1, pp. 91-134.

Booth, A. (1995). *The Economics of the Trade Union.* Cambridge University Press, Cambridge, U.K..

Bruno, M. and J. Sachs (1985*), The Economics of Worldwide Stagnation*, Harvard University Press, Cambridge MA.

Calmfors, L. (1993), *Centralization of Wage Bargaining and Macroeconomics Performance: A Survey.* Seminar Paper No. 536, Institute for International Economic Studies, Stockholm University.

Calmfors, L. (ed.) (1990*), Wage Formation and Macroeconomic Policy in the Nordic Countries*, Oxford University Press, Oxford.

Calmfors, L. and A. Forslund (1990), "Wage formation in Sweden", in CALMFORS, L. (ed.), *Wage Formation and Macroeconomic Policy in the Nordic Countries*, Oxford University Press, Oxford.

Calmfors, L. and J. Driffill (1988), Bargaining Structure, Corporatism and Macroeconomic Performance. *Economic Policy*, 9, pp. 14-61.

Cameron, D.R. (1984), "Social democracy, corporatism, labour quiescence, and the representation of economic interest in advanced capitalist society", in GOLDTHORPE, J.H. (ed.), *Order and Conflict in Contemporary Capitalism*, Clarendon Press, Oxford..

Carneiro, F. (1998). Productivity Effects in Brazilian Wage Determination. *World Development* 26(1), pp. 139-153.

Carneiro, F. (1999), Insider Power in Wage Determination: Evidence from Brazilian Data. *Review of Development Economics* 3(2), pp. 55-169.

Carneiro, F. and A. Henley (1998), Wage Determination in Brazil: The Growth of Union Bargaining Power and Informal Employment. *The Journal of Development Studies* 34(4), pp. 117-138.

Collier, R.B and D. Collier (1979), "Inducements versus constraints: disaggregating corporatism", *The American Political Science Review*, 73(4):967-986.

Craven, J. (1979), *The Distribution of the Product*, George Allen and Unwin, London.

Crouch, C. (1985), "Conditions for trade union wage restraint", in LINDBERG, L.N. and C.S. MAIER (eds.), *The Politics of Inflation and Economic Stagnation: Theoretical Approaches and International Case Studies*, The Brookings Institution, Washington.

Cubitt, R.P. (1994), "Corporatism, monetary policy and macroeconomic performance: a simple game theoretic analysis", School of Economic and Social Studies, University of East Anglia, mimeo.

Daveri, F. and G. Tabellini (2000), Unemployment and Taxes – Do Taxes Affect the Rate of Unemployment?, *Economic Policy*, 30, pp. 47-88.

Elmeskov, J., J.P. Martin, and S. Scarpetta (1998), Key Lessons for Labour Market Reforms: Evidence from OECD Countries' Experiencies, *Swedish Economic Policy Review*, 5, pp. 205-52.

Fields, G., and H. Wan, Jr. (1989), Wage-Setting Institutions and Economic Growth. *World Development* 17, pp. 1471-1483.

Flanagan, R.J. (1990), "Centralised and decentralised pay determination in Nordic countries", in CALMFORS, L. (ed.), *Wage Formation and Macroeconomic Policy in the Nordic Countries*, Oxford University Press, Oxford.

Flanagan, R.J. (1999), Macroeconomic Performance and Collective Bargaining: An International Perspective. *Journal of Economic Perspective*, 37:1150-1175.

Forslund, A. (1994), "Wage setting at the firm level - insider versus outsider forces", *Oxford Economic Papers*, 46, pp. 245-261.

Freeman, R. (1988), Labor Market Institutions and Economic Performance. *Economic Policy* (3), pp. 64-78.

Freeman, R.B. (1988), "Labour market institutions and economic performance", *Economic Policy*, 6:64-80.

Guasch, J.L. (1999), Labor Market Reform and Job Creation: *The Unfinished Agenda in Latin American and Caribbean Countries, Directions in Development*, The World Bank, Washington.

Goldthorpe, J.H. (1987), "Problems of political economy after the post-war period", in MAIER, C.S. (ed.), *Changing Boundaries of the Political*, Cambridge University Press, Cambridge.

Goldthorpe, J.H. (ed.) (1984), Order and Conflict in Contemporary Capitalism, Clarendon Press, Oxford.

Henley, A., and Euclid Tsakalotos (1991), "Corporatism, profit squeeze and investment", Cambridge *Journal of Economics*, 15:425-450.

Henley, A., and Euclid Tsakalotos (1992), "Corporatism and the European labour market after 1992", *British Journal of Industrial Relations*, December.

Henley, A., and Euclid Tsakalotos (1995), "Unemployment experience and the institutional preconditions for full employment", in ARESTIS, P. and M. MARSHALL (eds.), *The Political Economy of Full Employment*, Edward Elgar.

Hicks, J.R. (1963), *The Theory of Wages*, (1st edn. 1932), London: Macmillan.

Hodgson, G. (1988), *Economics and Institutions*, Polity Press, Cambridge.

Holden, S. (1990a), "Wage drift in Norway: a bargaining approach", in CALMFORS, L. (ed.), *Wage Formation and Macroeconomic Policy in the Nordic Countries*, Oxford University Press, Oxford.

Holden, S. (1990b), "Insiders and outsiders in labour market models", *Journal of Economics*, 52(1):43-54.

Holmlund, B. and P. Skedinger (1990), "Wage bargaining and wage drift: evidence from the Swedish wood industry", in CALMFORS, L. (ed.), *Wage Formation and Macroeconomic Policy in the Nordic Countries,* Oxford University Press, Oxford.

Horst, F. (2003), Labor Market Regulation and Labor Market Performance: Evidence Based on Surveys among Senior Business Executives, *Kiklos,* 56, No. 4, pp. 509-39.

Jackman, R. (1990), "Wage formation in the Nordic countries viewed from an international perspective", in CALMFORS, L. (ed*.), Wage Formation and Macroeconomic Policy in the Nordic Countries*, Oxford University Press, Oxford.

Lange, P. (1984), "Unions, workers, and wage regulation: the rational bases of consent", in GOLDTHORPE, J.H. (ed.), *Order and Conflict in Contemporary Capitalism*, Clarendon Press, Oxford.

Layard, R., S. Nickell, and R. Jackman (1991), Unemployment. Oxford University Press.

Maloney, T. and J. Savage (1996), Labor Markets and Policy, in: Silverstone, B., Bollard, A., and R. Lattimore (eds.) *A Study of Economic Reform: The Case of New Zealand*, Amsterdam, Elsevier.

McCallum, J. (1986), "Unemployment in OECD countries in the 1980s", *Economic Journal*, 92, N° 384.

Newell, A.T. and J. Symons (1987), "Corporatism, laissez-faire and the rise in unemployment", *European Economic Review*, 31, N° 3.

Nickell, S. (1997). Unemployment and Labor Market Rigidities: Europe versus North America. *Journal of Economic Perspectives* 11(3), pp. 55-74.

Nickell, S., and R. Layard (1997). *Labor Market Institutions and Economic Performance. Center for Economic Performance*, Discussion paper series no. 23, Oxford University.

OECD (1997). *Employment Outlook*. Paris.

Olson, M. (1965), *The Logic of Collective Action*, Harvard University Press, Cambridge, MA.

Olson, M. (1982). *The Rise and Decline of Nations. Economic Growth, Stagflation, and Social Rigidities*. New Haven/London: Yale University Press.

Padovano, F. and E. Galli (2003), Corporatism, Policies and Growth, *Economics of Governance*, 4, No. 3, pp. 245-60.

Panitch, L. (1980), "Recent theorisations of corporatism: reflections on a growth industry", *British Journal of Sociology*, 31, N° 2.

Pekkarinen, J., M. Pohjula and R.E. Rowthorn (eds.) (1992), *Social Corporatism: A Superior Economic System?*, Clarendon Press, Oxford.

Rama, M. (1995). Do Labor Market Policies and Institutions Matter? The Adjustment Experience in Latin America and the Caribbean. Labour, special issue, pp. 243-268.

Rama, M. (1997), Trade Unions and Economic Performance: East Asia And Latin America, in J. McGuire, (ed.), *Rethinking Development In East Asia and Latin America*. Center for International Studies, University of Southern California.

Rowthorn, R.E. (1980), *Capitalism, Conflict and Inflation*, Lawrence and Wishart, London.

Sawyer, M.C. (1989), *The Challenge of Radical Political Economy: An Introduction to to the Alternatives to Neo-Classical Economics*, Harvester Wheatsheaf, London.

Scarpetta, S. (1996), Assessing the Role of Labor Market Policies and Institutional Settings on Unemployment: A Cross-Country Study. *OECD Economic Studies*, 26, pp. 43-98.

Scarpetta, S. P. Hemmings, T. Tressel and J. Woo (2002), The Role of Policy and Institutions for Productivity and Firm Dynamics: Evidence from Micro and Industry Data, OECD Working Paper No. 329.

Schimitter, P.C. (1974), "Still the century of corporatism", *Review of Politics*, 36, no. 1, January.

Siebert, H. (1997), Labor Rigidities: At the Root of Unemployment in Europe. *Journal of Economic Perspectives*, 11(3), pp. 37-54.

Soskice, D. (1983), "Collective bargaining and economic policies", Manpower and Social Affairs Committee, OECD, MAS (83)23, quoted in CALMFORS, L. and J. DRIFFILL (1988), "Bargaining structure, corporatism and macroeconomic performance", *Economic Policy*, 6:13-61.

Soskice, D. (1990), "Wage determination: the changing role of institutions in advanced industrialised countries", *Oxford Review of Economic Policy*, 6, N° 4.

Taylor, M. (1976), *Anarchy and Cooperation*, New York, Wiley.

In: Economics of Unemployment
Editor: Mary I. Marshalle, pp. 17-50

ISBN: 1-60021-138-0
© 2006 Nova Science Publishers, Inc.

*Chapter 2*

# MAKING THE UNUSED LABOUR FORCE WORK: ASSESSING THE FACTS FOR THE NETHERLANDS

## *Lourens Broersma[1], Jouke van Dijk and Leo van Wissen*

University of Groningen, The Netherlands

## ABSTRACT

This paper identifies a broad concept of unused labour force. This concept can be related to the transitional labour market theory. It is next reviewed in the light of economic studies using a similar construct. Pro's and con's of our approach are discussed and the literature is used to assess characteristics of groups building this concept and to identify transition from these groups to (more) employment. A first assessment of the size and some of the main characteristics of such groups is made using the Dutch Labour Force Surveyof Statistics Netherlands. As far as transitions are concerned, international studies imply flows of persons from such different groups into labour will almost unavoidably have to be identified using linked longitudinal surveys among individuals. These are currently under construction at Statistics Netherlands.

## 1. INTRODUCTION

Labour supply decisions affect the well being of individuals and when aggregated, the welfare of an entire society in two ways. First, labour is a production factor so labour supply – in conjunction with labour demand – affects the production of goods and services available for consumption. Second, labour time itself, or its counterpart leisure, directly affects an individual's well being. A society is better off when it can produce a given amount of goods and services at lower costs in terms of labour time, i.e. with greater leisure.

---

[1] Corresponding author: University of Groningen, Department of Economics, Department of Spatial Science, P.O. Box 800, 9700 AV Groningen, The Netherlands and The Conference Board New York. Tel. +31 50 363 7053, Fax. +31 50 363 7337, E-mail: l.broersma@eco.rug.nl

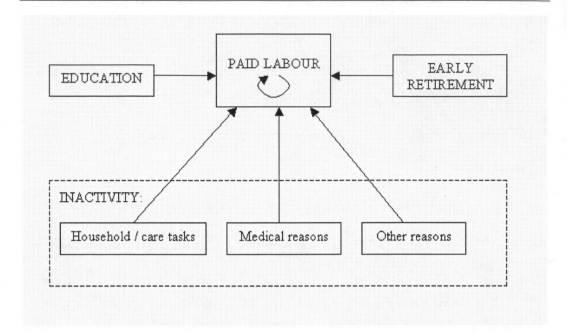

Figure 1. Life cycle stages and labour market flows into paid labour in a transitional labour market setting.

This means that labour can be regarded as a scarce product in an economic sense. Nevertheless in the past decades labour has been abundantly available, i.e. labour supply exceeded demand resulting in substantial levels of unemployment. Recently we have seen the opposite picture emerging, where in some sectors labour has indeed become scarce. Even in the current recession this scarcity remains in sectors like education and health care. Next to these purely cyclical effects, we should also realise that in the longer run labour could become a scarce factor on a more structural basis, because of the simultaneous ageing and declining rejuvenation of the population. This process will occur throughout the industrialised world.

Instead of focusing on labour solely as an economic good, stressing the choice between leisure and money, scarcity or abundance and factors influencing it, like wages, labour can also be considered in relation to a wider range of alternatives to choose from besides leisure. From the viewpoint of the so-called transitional labour market (Schmid and Gazier, 2002; Taylor 2002) labour is only one of the states a person can be in during his lifetime. Moreover, from a dynamical perspective, the transitional labour market concept considers much more than just the 'economic' transition from the state of being not employed (leisure) into employment. The transitional labour market approach starts from the observation that present day individuals choose different combinations of labour, education, care tasks and leisure at different stages in their lives. Each stage will have its own combinations.

In figure 1 an outline of this approach, based on Schmid and Gazier but adapted by us to give an adequate description of the Dutch situation. This adaptation is helpful in making this transitional labour market operational to the Dutch situation. Basically, it distinguishes four stages in the life cycle for an average person: education, paid labour, inactive on the labour market (due to various reasons) and early retirement. The most eye-catching aspect of figure 1 is the fact that inactivity is split by reason of inactivity. One of them is inactivity due to medical reasons, i.e. sickness or disability. This is an important group in The Netherlands. About 1 in every 10 persons between 15 and 64 years of age is entitled for a disability benefit. Another important group consists of persons inactive on the labour market due to care tasks, usually for young children. The third group consists of persons being inactive for other reasons, like being unemployed.

Between each of these stages in the course of life there exist transitions (flows) from one stage to the next. In this paper we will only focus on *transitions from each of the stages into paid labour*. This implies six transitions: (i) from education to a job, (ii) from job to job; (iii) from inactivity due to care tasks to a job; (iv) from inactivity for medical reasons to a job; (v) from inactivity due other reasons to a job and (vi) from early retirement to a job.

In this transitional labour market concept, policy measures are important to facilitate smooth transitions between each of these life cycle stages. A central issue of this paper is the possible transition from either stage into paid labour. Because of the ageing problem these transitions are becoming increasingly important to at least maintain current labour participation rates. Participation involves some definition of the labour force, which refers to both employed and unemployed persons. This means that transitions into paid labour may originate from the labour force itself, e.g. when an unemployed person finds a job, but it is not the only source for inflow into labour. When e.g. a student decides to accept an offer for a part-time job, this does involve a transition into paid labour, but not a transition originating from the pool of unemployed persons. It is therefore not only necessary to have a clear idea of what the labour force is, but also how this alternative source, the so-called unused labour force, is defined.

The flow chart of the transitional labour market theory in figure 1 shows possible sources from which this unused labour force can emerge. In fact, it can be part of all five stages of figure 1. In the sequel of this paper these stages will be studied, with the aim to get more information on the characteristics of persons in each stage who are part of the unused labour force. In addition this information provides possible incentives to make the unused labour force (move to) work. We therefore see the unused labour force a central issue in studying the empirical consequences of the transitional labour market theory.

The transitional labour market model is used as starting point in the strategic research programme "Social and Labour Market Dynamics" of Statistics Netherlands. This paper is the result of a joint effort of the University of Groningen en Statistics Netherlands within that programme with the aim to explore, quantify and characterise the unused labour force in The Netherlands. It surveys related academic literature on this topic, which will be used to give an assessment of the characteristics of groups of persons in different stages in their course of life who are part of the unused labour force. This may help to identify policy incentives that stimulate labour supply of unused labour and so mitigate the ageing problem.

The outline of this paper is as follows. Section 2 defines our concept of unused labour force. This is viewed from an international and from a Dutch perspective. Section 3 reviews both internationals and Dutch studies concerned with some concept of an unused labour force and with transitions (flows) from that unused labour force into paid labour. Despite the fact that each study has its own denomination and its own definition of unused labour force, this review can help to identify characteristics for our concept of unused labour force. Based on these results section 4 shows groups that matter for characterising our concept of unused labour force in The Netherlands based on the literature and makes a first assessment bout size and characteristics of these groups. Finally section 5 concludes.

## 2. OPERATIONAL DEFINITION OF UNUSED LABOUR FORCE

### 2.1. International Conventions on Labour Force Definition

As we have argued, transitions into paid labour from different stages of the transitional labour market theory do not only require a definition of the labour force, but also of the unused labour force. Obviously these two concepts are related so the unused labour force is best identified when first a definition is given of the labour force itself. The labour force comprises the employed and unemployed labour force. Progress has been made to come to international standards of a common definition of the labour force. Still differences between countries remain. One important issue is whether or not to impose a restriction on the number of hours per week a person should be employed in order to be part of the employed labour force. Such a restriction would by implication also apply to the unemployed labour force. As an international benchmark we take the definitions and conventions of Eurostat, the statistical agency of the European Union, which in fact are largely in accordance with ILO standards. Eurostat defines the *employed labour force* as

> ... persons over 15 years of age living in private households stating they are 'currently' working for pay or profit in a job or business *for at least one hour*, or not currently working but with a job or business from which they are temporarily absent. Persons 'at work' comprise therefore 'paid employees', 'self-employed (together with employers)', persons in 'training under special scheme related to employment' or in 'paid apprenticeship'. Persons 'working unpaid in family enterprise' are also included.[2]

Hence, according to international standards there is no hour's restriction on being counted as employed. The definition of the *unemployed labour force* is more complicated. Eurostat[3] defines the unemployed labour force as persons, between 15 an 74 years of age who are:

(i)     without work, i.e. neither had a job nor were at work (for 1 hour or more) in paid employment or self-employment and

(ii)    are available for work at short notice (within two weeks) and

(iii)   have actively seeking work during the past four weeks or have found a job to start later.

Even though an hour's restriction is not mentioned explicitly, by implication it has to be the same as its counterpart, the employed labour force. Hence persons fulfilling the criteria and search for a job of 1 hour a week are a part of the unemployed labour force. To conclude: the most common international definitions of labour force do not impose an hour's restriction.

---

[2] See: http://forum.europa.eu.int/irc/dsis/coded/info/data/coded/en/gl009302.htm.

[3] See: http://forum.europa.eu.int/irc/dsis/coded/info/data/coded/en/gl009302.htm and Eurostat (2002)

## 2.2. Dutch Conventions on Labour Force Definition

Statistics Netherlands follows these international conventions, but takes its own stance with respect to a definition of the labour force for domestic use that suits specific problems not (yet) solved internationally.

Until 1981 the Dutch labour force in The Netherlands was based on the number of persons stating that labour was their main societal activity. After 1981 the total number of persons with paid employment replaced this definition.[4] This latter definition was not satisfactory, because

(i)     it was no longer linked to what respondents felt to be their main activity,
(ii)    it was (therefore) hard to be used outside labour statistics and
(iii)   it was susceptible to measurement error, because
- persons holding small jobs of a few hours a week were observed poorly
- these small jobs are associated with high dynamics (large in- and outflows of persons and jobs). This implies that use of retrospective data to construct labour market flows, became unreliable.

See also Bierings et al. (1991) and Statistics Netherlands (2000).

This labour force definition implied that labour was seen purely as an economic phenomenon. A more sensible labour force definition starts from labour as a *social* phenomenon. This allows the 'labour force' also to be used outside economics, such as in social-economic surveys and surveys on state of life. Being in the labour force is now one of the activities next to school/college, disability, housekeeping or care tasks and (early) retirement. Hence this labour force concept neatly fits into that transitional labour market theory. Starting point is the fact that labour, or acquiring labour, corresponds to a person's main societal activity.

Therefore in 1991 a new labour force definition was established by Statistics Netherlands, capable of counteracting these drawbacks. This definition contained a lower bound restricting the labour force to a minimum of 12 hours a week. Introduction of this lower bound was based on what the respondents to the Labour Force Survey (LFS) stated to be their main activity in relation to the number of hours per week they worked or wanted to work. Work of less then 12 hours a week did not correspond to 'labour' as being the main activity to a majority of respondents. From 1991 the Dutch labour force is defined as

> ... comprising all persons in the resident population who are either employed for at least 12 hours a week or want to be employed, are available at short notice and are actively searching for work of at least 12 hours a week.[5]

The labour force consists of two groups of persons. First, the employed labour force consisting of all persons employed for at least 12 hours a week. Notice that use of the word 'job' is not mentioned. A job is the smallest unit of employment defined as "... an explicit of implicit

---

[4] In fact there was no hours restricttion. There was a boundary of labour of 20 hour a week or more for the so-called formal labour force, which was needed to construct the registered unemployment rate. Registered unemployment, at employment agencies, also had this lower bound.

[5] See: http://www.cbs.nl/nl/standaarden/begrippen/werken-leren/begrippenlijst.htm. See also Bierings et al (1991) for a justification of moving to an hours-restricted labour force concept. Note that there is no formal age restriction, but to assess participation rates an age restriction of 15-64 years of age in used.

contract between a person and an institutional unit to perform work in return for compensation for a definite period or until further notice" (Colledge, 2000), without an hours restriction involved. So a person who holds a job is not necessarily part of the employed labour force.

Second, the unemployed labour force (ULF) is determined by those who

(i)      are not employed or employed for less than 12 hours a week, and
(ii)     have accepted work for at least 12 hours a week, or
(iii)    want employment for at least 12 hours a week, and
(iv)     are available, i.e. can start at short notice (within two weeks) and
(v)      display active search effort in the past four weeks.

Notice that under Dutch conventions a persons working for less then 12 hours a week can be part of the unemployed labour force when he fulfils (i)-(v), while that same person would be part of the employed labour force under the Eurostat/ILO definition.

The Dutch definition of the unemployed labour force also takes the unemployed person's *preference* into account of whishing to be employed. Other countries also include such a preference criterion (Jones and Riddell, 1999, 2001). The point regarding active search needs further precision.[6] According to Eurostat, active search consists of either of the following steps:[7]

- having been in contact with a public employment office to find work, whoever took the initiative (renewing registration for administrative reasons is not an active step);
- having been in contact with a private agency (temporary work agency, firm specialising in recruitment, etc.) to find work;
- applying to employers directly
- asking among friends, relatives, unions, etc. to find work;
- placing or answering job advertisements;
- studying job advertisements;
- taking a recruitment test or examination or being interviewed
- looking for land, premises or equipment;
- applying for permits, licenses or financial resources.

These steps also apply to The Netherlands, as argued by Bierings et al. (1991). Notice that the latter two points of the list refer specifically to persons seeking self-employment. However, these 'active' search steps also contain a 'passive' step in the sense that persons just looking at job ads in newspapers without undertaking any action are included. This is not considered to be active job search in the US unemployment definition (Jones and Riddell, 1999, 2001).

The definition used by Statistics Netherlands also determines that a person is not in the labour force when he:

(i)      does not want employment for at least 12 hours a week, or
(ii)     does want employment, but cannot start at short notice, or
(iii)    does want employment and can start at short notice but not searches actively.

---

[6] On http://www.hrdc-drhc.gc.ca/sp-ps/arb-dgra/publications/research/r96-15eb.pdf a comprehensive discussion of this topic is found (page 64). See also Macredie (1997), Jones and Riddell (1999, 2001).
[7] See e.g. Eurostat (2002).

## 2.3. Composition of the Unused Labour Force

The concept of the labour force is prone to different and sometime conflicting requirements, so the same might be true for the unused labour force. When it comes to defining this unused labour force we take a broad stance that it should cover every hour of labour that can be supplied by persons, whether present in the labour force or not. This means our unused labour force concept consists of

*all persons of 15 years of age and older working 0 hours a week or more, who in principle can expand their number of weekly hours of employment.*

This definition has a number of implications. First, persons below 15 years are not taken into account due to compulsory education. Second, the definition has no preference restriction. Hence, whether a person *wants* to work (more hours) is not at stake here. Even if a person has no desire to work, this does not mean that he or she cannot work. Given the characteristics of such a person there may very well be circumstances under which he would be willing to accept a job. In that sense he can be seen as part of the unused labour force. Third, persons in the employed labour force can also be part of the unused labour force as long as their actual number of weekly hours of employment is more than 12, but less than a maximum number of weekly hours of employment, above which additional supply of labour hours is unwanted. We set this maximum number of weekly hours work at 35. So anyone already working 35 hours a week or more is assumed not to want to expand his or her weekly working hours. Hence, a large part of the employed labour force working part-time is in fact part of the unused labour force, because they *can* increase their hours of work. The same goes for persons working less then 12 hours a week, who are formally not in the Dutch labour force as we have seen. Some may already have a desire to work more hours, while under the right circumstances; others could be persuaded to expand their hours of employment. Fourth, the unemployed labour force is of course part of the unused labour force. Fifth, there is no timing aspect concerning availability, so persons who can and want employment but are not available at short notice are also included. This unused labour force can be expressed in number of persons, but it would best be expressed in number of hours available to fill a full-time job.[8]

This definition is obviously a very broad concept in which only those persons are excluded who *cannot* work. One is inclined to think that this refers to persons with a disability benefit, the number of which in The Netherlands approaches 1 million. This is however not the case. First, because roughly one quarter of the disabled is known to have a job and hence *can* work, perhaps in other circumstances than the ones in which they were declared disabled (Lisv, 2000). This number is recently corroborated by Weidum and Linder (2002), who studied the employment position of persons with a social benefit. They also found that 22% of all persons with a disability benefit are in fact part of the employed labour force, i.e. work 12 hours a week or more. Second, about one third of the persons with a disability benefit is only partly disabled and *can* thus (partly) work.[9] Of those who are fully disabled it depends on the type of disorder they have whether or not a(nother) job can be filled. So persons who cannot work clearly do not

---

[8] A full-time job is assumed to refer to a job of 35 hours a week or more.
[9] Of the partly disabled in 1998 almost 50% held a job, against 17% of the fully disabled (Lisv, 2000).

coincide with disabled. It is perhaps better to speak of the group of persons not in the unused labour force as those persons who *can never* work.

Not everyone in the unused labour force may in reality offer time for labour. Our concept merely gives an indication of the number of persons who potentially could work (more hours) and assesses the basic characteristics of some broad, homogeneous, groups within this concept. Each group has its own incentives (not) to (search for) work. The idea is that by identifying common characteristics such incentives may also become visible, which in turn may lead to specific policy measures to enhance participation of the group under consideration.

Figure 2 gives a graphical representation of the way our unused labour force concept is structured in broad categories and, where available, presents the number of persons in each group according to the Dutch Labour Force Survey of 2002. In the LFS-framework, the unused labour force consists of persons who can expand their weekly working hours and at the same time are part of any of the following three labour effort categories.

(i)     Persons with employment for 12 hours or more a week who work 12-34 hours a week. This is the group of part-time employed
(ii)    Persons with employment of 1 to 11 hours a week. This is the group of persons holding small jobs, not being part of the employed labour force.
(iii)   Persons with no employment (0 hours a week).

In all three cases the size of the unused labour force is determined by the number of persons in each of the three labour effort groups who can increase their weekly working hours. Effectively this boils down to identifying the unused labour force based on a transition in the weekly hours worked.

The groups of small (1-11 hours a week) job holders is distinguished as a separate group here because in many cases a small job is seen as a stepping stone towards a more substantial job in terms of weekly hours work. So this group is regarded to be important in our unused labour force concept and is therefore studied as a separate group. When additional information for these three building groups becomes available it may be possible to assess if and how this unused labour force can be deployed in a useful way. These three categories can be differentiated into the four life cycle stages of figure 1 from which flows into employment occur: education, employment (job to job movement), inactivity and early retirement.

Some persons in these groups may already work for some hours, while other may not. Students may have small or part-time jobs to supplement their tuition. The same applies to persons who are not active at the labour market. We already mentioned the fact that in The Netherlands many persons with a disability benefit do in fact hold a job. Also housewives may fill a small job or do (unpaid) voluntary work and even early retired may still occupy a part-time job. See also Das et al. (2002), Weidum and Linder (2002) and Arts et al. (2002). In the next section we will review the international literature on identification of the unused labour force and provide a first assessment of the numbers in each of these groups in the unused labour force in The Netherlands.

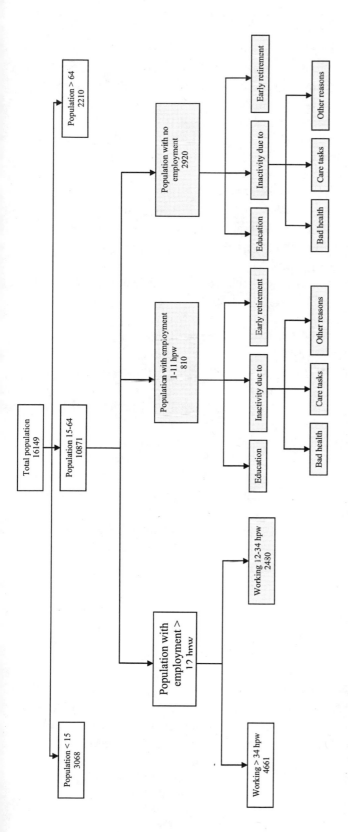

Figure 2 – Structure of unused labour force in shaded cells, with number of persons (x 1000) in each category in 2002 when available.

# 3. REVIEWING STUDIES OF UNUSED LABOUR FORCE

This section reviews the international literature on identifying concepts of an unused labour force in the vain of our definition. In a theoretical sense hidden unemployment is the denomination that comes closest to our idea of an unused labour force. These theoretical considerations usually start from the so-called discouraged worker effect. This is based on the premise that participation in the labour force is affected by variations in the business cycle. In a business cycle downturn, for some unemployed persons looking for work becomes so disheartening that they give up search and withdraw from the labour force and that persons who under normal circumstances would enter the labour force abstain from doing so. These are all labelled discouraged workers. Hidden unemployment is usually identified as the group of discouraged workers (Hamermesh and Rees, 1993, pp. 36-38). Search effort and search motivation are essential in this respect. In a neoclassical setting this means that wage and social benefit differentials are not large enough to persuade (discouraged) unemployed to search for work. See van der Wiel (1998).

The number of discouraged unemployed in The Netherlands averaged some 50 thousand persons in 2002, or 15% of the unemployed labour force, primarily women, elderly and lower educated. Notice however that our concept of an unused labour force discussed in the previous section is much broader than just the number of discouraged workers. Table 1 gives an overview of the definitions and denominations in various relevant economic studies in this field. We will discuss some these studies and provide a first assessment of the numbers of the associated unused labour force.

As far as measurement of the unused labour force is concerned we can distinguish two different methods in the international literature. First a macro approach where the unused labour force is estimated indirectly using aggregate data. In this approach the unused labour force is defined as the potential labour force, defined as the population between 15-64 that exists in addition to the actual labour force. Second, there is a micro approach in which the unused labour force is drawn from longitudinal surveys among households or individuals. In this paper we only consider this micro concept of the unused labour force.

Due to differences in the definition of the labour force in the Netherlands and the most of the industrialised world, also discussed in the previous section, we distinguish studies pertaining to The Netherlands and studies pertaining to other countries. Since research is hardly ever of a theoretical nature emphasis in the sequel is on empirical studies

## 3.1. International Studies

### Size of Unused Labour Force

As far as empirics is concerned two research groups have carried out most of the foreign studies on unused labour supply. First a group of German researchers centred around Elke Holst, who study aspects of the unused labour force in Germany (Holst and Schupp, 2000) and in some European countries (Holst and Spieß, 2001, 2002). In their work for Germany, micro level data from the *Sozio-oekonomische Panel* (SOEP), an annual survey among German households, are used. For the European work the European Community Household Panel (ECHP) is used.

**Table 1. Some measures of unused labour force in economic literature**

| Author(s) | Definition of unused labour force | Drawn directly from survey | Country |
|---|---|---|---|
| Jones and Riddell, 1999<br>Jones and Riddell, 2000<br>Jones and Riddell, 2001 | 'Marginally attached' non-participants: persons who want a job but are currently not searching. | Yes | Canada, USA |
| Holst and Spieß, 2001<br>Holst and Spieß, 2002 | 'Marginally attached' non-participants: (i) persons not pursuing paid work in past 7 days but searching (e.g. unavailable at short notice, not searching in past 4 weeks, not registered as unemployed); or (ii) persons not pursuing paid work in past 7 days and not searching due to discouragement | Yes | EU-countries |
| Holst and Schupp, 2000 | 'Hidden labour force'; various measures:<br>(i) non-participants who definitely or probably want to enter employment within 5 years<br>(ii) non-participants who want to enter employment in the future<br>(iii) non-participants who want to enter employment immediately<br>(iv) non-employed searching without employment office or persons not searching but immediately available and who would accept a job if employment situation would improve<br>(v) persons in training or reintegration projects and benefit recipients | Yes | Germany |
| CofFEE, 2002 | Persons 'marginally attached' to the labour market: persons wanting for work, but (i) not available in the reference week, or (ii) not searching because of discouragement | Yes | Australia |

**Table 1. (Continued)**

| Author(s) | Definition of unused labour force | Drawn directly from survey | Country |
|---|---|---|---|
| FAS, 2002 http://www.fas.ie/FAS_Review/ | 'Potential work force': (i) discouraged workers, (ii) passive job searchers, (iii) persons not in education but wanting to work | Yes | Ireland |
| Brummelkamp and van Driel 2003 | 'Silent reserve force': person between 15-64, without a job of 12 hours a week or more, who <br> - want to work for at least 12 hours a week <br> - can start within two weeks <br> - are not registered at employment agency <br> - are not school pupils of students | Yes | Netherlands |
| Bijsterbosch and Nahuis, 2001 | 'Favourable potential labour supply': (i) persons below 54 with working experience and (ii) school leavers | No, estimated | Netherlands |
| NAP, 2001 | 'Non-searching labour reserve': persons available for work at short notice, but not searching in past 4 weeks | Yes | Netherlands |
| De Grip et al 1999 | 'Not actively searching' | unknown | Netherlands |
| Dutch Ministry of SZW | ''Persons not searching, but wanting to work' | Yes | Netherlands |
| Statistics Netherlands | Various indicators: <br> (i) unemployed labour force <br> (ii) registered unemployment <br> (iii) persons wanting work for at least 12 hr/w <br> (iv) unemployment insurance benefits <br> (v) social assistance benefits | Yes | Netherlands |
| Taylor 2002 | Transition rates | unknown | EU |
| RvB, 2001 | Job searchers without a job, minus friction unemployment and school-leavers | unknown | Netherlands |

The second group of researchers involved in analysis of the unused labour force is centred around Stephen Jones and Craigh Riddell. They study the situation in Canada and the USA using the Canadian LFS and the US Current Population Survey (CPS). Sec Jones and Riddell (1998, 1999, 2001).

Starting in more detail with the study for Germany by Holst and Schupp (2000), the unused – or in their terminology: hidden – labour force is found in the non-employed population, *i.e.* all persons with 0 hours of weekly employment. This population is next subdivided into five groups:

(i)      non-employed who report they are registered as unemployed
(ii)     non-employed in education aged 15-24
(iii)    non-employed who wish definitely or probably to take up employment immediately or within one year (non-employed with a strong interest in employment)
(iv)     non-employed who wish definitely of probably to take up employment within one to five years (non-employed with moderate interest in employment)
(v)      all other non-employed who do not wish to take up employment after five or more years (non-employed with no interest in employment)

The unused (hidden) labour force in their approach is consists of groups (iii) and (iv) and amounts to some 1.8 million persons, or 3% of the population between 15-64, in 1998 in Germany.[1]

The unused (hidden) labour force in a number of European countries, analysed by Holst and Spieß (2002), is identified by the group of non-employed persons in the ECHP that is 'closer to the labour market then other non-employed groups' (Holst and Spieß, 2002, p. 5). These are labelled 'attached' to the labour market. The distance to the labour market is based only on the respondent answer to specific questions in the ECHP-questionnaire:

(i)      the group of persons that want employment for at least 1 hour a week but are not available on short notice and
(ii)     the discouraged unemployed, defined as persons wanting work, available at short notice but showing no active search effort due to low expectations (Holst and Spieß, p. 19).

The design of the ECHP does not allow a similar definition for the unused labour force as the one of Holst and Schupp (2000). The number of attached in the EU averages about 2% of the population between 15-59 years of age (Holst and Spieß, 2002, table 8), which implies some 4.6 million persons.[2]

Analysis of the marginally attached by Jones and Riddell (1998, 1999, 2001) is similar to what Holst and Spieß have been doing for Europe. The answers to specific questions in the Canadian LFS and the US Current Population Survey (CPS) are used to identify the unused labour force, they refer to as marginally attached. Marginally attached are identified by

(i)      the number of persons expressing they want to work, net of the unemployed labour force.

---

[1] When unemployed are included it increases to 5.9 million persons (13% of population 15-64).
[2] Based on Eurostat data of the population by age for 1996.

In fact this is the group of persons under (i) in the study of Holst and Spieß (2002). Distinctive characteristics of this group are gender, different unemployment states (temporary layoff, job searcher, future job start) and different reasons for being marginally attached (waiting, personal, discouraged). The actual number of persons being marginally attached to the labour market – and hence the size of the unused labour force in their approach – is not given. In fact their analysis focuses only on transitions from marginally attached into employment.

What all international studies reviewed here have in common is the fact that the unused labour force – irrespective of definition or denomination – is based on data availability rather than theoretical considerations. When theoretical aspects are mentioned they are usually just the discouraged worker hypothesis even when the empirical completion of the unused labour force encompasses more than just discouraged unemployed. Our concept of an unused labour force introduced in the previous section is based on a much broader concept than the above studies. The latter consider an unused labour force concept that can be made to use at relatively short notice. Only Holst and Schupp (2000) consider a longer period of five years in their definition.

Our concept of unused labour force is even wider than that of Holst and Schupp. It does not contain a specific time period after which entering the labour force should be effectuated. Neither does it exempt persons already in the labour force who work part-time. Core of our concept is the possibility of expansion of the number of hours worked, while most studies are concerned with expansion of the number of workers.

**Labour Market Flows**

What both Holst and Spieß and Jones and Riddell emphasise are transitions from the state of being (marginally) attached to the labour market into employment. Hence, essentially these studies are about the extent to which the unused labour force is made to use (i.e. has moved into paid labour). In order to get a flavour of their size, table 2 shows the transitions per month of persons from the state of being unemployed, marginally attached and other inactivity, respectively, to the state of being employed for the EU.[3] Table 2 shows that every month roughly 2.8% of the unemployed pass through to the employed. This is a higher transition rate than the 1.8% of the (marginally) attached that move into employment. The transition rates of other non-active persons is even smaller depending on the reason for being not active, ranging from 1.3% for students to 0.8% for non-participants due to household and care tasks.

**Table 2. Monthly transition rates into employment from five different states for the EU (12 countries), in % of the initial category***

| From: | Unemployed | Marginally attached | Not attached and in education | housekeeping | other |
|---|---|---|---|---|---|
| To: | Employed | Employed | Employed | Employed | Employed |
| EU-12: | | | | | |
| 1994/1995 | 2.9 | 1.9 | 1.3 | 0.8 | 1.0 |
| 1995/1996 | 2.7 | 1.8 | 1.3 | 0.7 | 0.8 |

*Transition rates refer to monthly figures, derived by divding annual figures by 12.
Source: Holstand Spieß (2002), tables 10 and 11.

**Table 3. Monthly transition rate into employment from three different states for Canada and the USA, in % of the initial category**

| From:<br>To: | Unemployed<br>Employed | Marginally attached<br>Employed | Not attached<br>Employed |
|---|---|---|---|
| Canada;<br>April 1997-April 1999 | 22.1 | 12.0 | 3.2 |
| USA;<br>Jan. 1994-Feb. 1994 | 22.2 | 8.7 | 3.6 |

Source: Jones and Riddell (2001), table 1 and Jones and Riddell (2000), table 1.

The monthly transition rates reported by Jones and Riddell are much larger than the ones from Holst and Spieß (table 3). Different survey designs of the panels involved, different data frequency and different populations and countries hamper comparison between the group around Holst and Jones and Riddell. Holst and Spieß analyse annual transitions, while Jones and Riddell analyse monthly transitions. Furthermore, labour markets are known to be much more flexible – and hence labour market dynamics is much larger – in the USA and Canada then in Europe. However, this explains only part of the difference. The fact that transition rates in the US and Canada are 5-8 times larger then the European ones is also related to the design and structure of the different databases. A Labour Force Survey is probably much more tailored to labour market issues then a household panel.[4]

**Table 4. Average monthly flows of persons between employment, unemployment and non- participation, in % of the initial category**

| From:<br>To: | Unemployed<br>Employed | Non-participants<br>all<br>Employed | attached[‡]<br>Employed |
|---|---|---|---|
| Blanchard and Diamond (1990)<br>USA; Jan. 1968-May 1986 | 24.6 | 2.8 | 34.0 |
| Burda and Wyplosz (1994)[†]<br>Germany; Jan.-Dec. 1987<br>France[*] Jan.-Dec. 1987 | 8.4<br>9.2 - 12.2 | -<br>- | -<br>- |
| Kock (2002)[†]<br>Netherlands; Jan.-Dec. 1999 | 7.4 | 0.7 | |

- is not available

[‡] Attached in this study refers to those non-participants indicating they want employment.

[†] Flow rates refer to monthly figures, derived by dividing annual figures by 12.

[*] For France two sources for unemployment flows are available, hence two figures.

---

[3] These monthly transistions are derived by dividing the original annual transitions by 12. See also Burda and Wyplosz (1994) for a similar approach.

[4] Furthermore, both the Canadian LFS and the US CPS each individual is questioned a number of consecutive month (LFS: 6; CPS: 4). This rotation group structure is utilised by Jones and Riddell in order to construct their panel. This is not possible in the ECHP.

Summarising, the unused labour force is mainly addressed in terms of data availability rather than for theoretical reasons. The actual size of the unused labour force in international studies ranges from about 2% to some 15% of the potential labour force (i.e. the population between 15-64), depending on the definition and the fact whether unemployed are included or not. An important issue obviously concerns the number of persons moving from this unused labour force into employment. These flows depend crucially on the data used.

A related area of research in which the unused labour force is important is on the ageing problem that faces many European countries. One way of coping with an ageing labour force population is by activating the unused labour force in order to keep participation rates from falling. Many of these studies also start from a transitional labour market concept in which similar groups as in our study are distinguished. See the Finish Ministry of Labour (2003) for an excellent review.

Another related research area is specifying and estimating a so-called matching functions, where a worker or job flows (like new hires or filled vacancies, respectively) are explained by both labour supply and is labour demand.[5] Usually labour supply is covered by the stock of unemployed and labour demand by the stock of vacancies. In most empirical studies the worker or job flow that is explained by these two stocks is chosen rather arbitrary. Broersma and van Ours (1999) provide an overview of these different flow measures and show that the choice of the flow that enters the matching function fixes the two explanatory stocks. The stock of unemployed to represent unused labour supply does not suffice in many cases.

Some matching studies provide information on the actual size of the flows they analyse, which gives us another comparison with flow rates presented so far. Comparison can only be adequate when the same data frequency is considered. Blanchard and Diamond (1990) present average monthly flows of US workers, while Burda and Wyplosz (1994) show annual flows for Germany, France, Spain and the UK and Kock (2002) provides annual flows for The Netherlands. Burda and Wyplosz mention annual flows can be compared to monthly flows by dividing by 12. Of their countries under study only Germany and France can be compared to the US.

Table 4 shows that the monthly unemployment to employment flow of Blanchard and Diamond for the US is close to the value reported by Riddell and Jones. The same is true for the employment flow from non-participation, but not for the attached. The flows from unemployment into employment for European countries are still 2-3 times smaller than those for the US, but they are also 3-4 times larger than the ones reported by Holst and Spieß. One the one hand this is related to well-known high dynamics of the US labour market relative to Europe. On the other hand, it provides an additional argument against using the ECHP for labour force transitions.

**Labour Supply Studies**
Finally, we mention a specific type of studies into the analysis of work behaviour, the labour supply studies of different groups of persons. In practically all labour supply studies the phenomenon being analysed is not related to labour market flows (transitions) in any sense. It is merely a 'stock' at a given point in time representing either

a)   a Boolean variable (employed vs. not employed, or participating vs. not participating)

---

[5] A recent overview of the matching literature is found in Petrongolo and Pissarides (2000)

b)  a continuous variable concerning weekly or annual number of hours of work (derived from a standard household utility function)

c)  a continuous variable representing the (net or gross) labour participation rate, i.e. employment (or participation) relative to the population between 15-64.

or a (simultaneously estimated) combination of these variables.

Usually the analysis is based on (pooled) cross section data from some household survey (sometimes: panel) of the country or region under consideration. Explanatory variables are numerous, depending on the aspect of labour supply being studied. In most cases they cover one or more of the following variables, including squares and combinations of variables (see next page). Such variables can of course also be used to identify specific categories of our unused labour force.

In most studies the various aspects refer to labour supply decisions of specific groups of persons, like

- elderly (Taylor and Urwin, 1999; O'Brien, 2000-01),
- students (Demeuelmeester and Rochat, 2000)
- disabled (Wilson, 2001)
- women, with or without children (Miller and Volker, 1983, Fayissa and Fessehatzion, 1990, Powell, 1997, Del Boca et al, 2000, Ribar, 2001).

| |
|---|
| Gender |
| Age |
| Education level |
| Education duration (years) |
| Nationality/Race |
| Residential region/area |
| Household position |
| Age youngest child |
| Child care costs |
| History of employment |
| Work experience |
| Income (wage) |
| Income partner |
| Tax regime |
| Education partner |
| Housing status |
| Health status |
| Health status partner |
| Desired job |
| Desired hours work per week |

## 3.2. Studies for the Netherlands

### Size of the Unused Labour Force

There are at least two major studies that address the identification of marginally attached in The Netherlands. Firstly, Bijsterbosch and Nahuis (2001) estimate the size of what they call the 'favourable potential labour supply'. Relevant data are drawn from the Dutch LFS. Like the international studies of 'marginally attached' this 'potential labour supply' is established by respondent's answers to specific questions in the LFS. Starting point is the group of persons who 'want employment for 12 hours a week or more'. Next the number of persons within this category, whose success of finding employment is 'favourable', can be estimated using two characteristics: age and work experience. This favourable potential labour supply amounted to 544 thousand persons in 1999, or 5.1% of the population between 15-64. In a frequency distribution for different characteristics, they report that the largest groups within this 'favourable potential labour supply' have the following characteristics: women, married, parents and wishing to work 20-34 hours a week. Cross tabulations were not reported.

The second major study is by Brummelkamp and van Driel (2003) who also use the LFS to assess what they call the 'silent reserve force'. Construction of this group is solely based on survey response and is defined by persons between 15 and 64 years old who:

1. do not work or work less than 12 hours a week and
2. want to work more than 12 hours a week and
3. can start at short notice (i.e. within two weeks) and
4. are not registered at the employment agency and
5. are not students or school pupils

When these requirements are fulfilled, their 'silent reserve force' has some 212 thousand persons in 2000 and 190 thousand in 2001, or 2.0%, respectively 1.8% of the population between 15-64. This concept is thus much smaller that the one of Bijsterbosch and Nahuis.

The main reason for this difference in size is the timing of availability. The concept of Brummelkamp and van Driel is a short-term concept focusing on the group of persons than can begin at short notice. The concept of Bijsterbosch and Nahuis is a based on a longer run principle, solely based on the desire for employment, irrespective of immediate availability. Our unused labour force definition – where the issue is neither availability, nor preference but potency: *can* a person work (more hours) – encompasses both. We view the unused labour force as a long run potential source to keep labour participation on track in view of the ageing in the coming decade.

Brummelkamp and van Driel (2003) also provide characteristics of their 'silent reserve force'. Its distribution over both sex and age is skewed, with an over-representation of females (70%) and of age group 35-54 (55%). Most females (60%) characterise themselves as housewives, many without small jobs or volunteer labour. Males characterise themselves in a wider variety of states: 25% state they are disabled, 20% states they are unemployed and only 9% label themselves as 'houseman'. The level of education of the unused labour force is not very different between sexes. More than half of them have followed secondary or tertiary education, so this is quite high. The education discipline most females have followed is (health) care. The distribution over disciplines for males is more spread. There is also an evenly spread of the unused labour force over the Dutch provinces, with slightly higher rates in the peripherical regions and lower rates in the economic heart. All in all, about three quarters of the unused labour force consist of three groups: (i) females (housewives), (ii) elderly (above 55) men and (iii) youngsters (15-24 years of age).

## Labour Supply Studies

These groups have also been the subject of standard labour supply studies, particularly females, like Ministry of Social Affairs (2001), Janssen (2001), Vlasblom et al. (2001) in table 1. Besides these standard labour supply studies, there has also been research in the field of labour supply in a more spatial context for The Netherlands. Ekamper and van Wissen (2000) study the effects of changes in regional labour markets on (labour) migration and commuting. The latter can be seen as 'spatial' labour supply. Broersma and van Dijk (2002) distinguish a similar spatial type of labour supply when analysing the total labour supply response to a labour demand shock in a regional setting. Central issue is here where the labour supply originates from (moves out to) when a positive (negative) labour demand shock hits a region: unemployment in that region, non-participation in that region or spatial adjustment. The latter are employed, unemployed or non-participants in other regions who move into (out of) or commute into (out of) the 'shocked' region for employment.

## Labour Market Flows

The problem with most studies so far, both international and referring to the Dutch situation, is their preoccupation with an unused labour force that can be put into service immediately. None of the above studies is concerned with investigating the full potential labour force. The only research that tackles this issue is a study into the full system of labour market flows initiated by Broersma and den Butter (1994) and later extended by Kock (2002).[6] Here the total system of labour market flows between different labour market states is at stake: employment, unemployment and non-participant. Between these states and the stock of vacancies all in- and outflows of both persons and jobs are identified and quantified in a consistent way.[7]

However, the flows in Kock (2002) stem from a variety of sources of both surveys and administrative databases. In some cases flows are identified by the stock-flow definition, while for others specific assumptions were required.[8] The novelty of this research is that all flows are identified at the macro level in a consistent way very much like in a National Accounting system. It fails the problems of flows identified by micro-level surveys. Firstly, it is based on continuous measurement of flows and not at discrete interval in time. Continuous measurement is a characteristic of administrative data. Secondly, micro surveys usually refer to only a part of the economy, like a single industry or only unemployed moving to the state of employment, without knowledge of other flows.

The approach of Kock et al. was criticized by Allaart and van Ours (2001) who showed that many of the flows in the system are in fact dominated by observable flows, in particular the flow of employment to unemployment, because it re-appears in many other labour market flows due to use of the stock-flow definition and some of the assumptions made. They found a different magnitude of flows using the OSA-labour supply panel.

---

[6] See also Broersma, den Butter and Kock (2000).
[7] Recently, Klein et al. (2002) have proposed a similar system of labour market flows.
[8] The stock-flow definition means the fact that the change in a stock equals the inflow minus outflow. When for example only an inflow is known and the change in the corresponding stock, the outflow follows simply from the stock-flow definition

Table 5 makes a comparison between the flows in Kock (2002) and those of Allaart and van Ours (2001) based on the OSA labour supply panel. For reasons of completeness we also report comparable flows of the work of Blanchard and Diamond and of Burda and Wyplosz mentioned earlier. We only present *monthly* flows from unemployment to employment and *vice versa* and from non-participation to employment and *vice versa*. All figures are in percentages of employment. Table 5 shows that the flows (relative to employment) are much larger in the approach of Kock than those derived from the OSA panel. However, the flows for The Netherlands are much smaller, particularly for Allaart and van Ours, than values for other countries. This implies a less flexibly operating Dutch labour market than is often assumed. The difference between Kock and Allaart and van Ours is related to continuous measurement of flows in administrative data sources we spoke of. The implications are also different: in the approach of Kock the net increase of employment stems from particularly from non-participation. In Allaart and van Ours the net increase in employment stems mainly from unemployed.

**Table 5. Comparison of the average monthly flows of persons between employment, unemployment and non-participation, in % of the employment stock**

| Country: | Netherlands | Netherlands | USA | Germany | France[†] |
|---|---|---|---|---|---|
| Authors: | Kock (2002) table 4.1 | Allaart and van Ours (2001) figures 4.3 and 4.4 | Blanchard and Diamond (1990) | Burda and Wypl osz (1994) | Burda and Wypl osz (1994) |
| Monthly flows pertaining to [*]: | 1999 | 1997 | 1968- 1986 | 1987 | 1987 |
| in % of employment Flows from | | | | | |
| - employment to unemployment | 0.4 | 0.1 | 1.7 | 0.9 | 1.8 |
| - unemployment to employment | 0.5 | 0.1 | 1.3 | 0.8 | 1.6-2.1 |
| - employment to non-participation | 0.2 | 0.1 | 1.6 | 0.7 | 0.6 |
| - non-participation to employment | 0.4 | 0.1 | 2.8 | 0.8 | 0.0-0.6 |

[*] Monthly flow rates for The Netherlands, Germany and France are derived by dividing annual figures by 12.

[†] For France two sources for flows of non-participation to and from employment are available, hence two figures.

Apart from these studies no equal international investigation has been found yet that has treated labour market flows in the same way. Nevertheless in terms of the life cycle stages of figure 1 both most studies stick to the standard distinction between employed, unemployed and non-participation. Both Kock and Allaart and van Ours do identify the flow of school leavers into each of these states, but school leavers are considered to be part of non-participants (inactivity). Kock divides non-participants into disabled and all others including retired.

Returning to figure 1 both studies particularly leave flows into employment from inactivity due to care tasks and early retirement untreated. Only Holst and Spieß come close to figure 1 with categories: employment, unemployment, education, housekeeping/care tasks and other. Our study tries to get a hold on all six flows of figure 1.

## 4. ASSESSING THE FACTS FOR THE NETHERLANDS

So far we have made a definition of the unused labour force, based on an individual's labour effort in terms of weekly hours work and the potential for expansion of these hours. This property led to three distinctive labour effort categories in figure 2 based on the LFS framework. With additional information on these three building groups it may be possible to assess if and how this unused labour force can be made to use, in terms of raising the number of working hours. Using the life cycle stages of an individual (in figure 1), each of the three building categories of the unused labour force (in figure 2) can be differentiated into the four life cycle stages: education, work, inactivity and early retirement. This gives rise to the illustration of figure 3, combining each of the three building blocks in terms of labour effort with the flow chart of transitional labour markets.

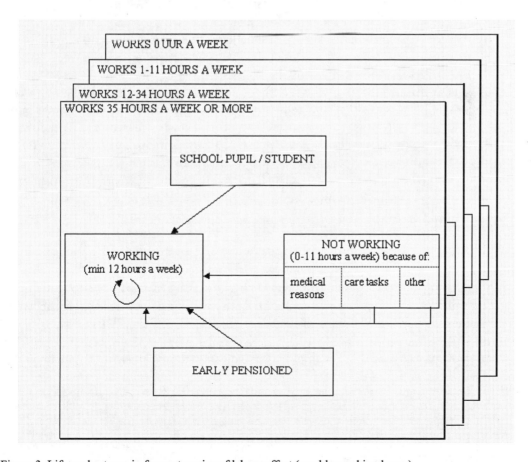

Figure 3. Life cycle stages in four categories of labour effort (weekly working hours).

The category of labour of 35 hours a week or more is assumed not expand its hours of work. This group is only present in figure 3 for the sake of completeness. It is not part of the unused labour force. Of the remaining three labour effort groups and for each of the positions in the life cycle stage different characteristics should be distinguished. These characteristics can be drawn from many standard labour supply studies mentioned earlier.

1. Personal characteristics:
- gender
- age
- education
- nationality
- residential region

2. Structural characteristics:
- household position
- history of employment
- working experience (duration)
- presence of children/age of youngest child
- availability of childcare provisions
- main source of income
- household income / partner income
- health status (chronical diseases)
- health status partner

3. Behavioural characteristics:
- desired job type (fixed vs. flexible)
- desired number of working hours a week

These characteristics, together with the life cycle position and the actual labour effort in terms of working hours a week, should be used to establish the size of the main groups in the unused labour force. Obviously choices have to be made with respect to the individual characteristics, because there are simply not enough observations available to study all characteristics simultaneously. [9] As a first step we want to assess the number of persons that can be attributed to each stage of the transitional labour market model of figure 1, irrespective of their characteristics. This provides information about the absolute size of each stage and, hence, of the source for transitions. The larger the number of persons in each stage, the larger are possible transitions from that source.

This implies that our unused labour force concept is empirically filled in terms of numbers of persons instead of number of hours, because adequate data on hours are not available. Figure 4 fills the cells of figure 1 and distinguishes the number of persons by weekly working hours: 35 hours a week or more, 12-34 hours a week, 1-12 hours a week and none. [10] This figure shows that each of the stages comprises a substantial number of persons, ranging from 370 thousand persons between 15-64, who are early retired, to 7.1 million persons in the employed labour force. [11] The number of persons with some kind of employment indicates the attachment to the labour market

---

[9] Very recent a start has been made to identify the unused labour force in The Netherlands with some of these characteristics. Van der Valk (2004) links unused labour supply, defined as persons willing to work for at least 12 hour a week, with history of employment. Lucassen (2004) studies females for whom the presence of young children was a reason to stop working in their effort to re-enter the labour force after raising their children.

[10] This cell filling is drawn from the Dutch LFS of 2002 and is based on the respondents' answer to what they consider to be their main societal activity.

in each life cycle stage. In this study we will label inactive persons holding a small job of less than 12 hours a week as 'attached to the labour market'. This is an entirely different definition of (marginally) attached than used by researchers like Holst and Spieß and Jones and Riddell discussed earlier. They focus on the willingness to work to express attachment; we focus on having a small job.

Attachment to the labour market outside the employed labour force is relatively high for persons in education, where 43% hold a small job, and low for inactive persons due to early retirement, where a mere 6% holds a small job. Hence labour market attachment is high for inactive persons in education and low for early retired.

Youths and elderly persons are two important groups in our unused labour force concept, because the participation rate of these two groups is known to be particularly low in comparison to other age groups. Figures 5 and 6 present male and female participation rates per age group and show that particularly at young ages (education) and old ages (early retirement) participation is very low. Apart from these extreme ends, figures 5 and 6 also show that female participation on the whole is below that of males. For ages between 25 and 50 there is a gap with male participation rates of 10 to 25 percentage point.12 This provides a first handle for policy measures to enhance participation. What we then need is further information about characteristics of persons within these three groups.

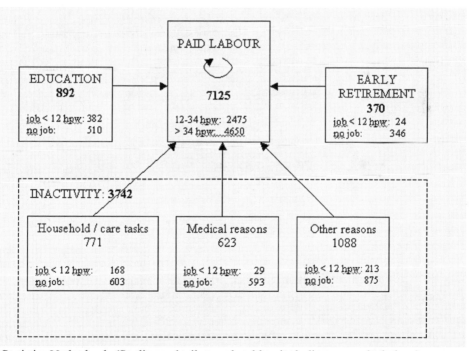

Source: Statistics Netherlands (Statline and tailor-made tables, including own calculations)

Figure 4. Number of persons between 15-64 years of age in each life cycle stage of the transitional labour market model by employment in hours per week (hpw), The Netherlands 2002 (× 1000).

---

[11] Note that the cell of persons being inactive for 'other reasons' includes unemployed. Of the 1.1 million persons being inactive for other reasons, some 300.000 comprise the unemployed labour force.

12 The steep fall in participation after age 50 occurs by both males and females and corresponds to the early retirement age.

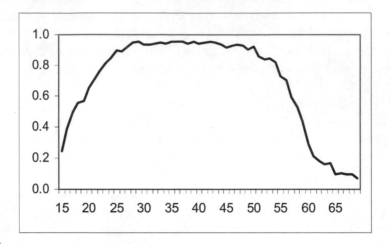

Source: NIDI

Figure 5. Male labour force participation by age, 2000.

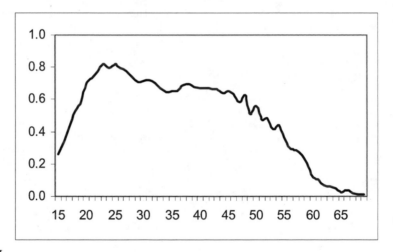

Source: NIDI

Figure 6. Female labour force participation by age, 2000.

The relatively high labour market attachment of (young) persons in education is a reassuring thought, because it means that many of them are already close to the labour market. Specific policy measures to further enhance participation or incentive to take on small jobs are not necessary. 13 Their main activity is their study and young persons will find their way on the labour market anyhow after they completed their education.14 The group of early retired is hardly attached to the labour market. The question is if there are policy measures to make them take up work again. The low participation rate of older workers has already invoked policy measures to make early retirement more difficult. If these measures have an effect the

---

13 Under the Dutch definition of labour force, mentioned earlier, labour force participation refers only to persons working 12 hours a week or more. Persons with a small job of less than 12 hours a week are not counted in the participation rate.
14 Completion of school or study is of course an important prerequisite for school-leavers for finding employment. Policy measures to counteract drop-out from school is important for participation of school-leavers.

participation of older workers will rise eventually.[15] The most promising group to direct policy measures to in order to enhance participation is the group of females between roughly 25-45 years of age. There exists a 'participation-gap' with males of the same age. In order to fill that gap, we first need more information about the characteristics of these age groups.

We will distinguish three characteristics: gender, age and education for the following groups:[16]

- persons in the employed labour force by weekly working hours;
- persons who are inactive for various reasons[17] holding a small job, thereby showing some attachment to the labour market;
- persons who are inactive without any attachment to the labour market.

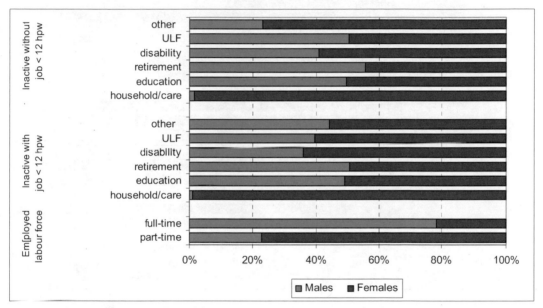

Source: Statistics Netherlands (Statline and tailor-made tables, including own calculations)

Figure 7. Distribution of life cycle and labour market stages by gender, The Netherlands 2002.

Figures 7, 8 and 9 present the distribution by gender, age and education over these three groups. The pattern for gender in each of these groups is familiar. Full-time workers primarily consist of males and part-timers are mostly females. It is more interesting to view the distribution for inactive person by reason for inactivity and by labour market attachment. Inactivity due to household and care tasks is predominantly a female thing, without any difference with respect to having a small job or not. There is also hardly any difference between gender and labour market attachment for inactivity due to education, disability, unemployment (ULF) and early retirement.

---

[15] This is due to the so-called cohort-effect, which means that a (permanent) change in the participation in certain age groups 'moves through' to the participation of higher ages as they become older and take with them this changed participation behaviour.

[16] Data for these groups is from the LFS 2002.

[17] We distinguish inactive persons in the unemployed labour force (ULF) separately from persons who are inactive for other reasons. The ULF is part of the (gross) participation rate and therefore does not need specific attention in

We do find a difference for inactivity due to other reasons. In this latter group, inactive males are more attached than inactive females.[18]

Figure 8 provides evidence of differences between active and inactive persons and labour force attachment by age. Again the obvious picture emerges for full-time versus part-time workers, where the latter group has slightly more young workers than the first group. The age pattern for inactivity due to education and early retirement is also in agreement with expectations: inactive persons in education are primarily in the youngest and early-retired persons are all in the oldest age group. This holds for inactivity with and without having a small job. Disabled persons are for more than half in the oldest age group of 50-64. The age group of 25-49 is, however, more often involved in small jobs than the oldest age group.

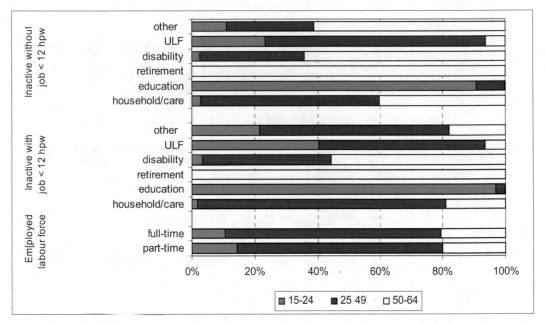

Source: Statistics Netherlands (Statline and tailor-made tables, including own calculations)

Figure 8. Distribution of life cycle and labour market stages by age, The Netherlands 2002.

The most eye-catching differences between age groups and extent of labour market attachment are at inactivity for household and care reasons, inactivity due to unemployment (ULF) and inactivity for other reasons. For the latter reason of inactivity, labour market attachment is high in the youngest and intermediate age group. For unemployed labour market attachment is limited to the youngest age category. Inactivity for household and care reasons by age, in conjunction with figure 7, shows that labour market attachment for females between 15-49 years of age still relatively high, while for age 50 and above it is relatively low. We can say that to a large extent this group of females between 25-49 being inactive for household and care reasons is responsible for the low female participation between 25-49 years of age (see also figure 6).

---

terms of policy measures to enhance participation. Inactivity for other reasons is a residual term consisting of a large number of different groups.

[18] We should, however, bear in mind that figure 4 showed that in absolute terms the majority of inactive persons for whatever reason is not attached to the labour market.

Finally, figure 9 gives the distribution of the level of education over the various life cycle stages. It shows that the pattern for employed labour by weekly working hours is hardly different. There are slightly more lower educated and slightly less higher educated workers working part-time. For all inactivity, apart from education, the share of low educated persons is slightly higher and that of persons with a high education is lower when there is no labour market attachment compared to some attachment.

Table 6 summarizes these results by indicating which of the characteristics involved here is clearly dominant over the others. This table provides information about characteristics of persons that are in the unused labour force as defined in this paper. Table 6 shows that females are dominant in many life cycle stages that determine the unused labour force. This not only the case for part-time employment and inactivity for household and care reasons, but also for unemployed and disabled, both holding small jobs. Hence, unemployed and disabled females are more often attached to the labour market than their male counterparts. They have already some working experience, which makes them less difficult to address in order to increase their working hours. Age is also distinctive between life cycle and labour market stages: inactive persons, apart from those in education, with some attachment to the labour market are more concentrated in younger age groups than those without labour market attachment. The same applies to inactivity by education, where low education levels far less dominate inactivity when some labour market attachment is involved than inactivity without labour market attachment.

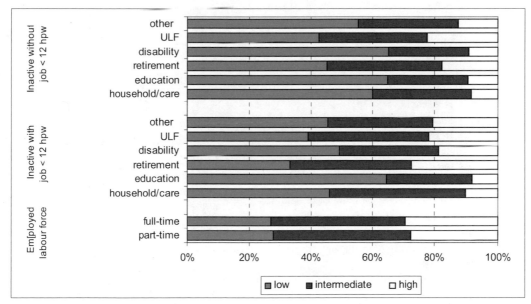

Source: Statistics Netherlands (Statline and tailor-made tables, including own calculations)

Figure 9. Distribution of life cycle and labour market stages by education level, The Netherlands 2002.

However, identifying groups with similar characteristics in each life cycle stage and labour effort category is one thing. Identification of flows between each of these stages and categories is quite another. In order to keep things simple we focus on those flows that enhance the labour participation rate. This means person formerly inactive moving into either the employed labour force or the unemployed labour force. Figure 10 shows that this boils down to five flows. We have already argued that the flow from education into either the employed or unemployed labour force will not need additional policy measures. We have also argued that it is hardly feasible to make persons who are early retired move back to work or job search again. Disincentives to early retirement and a cohort-effect will eventually raise participation of older age groups.

That leaves policy measures to stimulate persons who are inactive for various reasons to move into the labour force. The residual group of 'other' reasons is heterogeneous and it is difficult to pinpoint one dominant characteristic that makes this group stand out to the other two. When studying participation enhancing labour market flows, focus should be on the two remaining groups: women inactive for household and care reasons and men and women inactive for medical reasons.

### Table 6. Dominant characteristic by life cycle stage and labour market attachment in The Netherlands, 2002

| Labour market status | Life cycle stage | Gender | | Age class (years) | | | Level of education | | |
|---|---|---|---|---|---|---|---|---|---|
| | | Male | Female | 15-24 | 25-49 | 50-64 | Low | Interm. | High |
| Working | Part-time | | × | | | | | | |
| Inactive and attached | Education | | | × | | | × | | |
| | Household | × | | | × | | | | |
| | Disabled | × | | | | × | | | |
| | Retired | | | | | × | | | |
| | unemployed | × | | × | | | | | |
| | Other | | | | | | | | |
| Inactive and not attached | Education | | | × | | | × | | |
| | Household | × | | | | × | × | | |
| | Disabled | | | | | × | × | | |
| | Retired | | | | | × | | | |
| | Unemployed | | | | | | | | |
| | Other | × | | | | | × | | |

Dominance (×) is defined as:

Gender: share of 60% or more for male of female

Age: age groups 15-24 and 50-64 require a share of 40% or more and age group 25-49 requires a share of 75% or more

Education:  share of 50% or more for any of level of education

Source: Statistics Netherlands

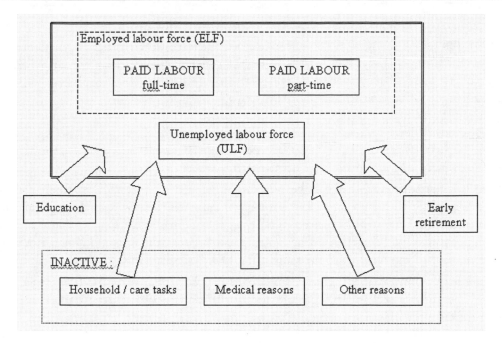

Figure 10. Labour market flows based on life cycle stages that stimulate labour force participation.

These are also the ones likely to be most relevant from a policy perspective. In terms of figures 5 and 6:

- the low participation at young age levels is probably unavoidable because of education.[19]
- the female participation gap for 25-49 year-olds can be cured by studying characteristics of women in that age group, who have moved from inactivity into the labour force or who have remained inactive, for that matter. When these characteristics are known we have a handle for policy to stimulate such flows. If for example the absence of childcare provisions is a hampering factor for these women to move into the labour force, then measures can be undertaken to make these provisions better accessible or less costly.
- the low participation at older age levels can be partly addressed by studying characteristics of disabled persons who have moved into the labour force, or who have remained inactive. If for example the presence of adjusted workplaces is lacking, so handicapped persons are unable to fill a job, this might also be a reason to undertake policy measures to ensure these adjustments.

## 5. CONCLUDING REMARKS

This paper is about the possibilities of getting the unused labour force to go to work. Different denominations of the unused labour force can be found in economic literature, like marginally attached, hidden labour force and silent reserve force. These are all closely related

---

[19] More and higher education in itself stimulates participation later on.

and have comparable definitions. They are all determined by respondent's answers to specific questions in the LFS. The definition of unused labour force of this paper is much broader. It covers the group of persons over 15, who can expand their number of (weekly) hours work. It not only covers person being inactive (working 0 hours a week), but also persons with some attachment the labour market, like those holding small jobs (1-11 hours a week) and part-time employed (12-34 hours a week).

This unused labour force concept is closely related to both the theory of transitional labour markets, where individuals are assumed to be in any typical stage of their life cycle depending on time: education, employed, inactive and early retired and move between stages at their own discretion. Narrowing down the stage of being employed by the actual number of weekly working hours supplied, means that four different labour effort categories are distinguished, three of which build the unused labour force. The category of persons working 35 hours a week or more are assumed to be at their maximum and do not expand their working hours. They are hence no part of the unused labour force. The other three categories, consisting of persons working 12-34 hour a week (employed labour force being part-time employed), persons working 1-11 hours a week and persons without employment, build the unused labour force.

We have found that the number of persons involved in each of the stages in our unused labour concept and of the transitional labour market is quite substantial in The Netherlands, ranging from some 2.5 million part-time workers, predominantly females, to 370 early-retired, whose main characteristic is their age. One group that can be distinguished here and which is usually absent in related studies is inactive persons due to household and care reasons, primarily females. Their age characteristic, however, depends on their labour market attachment in terms of holding a small job of less than 12 hours a week. Despite the fact that in absolute terms only few inactive persons are attached to the labour market, it does appear to be an important instrument to identify dominant groups of persons in the unused labour force.

We have come to the conclusion that studying labour market flows out of the various stages of inactivity into the labour force can best be determined in terms of policy relevance. This means that focus should be placed on factors that affect the flow of females between 25-50 years of age into the labour force and factors affecting the flow of disabled persons into the labour force.

## ACKNOWLEDGEMENTS

This paper is part of the Strategic Research Programme "SOCIAL AND LABOUR MARKET DYNAMICS" under auspices of Statistics Netherlands: *http://www.cbs.nl/nl/service/ onderzoek/strat-ondz/SDA/index-SDA.htm* and Dorien Manting, "Strategic Research Programme Social and Labour Market Dynamics", Statistics Netherlands, Voorburg, July 2002.

We gratefully acknowledge the many stimulating discussions with Dorien Manting and Jacques Thijssen, both of Statistics Netherlands, and comments and remarks of two anonymous referees. These have all improved the quality of this paper in many ways.

# REFERENCES

Allaart, Piet and Jan C. van Ours, 2001, *Stromen op de Nederlandse arbeidsmarkt*, OSA-publicatie A182, OSA, Tilburg. [in Dutch]

Arts, C.H., L. van Toor and S de Vries, 2002, "Stromen op de arbeidsmarkt, april-oktober 1999", *Sociaal-economische maandstatistiek*, December 2002, 66-71, Voorburg: CBS [in Dutch].

Bijsterbosch, M.G. and N.J. Nahuis, 2001, Vergroting arbeidsaanbod een uitdaging voor beleid", Amsterdam: Nederlandsche Bank NV. [in Dutch]

Blanchard, Oliver and Peter Diamond, 1990, "The Cyclical Behavior of Gross Flows of Workers in the US", *Brookings Papers on Economic Activity*, 2, 85-155.

Broersma, Lourens and Jouke van Dijk, 2002, "Regional Labour Market Dynamics in The Netherlands", *Papers in Regional Science*, 81 (3), 343-364.

Broersma, Lourens, Frank den Butter and Udo Kock, 2000, "A National Accounting System for Worker Flows", *Economics Letters*, 67, 331-336.

Broersma, Lourens and Jan C. van Ours, 1999, "Job Searchers, Job Matches and the Elasticiy of Matching", *Labour Economics*, 6, 77-93.

Broersma, Lourens and Frank den Butter, 1994, "A Consistent Set of Time Series Data on Labor Market Flows for The Netherlands", Research Memorandum No. 43, Free University Amsterdam.

Brummelkamp, G.W. and H.J. van Driel, 2003, "De stille reserve en het MKB", EIM Strategische Verkenning B200209, Zoetermeer: EIM [in Dutch].

Burda, Michael and Charles Wyplosz, 1994, "Gross Worker and Job Flows in Europe", *European Economic Review*, 38, 1287-1315.

Centre of Full Employment and Equity (CofFEE), 2002, "Labour Market Indicators: An Alternative View of the Labour Market", University of Newcastle, Australia, at *http://e1.newcastle.edu.au/coffee/docs/indicators/CLMI_July_2002.pdf*

Colledge, Michael, 2000, "Labour Force Indicators, Review of Standards and Practices, Statistics Directorate, OECD: Paris.

Das, M., L. van Toor and C.H. Arts, 2002, "Samenloop van banen en uitkeringen", *Sociaal-economische maandstatistiek*, December 2002, 22-28, Voorburg: CBS [in Dutch].

Demeulemeester, Jean-Luc and Denis Rochat, "Labour Participation of Higher Education Students", *Labour*, 14(3), 503-522.

Ekamper, Peter and Leo van Wissen, 2000, *Regionale arbeidsmarkten, migratie en woon-werk verkeer*, Den Haag: NIDI. [in Dutch]

Eurostat, 2002, "Euro Indicators", News Release No. 67/2002, 4 June 2002.

Finish Ministry of Labour, 2003, "Preparing for the Labour Market Change Caused by the Baby Boom Generation", Labour Administration Publication at *www.mol.fi/english/reports/babyboomgeneration.pdf*

Florquin, F.F., 2002, "Banen van studenten in het hoger onderwijs", *Sociaal-economische maandstatistiek*, December 2002, 59-65, Voorburg: CBS [in Dutch].

Haan, de H.F., A.A. Smit and M.J. van Gent, 2001, "Nieuwe schaarste? Nieuw aanbod Activerend arbeidsmarktbeleid op sectorniveau", TNO report 2590004/5570, Hoofddorp: TNO Arbeid [in Dutch].

Hamermesh, Daniel S. and Albert Rees, 1993, *The Economics of Work and Pay*, New York: Harper-Collins.

Holst, Elke and Jügen Schupp, 2000, "Hidden Labour Force in Germany", *Economic Bulletin*, 37 (9), p. 285-292.

Holst, Elke and C. Katharina Spieß, 2001, "Labour Market Attachment of 'Not Economically Active Persons': New Aspects of Hidden Labour Force in Europe", DIW Berlin.

Holst, Elke and C. Katharina Spieß, 2002, "Labour Market Attachment and People Outside the Labour Force: An Explorative Analysis of the Hidden Labour Fo0rce in Europe", *Journal of Applied Social Science Studies*, 122 (1), p. 55-83.

Hussmans, Ralf, Farhad, Mehran and Vijay Verma, 1990, "Survey of Economically Active Population, Employment, Unemployment and Underemployment, An ILO Manual on Concepts and Methods, Geneva: ILO.

Janssen, Mirjam M. 2001, "Ik ga niet betalen om te werken", Report for Dutch Ministry of Social Affairs. [in Dutch]

Jones, Stephen R.G. and W. Craigh Riddell, 1998, "Unemployment and Labour Force Attachment: A Multistate Analysis of Non-Employment, in: John Haltiwanger, Marilyn E. Topel and Robert Topel (eds), *Labor Statistics Measurement Issues*, Chicago: Chicago University Press.

Jones, Stephen R.G. and W. Craigh Riddell, 1999, "Unemployment and Labour Force Attachment: A Study of Canadian Experience 1997-1999", background paper prepared for Statistics Canada.

Jones, Stephen R.G. and W. Craigh Riddell, 2001, "Unemployment and Non-Employment: Heterogeneities in Labour Market States", University of British Columbia and CIAR, November 2001.

Klein, Michael W, Scott Schuh and Robert K. Triest, 2002, "Job Creation, Job Destruction and International Competition: A Literature Review", Tufts University, NBER and Federal Reserve; at: *http://www.bos.frb.org/economic/wp/wp2002/wp027.pdf*

Kock, Udo, 2002, *Social Benefits and the Flow Approachto the Labor Market*, Ph D Thesis, Amsterdam: Tinbergen Institute/Thela Thesis Publishers.

Landelijk instituut voor sociale verzekeringen (Lisv), 2000, "Signalement werkende ao-uitkeringsgerechtigden", Den Haag: Lisv. [in Dutch]

Lucassen, Sabine, 2004, "Herintreders op de arbeismarkt", *Sociaal-economische trends*, Voorburg: CBS. [in Dutch]

Macredie, Ian, 1997, "The Effects of Survey Instruments on the Canada/US Unemployment Rate Gap", Staff Report, Labour and Household Analysis Division, Statistics Canada.

Ministry of Social Affairs, 2001, "Plan van de aanpak herintredende vrouwen", Tweede Kamer, vergaderjaar 200-2001,27853, No. 1. [in Dutch]

Ministry of Social Affairs, 2003, site *www.szw.nl* [in Dutch]

O'Brien, Martin J. 2000-1, "Older Male Labour Force Participation: The Role of Social Security and Hidden Unemployment", *Australian Journal of Labour Economics*, 4(3), p. 206-223.

Petrongolo, Barabara and Chris Pissarides, 2001, "Looking into the Black Box: A Survey of the Matching Function", *Journal of Economic Literature*, 39 (2), 390-432.

Research voor Beleid, 2001, "Basaal: het blijvend tekort en de arbeidsreserve", website text. [in Dutch]

Schmid, Günther and Bernhard Glazier, 2002, *The Dynamics of Full Employment, Social Integration Through Transitional Labour Markets*, Cheltenham: Edward Elgar.

Statistics Netherlands (CBS), 2000, "Beroepsbevolkings- en werkloosheidscijfers: CAAS133", Voorburg: CBS [in Dutch].

Taylor, Mark 2002, "Labour Market Transitions in the context of Social Exclusion", A Report for the European Commission, DG Employment and Social Affairs.

Taylor, Philip and Peter Urwin, 1999 "Recent Trends in the Labour Force Participation of Older People in the UK", *Geneva Papers on Risk and Insurance*, 24 (4).

Valk, Johan van der, 2004, "Het onbenut arbeidsaanbod en hun arbeidsverleden", *Sociaal-economische trends*, Voorburg: CBS. [in Dutch]

Weidum, J. and F.S. Linder, 2002, "Arbeidspositie en opleidingsnievau van personen met een uitkering, 1998", *Sociaal-economische maandstatistiek*, December 2002, 82-95, Voorburg: CBS [in Dutch].

Wiel, Henry van der (1998), "Intr-industry Wage Differentials in The Netherlands", CPB-Report 98-4, at: *http://www.cpb.nl/nl/cpbreport/1998_4/s2_4.pdf*

Wilson, Sven E., 2002, "Work and Accommodation of Chronic Illness: A Re-Examination of the Health-Labour Supply Relationship, *Applied Economics*, 33, p. 1139-1156.

In: Economics of Unemployment
Editor: Mary I. Marshalle, pp. 51-62

ISBN: 1-60021-138-0

*Chapter 3*

# SOCIAL CAPITAL AND CULTURE: A CONCEPTUAL EXAMINATION OF YOUTH (UN) EMPLOYMENT IN CHINESE IMMIGRANT CONTEXT

*Miu Chung Yan and Ching Man Lam*

Dept of Social Work, The Chinese University of Hong Kong

Hong Kong SAR

## ABSTRACT

Youth unemployment has almost become a natural phenomenon in most industrial countries due to global economic restructuring. To resolve the problem of youth unemployment, numerous youth training and employment programs have been developed in many industrial countries. The main purpose of these programs has been largely to enhance the youths' human capital by improving their job skills. However, the effectiveness of these programs is uncertain, particularly their ability to link unemployed youth to the labour market, the entry into which is largely dependent on social capital (*i.e.* who one knows) rather than human capital. Drawing on empirical studies, this article will conceptually examine how the collective tradition within Chinese culture may prove a rich source of social capital for young people hoping to mount a successful job search. This article will also offer some practical and research recommendations for the social work profession in rethinking the roles of culture and social capitals in resolving youth unemployment issues in a Chinese context.

**Keywords:** Youth employment, Chinese culture, social capital

# INTRODUCTION

Youth[1] unemployment has almost become a natural phenomenon in most industrial countries due to global economic restructuring. To resolve the problem of youth unemployment, numerous youth training and employment programs have been developed in many industrial countries. The main purpose of these programs has been largely to enhance the youths' human capital by improving their job skills. However, the effectiveness of these programs is uncertain, particularly their ability to link unemployed youth to the labour market, the entry into which is largely depended on social capital (i.e. who one knows), rather than human capital.

Drawing on empirical studies from Canada, this article will conceptually examine how the collective tradition within Chinese culture may prove a rich source of social capital for young people hoping to mount a successful job search. The paper is contextualized in the Canadian context, within which the largest immigrant group is Chinese. As immigrants, Chinese youth may face additional barriers, compared to youth at large, when it comes to dealing with employment issues. This paper explores ways in which Chinese culture enhances and/or limits the use of social capital by unemployed youths when dealing with their unemployment issues. This article will also offer some practical and research recommendations for the social work profession in rethinking the roles of culture and social capitals in resolving youth unemployment issues in a Chinese context.

# YOUTH UNEMPLOYMENT: ISSUES AND CAUSES

Youth unemployment is not a local phenomenon. According to United Nations statistics[2], almost 60 million young people are unemployed worldwide. The statistics project that, in the next twenty years, over one hundred million additional jobs will be needed to meet youth employment demands. In many developed countries, including the United States, Canada, and many Western European countries, youth unemployment is at a constantly high level. Although numerous attempts have been made to investigate the causes and personal and social impacts of youth unemployment, the issue of youth unemployment continues to be overshadowed by adult unemployment problems. In Canada, unemployed youth are so invisible that they are called "hidden deficits" (Canadian Youth Foundation, 1995a).

In one of the classic books on youth unemployment, Jackson (1985) observes that "it would clearly be wrong... to suggest that youth unemployment can be explained simply by reference to one factor" (p.74). Youth unemployment is a complex social problem caused by various factors. These can be grouped into two main categories – personal and structural – although it can be difficult to distinguish between the impacts caused by each of these.

Personal factors are largely about youths being lacking in many of the qualities required in the labour market. Lack of maturity, lack of mobility (compared to adults) when looking for jobs elsewhere, low levels of education (Lynch, 1989; Hammer, 1997; White & Smith, 1994), health and mental health issues (e.g., Banks & Ullah, 1988; Winefield, Tiggemann, Winefield, &

---

[1] The age range of youth varies. In this paper, youth mainly means people who are 16 to 24 years old.
[2] Details please refer to United Nations (ILO) - World Bank, Brainstorming meeting on youth employment, United Nations Secretariat, New York, 25 August 2000, Background paper no. 2: United Nations Mandates on Youth Employment.

Goldney, 1993) are personal factors that may lead to and/or prolong unemployment periods for youths. In the eyes of adults, the youth is being criticized for their strong preference of leisure, their inability to adjust to the work culture (Jackson, 1985), their lack of proper attitude and their unacceptable personal appearance (Casson, 1979; Hammer, 1997). Thanks to the support of their family, the youth can afford to be 'picky' when job hunting and are reluctant to be accept employment involving low-wages or manual labour (Hammer, 1997). Gaining employment is a sign that a youth has successful made the transition to adulthood (Hutson, 1989).

Hammer's study (1997) shows that structural factors are critical to causing youth unemployment. Structural factors are the social and economic conditions that create, reinforce, and sustain barriers to young people gaining stable employment. Evans et al. (2000) and Marquardt (1998) point out that youth nowadays are living in a post-traditional society (Giddens, 1994) in which they can no longer expect a traditional smooth transition from school to work . The gap between the type of education youth receive and the knowledge that the workplace requires is a major cause of youth unemployment; rapid technological change has left formal education behind (White & Smith, 1994). As Marquardt (1998) notes, youth enter the job market "at their own risk", particularly those youth who are the least qualified school leavers (Gang, 2002). This technological impact is particularly severe for young people from the working class families, as they generally have less exposure to technology due to social deprivation.

Youth unemployment is affected by the structure of the adult workforce. In many western countries, baby bloomers have been major factors in contributing to youth unemployment, particularly in the 1980's (Blanchflower & Freeman, 2000a). In addition, aggregate economic conditions have caused critical fluctuations in it's the economy's ability to absorb young workers (Blanchflower & Freeman, 2000b), making youth unemployment a prolonged problem. Moreover, internal and external competition among countries in the global economic arena also puts youth at a disadvantage (White & Smith, 1994). With massive cuts to manufacturing in most developed countries, many low-wage entry-level jobs are disappearing as well. Youth can no longer obtain their first employment in the factories or industrial plants, or get a junior position that requires only minimal knowledge and skills.

Meanwhile, although research is not conclusive, pay structure may also be a cause of high youth unemployment. In a global economy where wages are racing down, it is argued that young people are "pricing themselves out of work" by asking for too high wages. This is particularly true in countries with strong union systems (Casson, 1979; M. White & Smith, 1994), or in countries where the wage level for youth is comparable to welfare benefit levels (White & Smith, 1994). Finally, long-term consequences of previous unemployment may result in ongoing youth unemployment. The concept of *hysteresis* (the lagging of an effect behind its cause) suggests that youth who are unable to enter the job market during periods of high unemployment may become unemployable over the long term due to a lack of training and the possession of outdated skills. Lynch's study (1989) indicates that there is strong negative correlation between the length of non-employment and probability of being re-employed. Hammer (1997) also indicates that the main problem for young people is how to obtain initial entry to the labour market – once they have managed to enter the labour market, the persistence of most youth has led them to stable employment in the end.

## CONVENTIONAL SOLUTIONS TO YOUTH UNEMPLOYMENT: WESTERN EXPERIENCE

To resolve a complex social problem, such as youth unemployment, society not only needs to deploy resources but also to develop a comprehensive set of social programs to tackle the various causes of the problem. In many developed countries, there are programs responding to the issue of youth unemployment, but most of these programs aim to enhance and generate human capitals. As Becker (1964) suggests, human capital is a form of assets generated by investments in education, training and medical care. To Becker, on-the-job-training and education are the most important forms of investment to improve one's human capital and lead to success in the labour market. In fact, most countries have adopted this concept as a guiding principle in formulating social programs to resolve youth (un)employment issues.

We can summarize at least three parallel social programs. The first is job creation. There are many ways for governments to create jobs, including using public funds to directly create temporary jobs. The government of Canada, for instance, fully subsidizes the widely-known youth training program FUTURES, which has served more than 20,000 unemployed young people in Ontario every year since 1984. Since 1997, the FUTURES program had been restructured due to funding constraints. A new training program, Job Connect, was created to provide financial support for employers to increase the number of training positions available to young people [3]. This kind of job creation program has been widely adopted in other countries, such as the Employment Assistance Programs (EPA) in Hong Kong and the Community Development Employment Projects (CDEP) in Australia. In an indirect way, helping young people to set up their own businesses creates jobs. A national focus group study in Canada indicates that youths believe that self-employment is a reasonable alternative to traditional employment (Canadian Youth Foundation, 1995b). Self-employment programs require not only financial support from both government and the private sector, but also training and mentorship.

At the personal level, the likelihood of youth gaining employment is determined by human capital variables, such as whether or not the individual has had sufficient training. With technological changes and increased global competition, the demand for highly qualified workers is increasing, and learning and upgrading have become on-going individual and collective endeavours. The solution, therefore, is to improve the quality and diversity of education and training programs. Education is an important means of increasing human capital by raising young people's learning capability and skill levels (Evans, Behrens, & Kaluza, 2000; White & Smith, 1994). Some countries have tried to integrate education, training and job market demands into the education system. In Canada, for example, co-operative education programs at the post-secondary level have grown rapidly. As Marquardt (1998) observes, cooperative education gives students a real sense of work life, and allows them to learn through direct experience. Very often, it may lead to a real job after graduation with the training employers.

For a variety of reasons, many youth have difficulty fitting into the formal education system. Youth dropping out of school has been a major cause of youth unemployment (Lynch, 1989). Therefore, various types of vocational training programs have been put in place to better-equip early school-leavers. Short-term on-the-job-training programs are useful, but limited in terms of transferability of skills and knowledge. Much can be learned from the experience in Germany,

---

[3] Details please refer to the program web-site at http://www.edu.gov.on.ca/eng/training/cepp/cepp.html.

where their apprenticeship program has proven a successful response to youth employment problems (White & Smith, 1994). The advantage of apprenticeship programs is that youth enter the labour force as interns of an apprenticeship program, and are able to earn formal qualifications, such as a certificate or diploma that can help them advance in fields that relate to their newly-gained skills and experiences.

Another measure is to provide counselling services to unemployed youth. In White and Smith's (1994) observation, intensive counselling programs help to reduce youth unemployment, as youth unemployment is in part caused by personal problems faced by the youth. Employment training that goes beyond job hunting and job matching to include personal counselling elements in the program is indeed essential. In our counselling experiences, we have observed that people seeking counselling for seemingly well-defined career issues may voluntarily raise other issues and turn out to have multiple problems. To incorporate personal counselling into employment programs may alleviate psychological tension and help youth to develop a more positive vision of their future. This integration of personal counselling with career has begun to be recognized by theorists such as Herr (1993, 1997). In Canada, the Ontario Job Connect program includes, as a major element, an employment planning program to help young people to understand their own interests, potentials and skills, and to assist them in developing both short-term employment goals and long-term career goals.

In brief, to resolve youth unemployment problems, many social programs have been developed. The majority of these programs focus on upgrading the human capital of youth. The assumption is that with greater human capital, youth will stand a greater chance of success in the job market. However, as Grannovetter (1974) has long pointed out, it is not who they are that matters when young people try to access the job market – instead, it is always who they know that determines their chances of success in the turbulent job market.

## BUILDING SOCIAL CAPITAL: AN ALTERNATIVE SOLUTION TO YOUTH UNEMPLOYMENT

The concept of social capital refers to those resources, based on social networks, that can contribute positively to one's success; it is a constantly expanding and contestable concept (Field, 2003), which may lose any distinct meaning (Portes, 1998). In general, there are two major discourses related to the idea of social capital. The first involves understanding social solidarity, integration and civil society. Putnam is perhaps its most prominent proponent, and his book, Bowling Alone (Putnam, 2000), is the foundation for many other studies on the revitalization of civil society (e.g., Edwards & Foley, 1998; Etzioni, 2001; Wilson, 2001). It is argued that, to revitalize civil society, we need to build trust and reciprocity among people by encouraging social participation in community organizations.

Economic sociologists generate the second major discourse. Coleman (1988; 1990), the most influential theorist on social capital, suggests that social capital, perhaps as much as physical capital and human capital, is critical to people's ability to achieve goals within the market. According to Coleman (1988, 1990), the concept of social capital relates to how social relationships of authority, of trust and of norms embedded in a child or young person through their family and their connections to community organizations affects his/her development of human capital.

Based on Coleman, Lin (2001) considers social capital, in its most basic form, to be a resource accessed by individuals through social ties to achieve purposive functions such as social mobility. Recently, social capital has become a key conceptual tools for understanding the educational, economic and political performance of immigrants and ethnic minorities (e.g., Aizelwood & Pendakur, 2004; Portes, 1995b; M. J. White & Glick, 2000; Zhou & Bankston, 1994), and labour market activities (e.g., Erickson, 2001; Fernandez & Castilla, 2001; Marsden, 2001). In terms of immigration study, Portes defines (1995a) social capital as "the capacity of individuals to command scarce resources by virtue of their membership in networks or broader social structures" (p.12). As Sander et al. (Sanders, Nee, & Sernau, 2000) observe, ties to ethnic groups contribute to the employment of immigrants, particularly in the metropolitan labour market. For many immigrant youths who have limited personal networks, extended networks accessed through family, peers, and ties to their ethnic community, represent social capital. In Putnam term (2000), it is their bonding social capital that reinforces specific reciprocity by mobilizing internal solidarity within groups. Although research results are not conclusive, some scholars attribute positive school performance among immigrant youth to their access to social capital at home, which emphasizes the norms of hard work and familial expectations of high educational achievement (e.g., Bankston, 2004; Kao, 2004; Noguera, 2004).

Although immigrant youths are strong in bonding capital, they are weak in bridging capital, a distinction drawn by Putnam (2000). Drawing on Coleman and Putnam, Burt (2001) argues that there are always gaps between different networks in society, as a result of people's strong ties to their own network. He calls these gaps as structural holes. Bridging social capital helps to fill these holes by linking social groups to external assets that connect to other networks. In terms of youth (un)employment, we can safely assume that youth, particularly immigrant youth, may lack of access to the social resources available to members of the larger society, and that they are connected to only a handful of networks that may or may not intersect. This is particularly true if social capital is not distributed evenly within the society.

Within a capitalist society, the distribution of social capital is uneven and is determined by one's access to cultural and economic capitals (Bourdieu, 1990). Also, the social position of the individual and their family may have great impact on their access to greater social resources, such as access to higher level jobs, information about job availability and, more important, the trust of those doing the hiring. Studies (Monitor, 2004; Yee, et al., 2003) indicate that immigrant status limits the ability of families to assist youth in job searches by providing bridging capital. Compared to youth in the larger community, immigrant youth faces additional structural barriers. The uprooting process of migration forces immigrant families to relinquish their pre-established networks and social capital, and re-establishing in a new country takes time. Lowered socio-economic status and such barriers as language, recognition of foreign credentials and education, access to information, culture shock and subtle racial discrimination (George, 2002; Isajiw, 1999) further handicap immigrants in their job searches (Shields & Rahi, 2002; Yee, et al., 2003). For immigrants, unemployment may run in families and continue over generations (Payne, 1987), as the unemployed family's lack of social contacts limits their ability to expand bridging social capital.

# SOCIAL CAPITAL AND CHINESE CULTURE:
# RESOURCES AND LIMITATIONS

Social capital is a useful metaphor for understanding the ways in which young people access the labour market. Social capital is embedded in the family, and mobilization of social capital by one's family to help youth is common practice in Chinese culture. Chinese culture is basically a familial culture with strong collectivistic characteristics (Bond, 1991; Hsu, 1972) and familial cohesion (Lam, 2003). A study investigating how Vietnamese Chinese youth cope with unemployment, indicates that Vietnamese Chinese immigrant families help their youth find jobs by mobilizing family resources (Yan, 2000). The majority of employed Chinese youth had secured their job through family connections, such as neighbours, relatives, sibling's boy- or girl friends or colleagues. Scholars conducting studies in mainland China (Yang, 1994), Taiwan (Monthly, 1990), Hong Kong (Wong & Salaff, 1998) and among overseas Chinese (Lam, 2005; Yan, 2000) reached similar conclusions, namely that networks of *guanxi* (relationships) are important in Chinese families and form the basis of a structure that facilitates job searching, recruitment and training (Coleman, 1988; Inglis & Stromback, 1986), and increased access to employment opportunities. The use of social relationships among Chinese has become a cultural art form that requires nurturing and planning (Yang, 1994). The strong bonding social capital within Chinese culture, if properly used, can definitely be a useful resource that facilitates young people's job searches.

No one with firsthand experience of Chinese society could fail to note that Chinese people are extremely sensitive to *guanxi,* and make deliberate efforts to establish *guanxi.* Social relationship among Chinese are a differential mode of association (Fei, 1983) which extends from the closest network – family – outward. As an old Chinese proverb said, "within the four seas [the whole world] people are all brothers." Colleagues, classmates, church members, playmates, etc. can all be included in this web and effectively turned into family members. Once this relationship is established, its benefits can be shared by other family members (Yan, 1998). However, the relationship must be reciprocal, and this reciprocity can be observed in delicate and unspecified ways. This extended network of relationships serve to expand social capital and bridging social capital. Day by day, being active network builders, Chinese cultivate connections and construct functional social networks to meet both employment and other emerging needs.

Paradoxically, Chinese social capital (social relationships) is both a resource and a constraint for youths. As mentioned earlier, Chinese have strong bonding social capital and the inclusion of a stranger into the family network requires certainly level of consensus among family members. Therefore, it is a censored and cautious process. One essential feature of social capital building is mutual trust (Coleman, 1988). A close network tends to discourage the building of trust relationships with strangers. In an immigrant situation, the social capital to which Chinese family may have access is largely limited to the ethnic community. According to Granovetter (1973), this kind of bonding social capital is strongly tied to the ethnic community, and is less effective for and beneficial to job searches in terms of dissemination of information and development of social contacts. Limiting actions to one's network may cause network closure (Coleman, 1988). As Portes (1995a) observes, however rich in bonding social capital a family might be, if it is closely tied to the immigrant community it may limit the opportunities of immigrant youth for upward mobility and expanded bridging social capital.

## IMPLICATIONS

This paper addresses the shortcomings in the existing youth employment programs, which focus on upgrading youths' human capital in terms of job skills. The effectiveness of these programs is uncertain particularly their ability to link unemployed youth to the labour market. Incorporating the idea of social capital enhances social workers' and employment service practitioners' awareness of the importance of network building. Employment services should go beyond the skills training and human capital enhancement level in order to help youths and their families access the pool of social resources available in the larger society, and to help families establish or strengthen relationships with others. In other words, service should be directed to fill the structural holes within our society.

Studies (Coleman, 1988) suggest that family is the main source of social capital for youths. Compared to youth in the larger community, immigrant youth face additional structural barriers when looking for jobs. As reported in the recent Statistics Canada report on immigrants in Canadian urban centres (Statistics Canada, 2004), immigrants tend to have lower employment rates and higher unemployment rates than Canadian-born individuals. Familial influence may be an added disadvantage to immigrant youths as the unemployed family may lack the necessary social contacts to secure jobs for their youths. This lack of bridging social capital may result in generational unemployment cycles of poverty. From the societal point of view, the price is high. The immigration policies of many countries, including Canada and Australia, have successfully attracted a large number of highly qualified immigrants (Wong & Salaff, 1998). Ensuring the proper utilization of immigrant talents and realizing the benefits of their experience would help not only the immigrants themselves, but also their next generation. In order to support immigrants and unemployed youths, agencies should play an advocacy role. Easily accessible job information for newcomers, mutual support programs, and bridging immigrants to the mainstream society in order to expand their social capital are among the many proactive ways to provide future-oriented employment services to immigrant youths.

The existing operation of employment programs and employment counselling reflects the Western model (Daniels, 1997) with strong emphasis on developing human capital and bridging social capital. As mentioned earlier, Chinese people define themselves through a web of interpersonal relationships (Bond, 1986; 1991; Lam, 2005) and with bonding social capital. However, bonding social capital can be either a resource or a constraint. Strong bonding social capital combined with a lack of bridging social capital may limit the access immigrant youth to the external resources necessary for upward social mobility. On the other hand, sole emphasis on bridging social capital without regard to bonding social capital does not fit the reality of Chinese culture. As employment counsellors, we need to understand clients' behaviour in terms of their own cultural environment and value system, and to develop culturally sensitive employment services that fit the environment, worldview and reality of our clients. Therefore, creating a balance between bonding and bridging social capital should be the direction our employment program take for immigrant youths.

As the result of changing immigration policies, many Anglophone countries Canada, Australia and New Zealand, have recruited large numbers of Chinese immigrants since the 1980s. These immigrants have gradually established their own communities, with steadily increasing numbers of one-and-a-half[4] and second-generation community members. However, as Portes (1994) notes, the growth and adaptation of the new generation has received very little attention in conventional immigration study. Some recent studies suggest that, with their better English skills (Kilbride, Anisef, Baichman-Anisef, & Khattar, 2004) and greater integration into mainstream society (Anisef, Sweet, & Frempong, 2003), the second generation may be better positioned to enter the job market (Maani, 1994). The findings, however, are not conclusive. Compared to studies on first generation immigrants, relatively few studies have been done on the job seeking experiences of the new generations. Further studies are needed, considering the increasing number of new-generation job seekers in the Chinese immigrant community.

In this global society, the world is becoming smaller and smaller. Recently, many Chinese Canadian youth have moved back to Hong Kong, Taiwan and Mainland China to look for jobs upon their graduation. There are many possible reasons to account for their behaviour; racism, strong familial ties, and uneven distribution of social capital are all possible reasons. It is likely that youths and their families are making use of both well-established bonding and bridging social capital resources in their homeland and emerging networks in their host countries. This practice is, in reality, a means of expanding social capital and is a possible solution to youth employment. Employment services thus should not be cultural- or geographically-limited in this global era. Unfortunately, this new phenomenon has not yet drawn much attention in the field of youth employment, and is an area worthy of further research.

## CONCLUSION

Youth employment is a chronic social problem. This problem is even more critical among immigrant youths who, due to their families having been uprooted and various forms of racism, face more challenges in accessing the labour market than do other youth. In this paper, we demonstrated that, for Chinese immigrants, the cultural emphasis on extended social relationships might provide resources for younger members seeking jobs. On the other hand, strong ties to their own ethnic (or familial) community may restrict their access to greater social resources and other, broader, networks. Adopting social capital frameworks in social work practices serving Chinese immigrant youth with issues of (un)employment helps us to expand our horizon, to creatively utilize our clients' existing resource, and to develop bridges to enable youths to reach out to greater social networks.

## REFERENCES

Aizelwood, A., & Pendakur, R. (2004). *Ethnicity and Social Capital in Canada*. Vancouver, BC: Research on Immigration and Integration in the Metropolis.

Anisef, P., Sweet, R., & Frempong, G. (2003). *Labour Market Outcomes of Immigrant and Racial Minority University Graduates in Canada*. Toronto, ON: Joint Centre of Excellence for Research on Immigration and Settlement -- Toronto.

---

[4] One-and-a-half generation is generally defined as those first-generation immigrants who came to the host country when they were very young and have gone through most of their education in the host country.

Banks, M. H., & Ullah, P. (1988). *Youth Unemployment in the 1980s: Its Psychological Effects*. London, UK: Croom Helm.

Bankston, C. L. I. (2004). Social capital, cultural values, immigration, and academic achievement: The host country context and contradictory consequences. *Sociology of Education, 77*(April), 176-179.

Becker, G. S. (1964). *Human Capital: A Theoretical and Empirical Analysis with Special Reference to Education*. New York, NY: National Bureau of Economic Research.

Blanchflower, D. G., & Freeman, R. B. (2000a). The declining economic status of young workers in OECD countries. In D. G. Blanchflower & R. B. Freeman (Eds.), *Youth Employment and Joblessness in Advanced Countries* (pp. 19-55). Chicago, IL: University of Chicago Press.

Blanchflower, D. G., & Freeman, R. B. (2000b). Introduction. In D. G. Blanchflower & R. B. Freeman (Eds.), *Youth Employment and Joblessness in Advanced Countries* (pp. 1-16). Chicago, IL: University of Chicago Press.

Bond, M. H. (1986). *The psychology of the Chinese people*. Hong Kong: Oxford Universtiy Press.

Bond, M. H. (1991). *Beyond the Chinese Face*. Hong Kong: Oxford University Press.

Bourdieu, P. (1990). *The Logic of Practice* (R. Nice, Trans.). Stanford, CA: Stanford University Press.

Burt, R. S. (2001). Structural holes versus network closure as social capital. In N. Lin, K. Cook & R. S. Burt (Eds.), *Social Capital: Theory and Research* (pp. 31-56). Hawthone, NY: Aldine De Gruyter.

Canadian Youth Foundation. (1995a). *Youth Unemployment: Canada's Hidden Deficit*. Ottawa: Canadian Youth Foundation.

Canadian Youth Foundation. (1995b). *Youth Unemployment: Canada's Rite of Passage*. Ottawa: Canadian Youth Foundation.

Casson, M. (1979). *Youth Unemployment*. London, UK: MacMillan.

Coleman, J. S. (1988). Social capital in the creation of human capital. *American Journal of Sociology, 96*(Supplement), S95-S120.

Coleman, J. S. (1990). *Foundations of Social Theory*. Cambridge, MA: Harvard University Press.

Daniels, S. (1997). Employee assistant programmes. *Work Study, 46* (7), 251-253.

Edwards, B., & Foley, M. W. (1998). Civil society and social capital beyond Putnam. *The American Behavioral Scientist, 42*(1), 124-139.

Erickson, B. H. (2001). Good networks and good jobs: The value of social capital to employers and employees. In N. Lin, K. Cook & R. S. Burt (Eds.), *Social Capital: Theory and Research* (pp. 127-158). Hawthorne, NY: Aldine de Gruyter.

Etzioni, A. (2001). Is bowling together sociological lite? *Contemporary Sociology, 30*(3), 223-224.

Evans, K., Behrens, M., & Kaluza, J. (2000). *Learning and Work in the Risk Society: Lessons for the Labour Markets of Europe from East Germany*. London, UK: MacMillan.

Fei, X. T. (1983). *Xiangtu Zhongguo (Folk China) (Reprint of 1947 version)*. Hong Kong: Phoenix Publishing Co.

Fernandez, R. M., & Castilla, E. J. (2001). How much is that network worth? Social capital in employee referral network. In N. Lin, K. Cook & R. S. Burt (Eds.), *Social Capital: Theory and Research* (pp. 85-104). Hawthorne, NY: Aldine de Gruyter.

Field, J. (2003). *Social Capital*. London and New York: Routledge.

Gang, M. (2002). Changing labour markets and early career outcomes: Labour market entry in Europe over the past decade. *Work, Employment and Society, 16*(1), 67-90.

Giddens, A. (1994). *Beyond Left and Right: the Future of Radical Politics*. Cambridge, UK: Polity Press.

Granovetter, M. S. (1974). *Getting a Job: A Study of Contacts and Careers*. Cambridge, MA: Harvard University Press.

Hammer, T. (1997). History dependence in youth unemployment. *European Sociological Review, 13*(1), 17-33.

Hsu, F. L. K. (1972). *Americans and Chinese: Reflections on Two Cultures and Their People*. New York, NY: American Museum of Science Books.

Hutson, S. a. J., R. (1989). *Taking the Strain: Families, unemployment and the Transition to Adulthood*. Milton Keynes, U.K: Open University Press.

Jackson, M. P. (1985). *Youth Unemployment*. Kent, UK: Croom Helm.

Kao, G. (2004). Social capital and its relevance to minority and immigrant population. *Sociology of Education, 77*(April), 172-175.

Kilbride, K. M., Anisef, P., Baichman-Anisef, E., & Khattar, R. (2004). *Between Two Worlds: The Experiences and Concerns of Immigrant Youth*. Retrieved 10/5/2004, 2004, from *http://ceris.metropolis.net/Virtual%20Library/other/kilbride2.html*

Lam, C. M. (2003). Covert parental control: Parent-adolescent interaction and adolescent development in a Chinese context. *International Journal of Adolescent Medicine and Health 15* (1), 63-77.

Lam, C. M. (2005, in press). Chinese construction of adolescent development outcome: Themes discerned in a qualitative study. *Child and Adolescent Social Work Journal 22,* (2)

Lin, N. (2001). *Social Capital: A Theory of Social Structure and Action*. Cambridge and New York: Cambridge University Press.

Maani, S. A. (1994). Are young first and second generation immigrants at a disadvantage in the Australian labor market? *International Migration Review, 28*(4, Special Issue: The New Second Generation), 865-882.

Marquardt, R. (1998). *Enter at Your Own Risk: Canadian Youth and the Labour Market*. Toronto, CAN: Between the Lines.

Marsden, P. V. (2001). Interpersonal ties, social capital, and employer and staff practices. In N. Lin, K. Cook & R. S. Burt (Eds.), *Social Capital: Theory and Research* (pp. 105-126). Hawthorne, NY: Aldine de Gruyter.

Monthly, E. B. (1990). *The Secular Game of Chinese -- Human Sentiments (Ren Qing) and Social Sensitivity (Shi Gu)*. Taiwan: Zhang Lao Shi Publishing Co.

Noguera, P. A. (2004). Social capital and education of immigrant students: Categories and generalizations. *Sociology of Education, 77*(April), 180-183.

Portes, A. (1994). Introduction: Immigration and Its Aftermath. *Journal of International Migration and Integration, xxviii*(4), 632-639.

Portes, A. (1995a). Economic sociology and the sociology of immigration: A conceptual overview. In *The Economic Sociology of Immigration: Essays on Networks, Ethnicity, and Entrepreneurship* (pp. 1-41). New York, NY: Russell Sage Foundation.

Portes, A. (1995b). *The Economic Sociology of Immigration: Essays on Networks, Ethnicity, and Entrepreneurship*. New York, NY: Russell Sage Foundation.

Portes, A. (1998). Social capital: Its origin and applications in modern sociology. *Annual Review of Sociology, 24*, 1-24.

Putnam, R. (2000). *Bowling Alone: The Collapse and Revival of American Community*. New York, NY: A Touchstone Book.

Sanders, J., Nee, V., & Sernau, S. (2000). "Asian immigrant's reliance on social ties in a multiethnic labor market. *Social Forces, 81*(1), 281-314.

Statistics Canada. (2004). *Study: Immigrants in Canada's Urban Centres*. Ottawa, ON: Statistics Canada.

White, M., & Smith, D. J. (1994). The causes of persistently high unemployment. In A. C. Peterssen & J. T. Mortimer (Eds.), *Youth Unemployment and Society* (pp. 95-144). Cambridge, UK: Cambridge University Press.

White, M. J., & Glick, J. E. (2000). Generation Status, social capital and the routes out of high school. *Sociological Forum, 15*(4), 671-691.

Wilson, J. (2001). Dr. Putnam's Social Lubricant. *Contemporary Sociology, 30*(3), 225-227.

Winefield, A. H., Tiggemann, M., Winefield, H. R., & Goldney, R. D. (1993). *Growing Up With Unemployment: A Longitudinal Study of Its Psychological Impact*. London, UK: Routledge.

Wong, S. L., & Salaff, J. W. (1998). Network capital: emigration from Hong Kong. *British Journal of Sociology, 49*(3), 358-374.

Yan, M. C. (1998). A social functioning discourse in Chinese context: implication of developing social work in mainland China. *International Social Work, 41*(2), 181-194.

Yan, M. C. (2000). Coping with unemployment: Some lessons to learn from a group of unemployed ethnic minority youths. *Canadian Social Work Review, 17*(1), 87-109.

Yang, M. M. H. (1994). *Gifts, Favors & Banquets: The Art of Social Relationships in China*. Ithaca & London: Cornell University Press.

Zhou, M., & Bankston, C. L. (1994). Social capital and the adaptation of the second generation: The case of Vietnamese Youth in New Orleans. *International Migration Review, 28*(4), 821-845.

In: Economics of Unemployment
Editor: Mary I. Marshalle, pp. 63-79
ISBN: 1-60021-138-0
© 2006 Nova Science Publishers, Inc.

*Chapter 4*

# LEAVING UNEMPLOYMENT WITH THE STATE ASSISTANCE: EVIDENCE FROM RUSSIA

*Ludmila Nivorozhkina*
Rostov State Economic University
*Eugene Nivorozhkin and Anton Nivorozhkin*
Göteborg University

## ABSTRACT

This chapter analyzes factors affecting the duration of registered unemployment and the likelihood of individual transition from unemployment. The results help to evaluate the process of population adaptation to the government system of employment assistance in Russia and the effects of this system on the relative chances of employment for various socio-demographic groups. The empirical modeling is done using transition data analysis. The results indicate significant effect of rules and regulations on incentives to find a job for unemployed individuals inquiring for the state assistance.

**JEL Classification:** J23, J24, J41, J64.
**Keywords:** unemployment duration; transition economy; urban Russia.

## 1. INTRODUCTION

One of the major characteristics of the economic transformation of the Russian Federation from a centralized system to a market-based one was the abandoning of the fundamental principle of the socialist system - full employment. In fact, the low efficiency of the old economic system was to a large extent explained by the excessive labor resources employed by the state-owned companies.

Economic restructuring and the rise of open unemployment tend to be closely linked in transition economies. Aghion and Blanchard (1994) provide theoretical grounds for analyzing unemployment in transition countries. Their model predicts that in the process of transition, the employment in the state sector is going to decline but it would be offset by the creation of new jobs in the private sector. However, some workers would remain unemployed. These individuals, especially long-term unemployed, are going to suffer the most during the economic transition.

Russian economic liberalization led to a massive reallocation of labor accompanied by expansion of the private sector. New spheres of economic activities and new forms of employment had emerged. At the same time, economic decline throughout most of the 1990s led to a rise in unemployment. However, the behavior of Russian labor market appeared to be rather different from transition economies of Central and Eastern Europe (CEE) which started reforms earlier. Employment reaction to the output shocks was substantially weaker in Russia relative to countries of CEE, open unemployment was increasing only slowly, the share of long-term unemployed remained relatively low while the intensity of labor turnover was very high.

In this chapter we investigate the mechanism of the population adaptation to the government system of employment assistance. We investigate the effects of this system on the duration of unemployment and the chances of obtaining employment for different socio-demographic groups. We investigate the impact of legislative rules for obtaining unemployment status and the effects of size and duration of unemployment benefits on the probability of individual employment.

## Background

The formation of the labor market in Russia was accompanied by the creation of an institutional infrastructure to deal with unemployment. Public Employment Offices (PEOs) were created by government decree in 1991 to assist in maintaining employment and render financial support to the registered unemployed. However, not all unemployed individuals chose to register with the PEOs, so government statistics report two indicators of unemployment, i.e. registered unemployment based on information provided by the PEOs and general unemployment based on surveys undertaken according to International Labour Organization (ILO) methodology.

The gap between general unemployment and registered unemployment is an interesting feature of the Russian labor market. Between 1992 and 2000, registered unemployment as a percentage of the total labor force averaged just 23% of general unemployment rate.

Definition of unemployment provided by the PEOs of Russia was criticized (e.g. Grogan and van den Berg (1999) and Kapelushnikov (2002)) since the population of registered unemployed reflects poorly the population of unemployed defined according to the ILO guidelines. However, large differences in levels of unemployment are not truly unique for Russia. Such difference persists in a large number of countries (ILO (1995), Hussmanns (1994, 2001)). In our opinion the major limitation of the information supplied by the PEOs is in the fact that the composition of the population of registered unemployed may depend on the rules and conditions governing eligibility to register as unemployed with the PEOs. Thus our results should be viewed as being conditional on current legislation. Yet, datasets supplied by the PEOs has three major virtues. First of all, it is inexpensive and easy to acquire, since it is a side product of functioning of the PEOs. Second, the data on benefit claimants can be collected quickly and frequently. Finally, information from the registries of the PEOs tends to be the only source of systematic information on unemployment in urban Russian.

From the policy standpoint, studying registered unemployment is important because the financial resources allocated by the Russian government (and international organizations) aim at dealing with registered unemployed. As these resources are limited and cannot be used for other social purposes, the studies of the incentives of the registered unemployed and the effects and efficiency of labor market programs conducted within the PEOs are justified.

## Literature Review

Various issues related to determinants of unemployment duration in transition economies have been previously considered in the economic literature. Ham, Svejnar, and Terrell (1998) investigate the differences in unemployment in the Czech Republic and Slovakia. The authors attempt to answer the question regarding the optimal balance between free market incentives with minimum involvement of the state and an adequate system of social protection for unemployed individuals. The issues raised are investigated by looking at the effect of the socio-demographic characteristics of the unemployed and the level of financial support rendered to them on the probability of transiting from unemployment. The paper adopts the transition data analysis and illustrates the advantage of this method for this type of study. Transition data analysis is also employed in a series of papers by Lubyova and van Ours (1999a, 1999b, 1998, 1997) in analyzing the effects of changes in the rules and regulations governing unemployment in Slovak Republic. The paper by Earl and Pauna (1996) deals with issues of unemployment in Romania. Micklewright and Nagy (2002, 1998, 1996) use non-parametric methods to study unemployment duration in Hungary.

Research on the determinants of unemployment duration in Russia is limited. Foley (1997) analyzes the early period of economic transition in Russia. He uses information provided by the Russian Longitudinal Monitoring Survey (RLMS) for the years 1994-1996 to investigate determinants of unemployment duration. The author defines unemployed as those who are temporary unemployed and searching for job. This definition of unemployment was criticized by Grogan and van den Berg (2001) as being too narrow. The authors suggest that in order to capture the complexity of unemployment problem in Russia one needs to use a broader definition of unemployment. Using the RLMS information for the years 1996-1998 Grogan and van den Berg (2001) extend the definition suggested by Foley (1997). They distinguish four distinct groups of unemployed, those who are temporary unemployed and searching for job, discouraged unemployed who do not actively search for job, individuals on unpaid leave and workers with wage arrears. Both studies contribute to the discussion of duration of unemployment in Russia. Yet, they lack careful analysis of the impact of registration with the PEOs in Russia. In fact small number of observations for unemployed registered with the PEOs in RLMS dataset does allow author to conduct separate analysis for these individuals.

Research of unemployment duration of registered unemployed in Russia is limited to a regional or city databases. To our knowledge the only existing statistical study of unemployment duration of individuals registered with the PEOs in Russia is Denisova (2002). The author investigates the determinants of the duration of registration with the PEOs in Voronezh province during the period of 1996-2000.

The distinct feature of a large number of the above mentioned papers is the usage of econometric methodology of transition data analysis. It allows one to estimate the probability of transition from unemployment as a function of various factors (e.g. time spent in unemployment, socio-demographic characteristics of unemployed, amount of unemployment benefits and changes in legislation).

In this chapter we use the transition data methodology to investigate the mechanism of population adaptation to the government system of employment assistance in urban Russia. We study the effects of the employment assistance system on the duration of unemployment and the chances of obtaining employment for different socio-demographic groups.

## 2. URBAN UNEMPLOYMENT IN RUSSIA AND LABOR MARKET OF ROSTOV-ON-DON

The objects of our investigation are the unemployed individuals registered at the PEOs of Rostov-on-Don during the period from January 1997 to December 1998. With its population of over one million, Rostov-on-Don is among top ten biggest cities in Russia and the biggest city in southern Russia.

In the context of our analysis, we suggest that the process of freeing and redistributing labor resources on the registered segment of the labor market of big industrial cities in Russia is determined by similar factors. The primary reasons for that are certain similarities in the economic environment of these cities as well as in factors driving the formation of local labor markets.

First, the all-Russian law governing registered unemployment specifies the rules for registering at the PEOs, the requirements for receiving unemployment status as well as the terms, duration and the size of unemployment benefits. In other words it creates a uniform legal framework for local labor markets and provides particular incentives for those searching for a job (see Appendix).

Second, big cities in Russia tend to have a diversified economy consisting of high-tech military-oriented enterprises, machine building, food, and light industries as well as many others. Moreover, they have a well-developed educational infrastructure and a system of on-the-job and off-the-job training adapted to the needs of the enterprises in the city and region. Another distinctive feature of these cities is the presence of a large industrial enterprise that historically accounted for a disproportionately large share of employment. In this context we argue that the processes of structural changes in the economies of the big cities would likely influence the behavior of the unemployed in a similar manner.

Third, a characteristic feature of the Russian labor market is low labor migration. The reasons for that are relatively high unemployment and the preserved system of population registration (*propiska*).

In our opinion, the similarity of the social and economic problems of the big cites and uniform legislative framework makes it possible to draw rather general conclusions from a study of one city.

The economic environment of Rostov-on-Don was characterized by a revival during the period under our investigation. Since 1997 the economy started to grow, leading to an increase in employment. The growth of business activity in the city decreased the number of registered unemployed. By the middle of 1999, the unemployment level in the city decreased to 1.2%.

During the period we study, the labor market of Rostov-on-Don was characterized by the presence of both officially registered vacancies and vacancies outside the PEOs. The structure of these vacancies differed significantly from the unemployment structure. For example, in 1998 there was one vacancy per every blue-collar worker unemployed, but only one vacancy per every two white-collar worker unemployed.

According to a survey of the unemployed undertaken by the Rostov's PEOs in October 1999, an unemployed individual received on average 13.3 offers of vacancies from the PEO, 3.5 of these vacancies were rejected by the unemployed while in the rest of the cases, the employer rejected the individual candidate.[1] In November 1999, the PEOs also undertook a survey of non-registered unemployed. The corresponding results were the following: 6 received vacancies on average, 3.7 positions were rejected by the unemployed and for the other positions, the applicant was rejected by the employer. The results indicate that the officially registered unemployed face higher probability of being rejected by a potential employer.

The dominating reasons for rejecting an offered vacancy are insufficient pay (60/70% in two surveys respectively), unsatisfactory working conditions (30/40%), and the commuting distance to work (20/25%). Only 13.2% indicated that the reason for rejecting a vacancy was the requirement to change a profession.

When it comes to the reasons why employers rejected potential candidates, the results of two surveys differed significantly (see Table 1). Of the registered unemployed, 71% indicated that the vacancy was already taken at the moment of their inquiry with the employer. This reason was only mentioned by 35.1% of the non-registered unemployed. Of the registered unemployed, 53.3% mentioned their insufficient qualifications and experience as a reason for rejection. The corresponding number for the non-registered unemployed is only 36.6%. Age discrimination was sited as a reason by 37% of the registered and 43.9% of the non-registered unemployed.

Table 1 shows that independently of time spent in unemployment the main reason for employer's rejection of an applicant is the unavailability of a vacancy. One explanation is that vacancy database is not updated in a timely fashion, so the job openings are already filled at the time of inquiry.

### Table 1. The Employer's Reasons for Rejecting the Registered Unemployed (% of respondents providing each reason)

| Rejection reason | Unemployment duration interval | | |
|---|---|---|---|
| | Up to 3 months | 3.1 to 7 months | 7.1 to 12 months |
| Unsatisfactory qualifications | 45.7 | 47.6 | 49.2 |
| Unsuitable profession | 15.0 | 23.6 | 20.0 |
| Unavailability of vacancy | 62.5 | 61.6 | 63.7 |
| Unsuitable age | 22.2 | 37.6 | 45.9 |
| Presence of children | 2.4 | 3.6 | 5.9 |
| Health conditions | 3.4 | 3.6 | 4.8 |
| Unsuitable gender | 3.4 | 8.8 | 8.2 |

---

1 The survey covered 932 unemployed individuals, which amounted to 22.4% of the officially registered unemployed at the time of the survey.

According to Table 1, an increase in unemployment duration leads to an increase in the number of cases when an employer rejects a candidate for reasons such as unsatisfactory qualifications or profession of the unemployed, unsuitable age of the unemployed, presence of young children or poor health. In other words, the process of vacancy fulfillment serves as a sorting device with "higher quality" workers leaving the unemployment pool earlier.

# 3. DATA AND METHODOLOGY

The data set we use is relatively rare for Russia. The PEOs were set up in 1991, but the computer database collection in most of the cities began only in 1996.[2] Our dataset includes complex information on all individuals inquiring to the PEOs for assistance in finding a job.

The dataset contains over 250 individual characteristics of unemployed. These characteristics include social-demographic information on a registered individual (e.g. age, gender, marital status, number of children), professional and qualification characteristics (e.g. working experience, education, profession and qualification), the reasons for entering unemployment ( e.g. voluntary leave, layoff). The database also contains some information related to the amounts and timing of unemployment benefits and extra transfers received by unemployed.

We form an inflow sample by selecting the individuals registering with the PEOs between January 1, 1997 and December 31, 1998. Individuals entering unemployment during the specified inflow period were followed until June 30, 1999. During the period under investigation, 72,010 individuals registered with the PEOs.

We measure the duration of unemployment in days from the start to the end of registration with the PEOs.

We distinguish the following reasons for termination of registration with the PEOs: Employment with the assistance of the PEOs; Termination of registration without finding employment at the PEOs (e.g. individuals finding a job without the PEOs assistance).

The unemployment period is incomplete (right-censored) if an unemployed individual was still registered with the PEOs at the end of our observation period. For analysis we selected variables reflecting socio-demographic and professional status of unemployed, variables describing the circumstances of entering unemployment and the size of unemployment benefits as well as other transfers. The definitions and sample statistics are reported in Table 2.

## Econometric Framework

In our empirical investigation we would like to model factors affecting the likelihood of individual transition from unemployment. The methods developed in the subject of transition data analysis appear to be the appropriate tools for our study. Transition data analysis deals with modeling time-to-event data, also known as duration data. The overviews of econometric aspects

---

[2] From 1992 to 1996, the electronic database contains data only for selected districts of Rostov-on-Don. The rest of the data is in paper form.

of transition data analysis can be found in van den Berg (2001), Tasiran (1996), Lancaster (1990) and Kiefer (1988).

**Table 2. Descriptive Statistics of Variables Used in the Analysis (in %)**

| Variables | Total Sample | Exit from the PEO with employment | Exit from the PEO without employment |
|---|---|---|---|
| Male | 32.80 | 35.21 | 31.61 |
| Age $\leq$ 20 | 10.33 | 11.11 | 10.03 |
| 20 < Age $\leq$ 30 | 26.54 | 29.06 | 23.24 |
| 30 < Age $\leq$ 40 | 24.91 | 24.99 | 25.24 |
| 40 < Age $\leq$ 50 | 27.36 | 25.66 | 29.37 |
| Age > 50 | 10.87 | 9.19 | 13.13 |
| University Education | 36.34 | 35.80 | 34.41 |
| Technical secondary education | 28.59 | 27.57 | 29.61 |
| General secondary education, | 18.90 | 19.62 | 19.71 |
| Only primary | 16.17 | 17.00 | 16.27 |
| Married | 53.42 | 53.32 | 54.83 |
| No profession | 11.61 | 13.04 | 10.45 |
| Blue-collar profession | 37.29 | 38.88 | 37.14 |
| White-collar profession | 51.10 | 48.08 | 52.40 |
| Minimum benefits recipient | 51.34 | 54.5 | 53.59 |
| Extra benefits recipient | 36.01 | 34.95 | 37.26 |
| From out of the labor force | 25.53 | 26.44 | 25.73 |
| Voluntary quit of last employment | 40.39 | 43.89 | 31.76 |
| Average duration of unemployment | 156.34 | 136.60 | 216.27 |

We consider a time domain for individuals, which can be partitioned into three mutually-exclusive states at each point in time – the status-quo state (continue to be unemployed), exit due to employment with the PEOs assistance and exit from the PEOs for other reasons (e.g. finding a job without the PEOs assistance).

A popular method allowing the estimation of the joint effect of factors affecting the risk of transition is a piece-wise constant exponential hazard model. The model captures individual chances of exiting unemployment at each time period condition on survival (remaining unemployed) until that period. The risk of transition from unemployment consists of two components – the time-varying baseline hazard component, $\lambda_0(t)$, and an individual specific component, $\varphi(x;\Theta)$. Formally,

$$\lambda(t|x;\Theta) = \lambda_0(t)\varphi(x;\Theta),\qquad(1)$$

where x is a vector of individual specific observable characteristics and $\Theta$ is a vector of parameters.

We choose a flexible way of specifying $\lambda_0(t)$ that allows for duration dependency by assuming that the baseline hazard is piece-wise constant (see Lancaster (1990)). This implies that time in unemployment can be divided into $k$ intervals:

$$\lambda_0(t) = \gamma_1 \qquad\qquad\qquad \text{if } 0 \leq t \leq c_1$$
$$\gamma_2 \qquad\qquad\qquad\quad \text{if } c_1 < t \leq c_2$$
$$\cdots \qquad\qquad\qquad\qquad \cdots$$
$$\gamma_k \qquad\qquad\qquad\quad\; \text{if } c_{k-1} < t < \infty$$

where $\gamma_k$ are parameters to be estimated, the $c_k$s are the points in time and $0 < c_1 < c_2 < ... < c_{K-1} < \infty$.

Assuming that $\gamma_k = \exp(\eta_k)$ and $\varphi(x;\Theta) = \exp(x'\Theta)$, the hazard function can be written as:

$$\lambda(t|x;\Theta) = \exp(d_k\eta_k)\varphi(x;\Theta) = \exp(d_k\eta_k + x'\Theta), \tag{2}$$

where $d_k$ equals one if $t$ falls within the interval $\left(c_{k-1},c_k\right]$ and equals zero otherwise. Assuming only time-invariant covariates in $x$, the integrated hazard is

$$\Lambda(t|x;\Theta) = \varphi(x;\Theta)\left[\sum_{l=0}^{k} b_l\gamma_l + (t - c_k)\gamma_{k+1}\right],$$

where $b_l = c_l - c_{l-1}, c_k < t \leq c_{k+1}$ и $k = 0,1,...,k-1$. The likelihood contribution of a given individual $i$ can now be written as

$$L_i^1(\Theta) = \lambda_i(t|x;\Theta)^{c_i} \exp[-\Lambda_i(t|x;\Theta)], \tag{3}$$

where $c_i$ is a binary variable equal to one if the observation is uncensored and equal to zero otherwise.

In our model we look at two types of competing risks of transition from the PEOs: exit due to employment with the PEOs assistance and exit from the PEOs for other reasons (e.g. finding a job without the PEOs assistance).

In a competing risks framework, the hazard rate from unemployment equals the sum of $J$ different hazard rates where $J$ denotes the number of different risks, or exit destinations. The observed duration can be written as

$$t = \min(t_1, t_2, ..., t_J),$$

and the individual contribution to the likelihood function is now

$$L_i^2(\Theta) = \prod_{j=1}^{J} \left\{ \lambda_i^j \left(t|x;\Theta\right)^{c_{ij}} \exp\left[- \Lambda_i^j \left(t|x;\Theta\right)\right]\right\},\tag{4}$$

where $c_{ij}$ is a binary variable that equals one if individual $I$ exits to state $j$ and it equals zero otherwise. Because of the assumption of independence among the risks, the estimation of the $J$ durations can be done separately and the contribution of observed exit to destination $m \neq j$ to the likelihood in (4) is the same as that of a censored observation in (3).

## 4. ESTIMATION RESULTS

We estimate a proportional hazard model with a flexible baseline hazard. The hazard rate is assumed to be constant within duration intervals but is allowed to differ among duration intervals. The piece-wise constant baseline hazard was specified by dividing the unemployment duration into 30-day intervals for the period of up to one year and the last interval include all individuals with unemployment duration exceeding one year.

We estimated competing risk model allowing exit to two destinations. The first destination is related to the risk of transition to employment with the assistance of the PEOs. The second destination considers the risk of transition from registration with the PEOs to other destinations. The results are reported in Table 3. The results of the competing risk model estimation (see Table 3) reveal significant differences in the exit rate to selected destinations. The risk of transition to employment with the assistance of the PEOs does not depend on the gender of the unemployed (see Model 1 in Table 3). In Model 2, the rate of exit from the PEOs for men is significantly greater than for women, which hints at the higher chances of men finding a job on their own.

To further investigate the gender effects we constructed two dummy variables capturing the risk of transition from unemployment for women. We control if women were married and if they had children. The results indicate that the risk of transition to employment with the assistance of the PEOs is lower for married women compared to other individuals and higher when women exit the PEOs for other reasons. The interaction variable for women with children is not significant in both models, but the presence of extra benefits for dependants, which may be more important for women, lowers the risk of transition to both destinations.

The results confirm that age is a significant determinant of the risk of transition to employment with the assistance of the PEOs. The reference group for the age variable is the group of unemployed over 50 years old. The risk of transition decreases with age in Model 1, while the results in Model 2 are insignificant.

Relative to unemployed with only primary education, individuals with general secondary education have the highest risk of transition to employment with the assistance of the PEOs. This can be explained by the fact that the absence of professional education (of any level) lowers the criteria for a suitable job offer for the latter group (see Appendix). The presence of university education or technical secondary education lowers the risk of transition relative to other groups in Model 2.

## Table 3. Results of the competing risk model

|  | Exit from the PEOs with employment (Model 1) | | Exit from the PEOs to other destinations (Model 2) | |
| --- | --- | --- | --- | --- |
|  | Parameter Estimate | Standard error | Parameter Estimate | Standard error |
| Constant | 6.6502*** | (0.0700) | 7.2812*** | (0.1384) |
| Male | -0.0005 | (0.0469) | 0.3028** | (0.1032) |
| Age $\leq$ 20 | 0.3089*** | (0.0483) | -0.0805 | (0.0972) |
| 20 < Age $\leq$ 30 | 0.3406*** | (0.0363) | -0.0464 | (0.0731) |
| 30 < Age $\leq$ 40 | 0.3000*** | (0.0362) | 0.0338 | (0.0730) |
| 40 < Age $\leq$ 50 | 0.1947*** | (0.0344) | -0.0472 | (0.0653) |
| University Education | -0.0202 | (0.4846) | -0.2925*** | (0.0617) |
| Technical secondary education | -0.0343 | (1.5109) | -0.1682** | (0.0579) |
| General secondary education | 0.0767** | (0.0289) | -0.0418 | (0.0603) |
| Married | 0.1514*** | (0.0357) | -0.1689** | (0.0784) |
| Married women | -0.1518*** | (0.0411) | 0.2460** | (0.0883) |
| Women with children | -0.0647 | (0.0410) | 0.0775 | (0.0921) |
| Blue-collar | -0.0988** | (0.0385) | 0.1567** | (0.0798) |
| White-collar | -0.1956*** | (0.0366) | 0.0378 | (0.0753) |
| Minimum benefits recipient. | 0.1314*** | (0.0205) | 0.6311*** | (0.0430) |
| Extra benefits recipient | -0.0793*** | (0.0232) | -0.1175** | (0.0489) |
| From out of the labor force | -0.0778** | (0.2939) | 0.0783 | (0.0569) |
| Voluntarily quit last job | 0.1828*** | (0.0192) | -0.0170 | (0.0407) |
| 0 <=duration<= 30 | 3.5429*** | (0.0398) | 0.6344*** | (0.1140) |
| 30 <duration<=60 | 2.1827*** | (0.0423) | 0.8488*** | (0.0764) |
| 60 <duration<=90 | 1.6470*** | (0.0433) | 0.5456*** | (0.0722) |
| 90 <duration<=120 | 1.3217*** | (0.4282) | 0.1549** | (0.0755) |
| 120 <duration<=150 | 1.1381*** | (0.0451) | 0.1086 | (0.0780) |
| 150 <duration<=180 | 0.9350*** | (0.0479) | -0.1015 | (0.0857) |
| 180 <duration<=210 | 0.8815*** | (0.0487) | -0.0850 | (0.0848) |
| 210 <duration<=240 | 0.7706*** | (0.0516) | -0.3637*** | (0.0984) |
| 240 <duration<=270 | 0.6619*** | (0.0527) | -0.4323*** | (0.0995) |
| 270 <duration<=300 | 0.6264*** | (0.0560) | -0.5248*** | (0.1118) |
| 300 <duration<=330 | 0.5380*** | (0.0584) | -0.6270*** | (0.1198) |
| 330 <duration<=365 | 0.2169*** | (0.0455) | 0.0044 | (0.0634) |
| duration> 365 | - |  | - |  |
| Log Likelihood | -19640.83 |  | -8147.35 |  |

Notes: *** indicates 1% significance, ** - 5% significance, and * - 10% significance.

Unemployed individuals without a profession (our reference group) are more likely to transit to employment with the assistance of the PEOs than individuals with a profession. One explanation for this fact could be that the rules for registering with the PEOs make it difficult for the former group of unemployed to discriminate among alternative vacancies. The results of

Model 2 show that higher labor demand for blue-collar workers results in their significantly higher chances to exit the PEOs without obtaining the job with its assistance.

The minimum size of unemployment benefits significantly increases the risk of transition from unemployment. Therefore, insufficient income support is likely to result in higher intensity of job search or lower reservation wage for the unemployed.

Individuals entering the PEOs out of the labor force have a lower risk of transiting to employment with the assistance of the PEOs (see Model 1) while the result in Model 2 is insignificant. The negative effect of coming from out of the labor force in Model 1 can be explained by the fact that a significant part of the individuals in this category are graduates with professional education which allows them to choose their employment according to their profession thus to stay unemployed longer. The complementary supply side explanation would be that potential employers are likely to prefer fulfilling vacancies with more experienced workers.

The risks for individuals who left their last job voluntarily differ between Model 1 and Model 2. For those who find employment with the assistance of the PEOs, the risk of transition is higher while Model 2 gives negative but insignificant result. This supports our hypothesis that the individuals who voluntary quit their employment anticipating their relative advantage in finding a job through the PEOs.

The rules of registering with the PEOs and receiving unemployment benefits highlight the possibility that the duration of registration with the PEOs could itself significantly affect the risk of transition from unemployment. The major factor encouraging an exit from unemployment tends to be the financial one – the amount of unemployment benefits is decreasing over time (see Appendix). Another reason encouraging a fast exit could be "the stigma" attached to being unemployed. Employers might prefer individuals with shorter unemployment duration, interpreting it as a signal of better quality of labor. On the other hand, some groups of the unemployed could be interested in retaining their unemployment status for a longer time.

To incorporate the above-mentioned factors into our model, we explicitly introduced variables accounting for the duration of unemployment. The duration dependence of the exit rate from unemployment in our model is captured by thirteen dummy variables, which corresponds to the unemployment duration intervals. The duration dependency coefficients indicate whether or not, conditional on the explanatory variables, the exit rate changes over the duration of unemployment. These changes may occur because of employers' behavior, workers' behavior or a combination of both. If employers prefer short-term unemployment to long-term unemployment then the exit rate to a job steadily declines over the duration of unemployment. If unemployed individuals are discouraged by remaining unemployed and decrease their job search intensity, the exit rate will also decline.

It may also be the case that the unemployment benefits rules influence the exit rate form the PEOs. Individuals may be inclined to leave the PEOs just before there is a drop in their benefits. In that case we can expect sharp increases in the exit rate prior to a decrease in the amount of the benefits. Therefore, the pattern of duration dependency may provide information about the effect of financial incentives, which change over the duration of unemployment.

The results in Model 1 indicate a decrease in the exit rate for longer duration periods. In Model 2, the exit rate from the PEO system increases in the second month and declines afterwards becoming insignificant after the fourth month of unemployment and decreasing again between the eighth and eleventh months.

**Table 4. Logit model for transition from the PEO within 10 days of registration**

| Explanatory Variables | Parameter Estimate | Standard Error | Risk Ratio |
|---|---|---|---|
| Intercept | 1.39*** | 0.05 | - |
| Male | 1.13*** | 0.02 | 1.14 |
| Age ≤ 20 | 0.85*** | 0.05 | 2.34 |
| 20 < Age ≤ 30 | 0.27*** | 0.04 | 1.32 |
| 30 < Age ≤ 40 | 0.36*** | 0.04 | 1.44 |
| 40 < Age ≤ 50 | 0.08** | 0.04 | 1.08 |
| University Education | -0.91*** | 0.04 | 0.40 |
| Technical secondary education | -0.82*** | 0.03 | 0.44 |
| General secondary education | -0.15*** | 0.02 | 0.86 |
| Married | 0.65*** | 0.03 | 0.92 |
| Number of children | -0.69*** | 0.02 | 0.50 |
| Blue-collar profession | -2.73*** | 0.03 | 0.07 |
| White-collar profession | -3.29*** | 0.04 | 0.04 |
| Voluntarily quit | 0.77*** | 0.03 | 2.17 |
| From out of the labor force | -1.62*** | 0.03 | 0.20 |
| -2 Log L=98042.01 | | | |

Note: *** indicates 1% significance, ** - 5% significance, and * - 10% significance

The pattern of duration dependency of the exit rate captured by Model 1 can be explained based on the personal observations of the authors of this article. The structure of vacancies available from the PEOs of Rostov-on-Don was quite homogeneous during the period under observation. Most of the vacancies available from the PEOs were not very attractive, often low-skilled jobs. In addition, a significant number of people registered with the PEOs do not have very high criteria for a suitable job. Therefore, the greatest exit rate is usually observed shortly after registration with the PEOs, which simply represents the process of fulfilling unattractive vacancies with individuals with lower criteria for a suitable job. The higher skilled unemployed individuals most likely have to stay with the PEOs longer to find a suitable job.

## An Extension of the Model: Accounting for Short Periods of Unemployment

As we already mentioned in introduction the general level of unemployment in Russia is greater than the level of registered unemployment. One reason contributing to the observed difference is that individuals who satisfy the criteria of being registered as unemployed but obtain a job during the first ten days of registration with the PEOs may not be included in the registered unemployment indicator.

In this section we use the logistic model to study the probability of leaving the PEOs within ten days. The dependant variable takes the value of one if an individual stayed with the PEOs for over ten days and zero otherwise. The regression results are in Table 4.

According to our results (see Table 4) men have higher chances of obtaining a job during the first ten days of unemployment than women. In fact, the group with unemployment duration of over ten days is dominated by women, which is confirmed by a high risk ratio.

Individuals younger than twenty have the highest probability of transiting to employment during the first ten days relative to other age groups. An increase in age tends to decrease the likelihood of finding a job within ten days. An increase in the level of education raises the chances of remaining in the PEOs for more than ten days. Unmarried individuals have lower probability of finding a job within ten days after registration with the PEOs. Having more children negatively affects the probability of leaving the PEOs within ten days. Individuals who were not in the labor force prior to entering the PEOs are less likely to leave it within ten days. Individuals with both blue - and white – collar professions have higher chances to remain unemployed for more than ten days relative to individuals with no profession. Individuals who voluntarily quit their jobs are more likely to exit the PEOs within ten days relative to other groups. It is worth mentioning that the odds ratio for this variable is very high indicating that this is one of the major determinants of fast transition from registered unemployment.

Overall the model indicates substantial heterogeneity between individuals who transit from the PEOs within ten days and those who remain unemployed longer. According to our model individuals who leave the registered unemployment within ten days tend to have relatively lower level of education and lower level of qualification. As a result these individuals face a wider array of suitable jobs from the PEOs vacancy bank and therefore fewer opportunities to discriminate among the jobs offered by the PEOs. Individuals with higher criteria of a suitable job are likely to face lower number of available vacancies. Therefore these individuals tend to remain registered unemployed longer.

# 5. CONCLUSION

The study of urban unemployment in Russia is a relatively new area of empirical research. We demonstrate the possibilities of empirical analysis using the data collected by the Public Employment Offices. We used the data from the largest city in the south of Russia – Rostov-on-Don.

We find that the rules and regulations governing registered unemployment and the size of unemployment benefits significantly affect the duration of unemployment and the likelihood of transition from unemployment. Our results indicate the likely existence of at least three distinct groups of unemployed with different motivations for registration with the PEOs. The first group consists of individuals who find a job within ten days of registration due to a higher demand for their labor or their low criteria of a suitable job. The second group includes individuals who claimed unemployment benefits and other forms of monetary support from the state and experience a transition within a year. The third group is long-term unemployed having few chances and/or incentives to find a job. These groups tend to differ in their socio-demographic and professional characteristics. The individuals with low suitable job criteria who are more likely to experience fast transition from unemployment tend to be young, entering the labor market from out of labor force and having little professional experience and skills. Our analysis reveals that unemployed women tend to be segregated within the PEOs. Other things equal, they have lower risk of transition to employment. A plausible explanation emerging from our study is that women may use their registration with the PEOs as a tool for maintaining social security benefits (both monetary and non-monetary) while continuing to work in the household. The size of unemployment benefits significantly affects the duration of unemployment. Individuals receiving the minimum benefits have higher chances of transition from registered unemployment.

The Public Employment Office is a relatively new institution in the Russian labor market. The rules of registration and receiving unemployment benefits as well as the economic environment significantly affect the behavior of registered unemployed. The need for broader institutional reforms of Russian labor market and social protection system calls for more research on the efficiency of existing institutions and their effects on the incentives of unemployed.

## ACKNOWLEDGEMENTS

The financial support from The Royal Swedish Academy of Sciences (Grant for Cooperation between Sweden and the Former Soviet Union) is gratefully acknowledged. The earlier version of this paper entitled "Modeling Labor Market Behavior of the Population of a Large Industrial City: Duration of Registered Unemployment" was written as part of the project funded by the Economic Education and Research Consortium Russia (EERC) - Grant №99-0821. The comments of anonymous referees are gratefully acknowledged. We are very thankful for the valuable advice of Martina Lubyova, Michael Sollogub, Ruben Gronau, Jan Svejnar, John Earle, and Klara Sabirianova. The usual disclaimer applies.

## REFERENCES

Aghion P., and O. J., Blanchard (1994), On the speed of transition in Central Europe, *NBER Macroeconomic annual* 1994, Cambridge and London: MIT Press, 283-320.

Chetvertina T. (1997), Polozhenie bezrabotnih I gosudarstvennaya politika na rinke truda, *Voprosi Ekonomiki*, v.2, 102-13.

Denisova I. (2002), Staying longer in unemployment registry in Russia: Lack of education, bad luck, or something else? CEFIR working paper.

Earle J. S. and C. Pauna (1996), Incidence and duration of unemployment in Romania, *European Economic Review, April,* v. 40, No. 3-5, 829-37.

Foley M. C. (1997), *Determinants of unemployment duration in Russia, Economic Growth Center Discussion* Paper No. 779, Yale University.

Goskomstat of Russia (2001a), *Russian statistical yearbook.*

Goskomstat of Russia (2001b), *Labor and employment in Russia, statistical Yearbook.*

Grogan L. and G. J. van den Berg (2001), The duration of unemployment in Russia, *Journal of Population Economics*, v. 14, No. 3, 549-68.

Grogan L. and G. J. van den Berg (1999), *The duration of unemployment in Russia*, Centre for Economic Policy Research Discussion Paper No. 2268, London.

Ham J. C., Svejnar, J., and K. Terrell (1998), Unemployment and the social safety net during transitions to a market economy: Evidence from the Czech and Slovak republics, *American Economic Review*, December, v. 88, No. 5, 1117-42.

Ham J. C., Svejnar, J., and K. Terrell (1999), Women's unemployment during transition: Evidence from Czech and Slovak micro-data, *Economics of Transition*, v. 7, No.1, 47-78.

Hussmanns R. (1994), International standards on the measurement of economic activity, employment, unemployment and underemployment, pp. 77-105, In *Labour statistics for a market economy: Challenges and solutions in the transition countries of Central and Eastern Europe and the former Soviet Union*, Budapest: Central European University Press in association with the International Labour Office.

Hussmanns R. (2001), *Unemployment statistics: Important issues*, Working Paper, Training Workshop on Labour Market Information and Analysis, Harare, Zimbabwe.

ILO (1995), World labour report, *International Labour Organization*, v.8, Geneva and Washington.

Kapelushnikov R. (2002), Obschaja i registrirujamaja bezrabotitsa: v chem. Prichiny razriva? Working paper, WP3/2002/03, State University Higher School of Economics, Moscow.

Kiefer N. (1988), Economic duration data and hazard function, *Journal of Economic Literature*, Vol. 26, No.2, 646-679.

Lancaster T. (1990) *The Econometric Analysis of Transition Data*, Cambridge University Press, Cambridge.

Lubyova M. and J. C. van Ours (1999a), Effects of active labor market programs on the transition rate from unemployment into regular jobs in the Slovak Republic, *Journal of Comparative Economics*, March, v. 27, No. 1, 90-112.

Lubyova M. and J.C. van Ours (1999b), Unemployment durations of job losers in a labour market in transition, *Economics of Transition*, v. 7, No. 3, 665-86.

Lubyova M. and J. C. van Ours (1998), Work incentives and other effects of the transition to social assistance: Evidence from the Slovak Republic, *Empirical Economics,* v. 23, No. 1-2, 121-53.

Lubyova M. and J. C. van Ours (1997), Unemployment dynamics and the restructuring of the Slovak unemployment benefit system, *European Economic Review*, April, v. 41, No. 3-5, 925-34.

Micklewright J. and G. Nagi (2002), The informational value of job-search data and the dynamics of search behavior: Evidence from Hungary, *Acta Oeconomica*, v. 52, No. 4, 399-419.

Micklewright J. and G. Nagi (1998), Unemployment assistance in Hungary, *Empirical Economics*, v. 23, No. 1-2, 155-75.

Micklewright J. and G. Nagi (1996), Labor Market Policy and the Unemployed in Hungary, *European Economic Review*, v. 40, No. 3-5, 819-28.

Russian Statistical Yearbook (2000) *Goskomstat Rossii.*

Rostov Statistical Office (2000) *Rostov-na-Donu v Tshifrah.*

Tasiran A. C. (1996), Fertility dynamics: Spacing and timing of births in Sweden and the United States, *Contributions to Economic Analysis*, v. 229, Amsterdam; New York and Tokyo: Elsevier Science, North-Holland.

Van den Berg G.J. (2001), Duration models: specification, identification, and multiple durations, *Handbooks in Economics*, vol. 2. Amsterdam; London and New York: Elsevier Science, North-Holland, 3381-460.

# APPENDIX: THE RULES AND REGULATIONS GOVERNING REGISTRATION WITH THE PEO AND RECEIVING UNEMPLOYMENT STATUS[3]

According to the Law of the Russian Federation "On Employment of the Population in the Russian Federation," an unemployed individual is the one who simultaneously satisfies the following criteria: (1) belongs to the labor force; (2) presently without a job and income; (3) actively searching for a job; (4) willing to take on a job; (5) inquiring to the PEOs for assistance in finding a job.

Unemployed individuals are registered with the PEO according to the procedure set by law and in the following sequence: (1) primary registration of unemployed individuals;[4] (2) registration of unemployed individuals seeking a suitable job; (3) registration of individuals with unemployed status.

The PEO is obliged to offer an individual two suitable jobs during the first ten days following the inquiry, subject to job availability. Suitable job offers can include both an offer of permanent employment as well as an offer of temporary employment. The individuals entering the labor market for the first time may receive two offers of professional training.

Unemployment status is awarded to an individual who is: (1) in the labor force; (2) does not have an income; (3) registered with the PEOs to find a suitable job; (4) unemployed following ten days after initial inquiry at the PEOs.

The nature of the suitable jobs offered by the PEO to an individual with unemployment status depends on the circumstances of becoming unemployed. The first criterion of a suitable job is the profession that can be demanded by an unemployed. Laid-off job seekers and those who voluntarily quit their last job should be offered a job in the same profession as their last employment irrespective of the profession stated on their education diploma. Graduates of universities and technical secondary schools should be offered a job corresponding to their diplomas. Graduates of secondary schools are typically sent to professional training. Individuals who did not work for an extended period of time (over 3 years) can be offered any job or sent for retraining. The second criterion is wage. The PEOs should offer an unemployed individual a wage that is not less that the one received at the last job. For those who had a high wage at their last job, a suitable wage offer should be at least the average wage for a given administrative territory (oblast, in our case). Suitable offers to individuals who did not work prior to registering at the PEOs are limited only by the minimum wage in the country. The third criterion is that the job should be located within the administrative border of the city and commuting to the job should not involve more than two transfers on public transportation.

## The Rules Governing the Amount and Duration of Unemployment Benefits

The amount of unemployment benefits is related to the wage unemployed individual received at the last employment. Unemployment benefits are awarded to individuals with unemployment status who left their last employment due to any reason. These benefits are

---

[3] The described rules are valid for the time period of our investigation.
[4] At this stage, the PEO offers "consulting services" to inquiring individuals without asking for identification.

calculated as a percent of the average wage during the preceding three months if the individual had a paid full-time job during at least 26 consecutive weeks (or the equivalent) in the 12 months prior to registering with the PEOs. Individuals entering the job market for the first time and those who do not fulfill the conditions above obtain unemployment benefits equal to the minimum wage. In the presence of dependants, unemployment benefits are increased by 50% of the minimum wage for each dependant, but the total amount cannot exceed 1.5 of the minimum wage. Individuals whose work experience is sufficiently long may receive benefits for twenty-four months cumulatively during thirty-six calendar months. In the absence of suitable jobs at the PEOs close to retirement age may be offered the early retirement, but not prior to two years before the retirement age set by the law.

Unemployed starts receiving benefit payments after obtaining unemployment status. Typically, duration of the benefit payments should not exceed twelve cumulative months during eighteen calendar months. Individuals who do not receive a suitable job during eighteen months can renew their application and obtain minimum unemployment benefits.

The amount of unemployment benefits during the first three month is equal to 75% of the wage received at the last employment, 60% during the next four months, and later on – 45%. In all cases, the benefits must not be below the minimum wage and not higher than the average wage in an administrative territory.

The PEOs were financed from the transfers of employers, employees, and if necessary contributions from the Federal and local budgets.

In: Economics of Unemployment
Editor: Mary I. Marshalle, pp. 81-107

ISBN: 1-60021-138-0
© 2006 Nova Science Publishers, Inc.

*Chapter 5*

# COUNTER-INTUITIVE EFFECTS OF UNEMPLOYMENT BENEFITS: BALANCED-BUDGET INCIDENCE

*Ko Sumino*[a]

Otaru University of Commerce, 3-5-21, Midori, Otaru, Hokkaido 047-8501, Japan

*Salim Rashid*[b]

University of Illinois at Urbana-Champaign, 309 Commerce West Building, 1206 South Sixth Street, Champaign, IL 61820, USA

## ABSTRACT

In the present paper, we analyze the effects of unemployment benefits on unemployment. Following Harris and Todaro (Harris, J. R. and Todaro, M. P., *American Economic Review* 60, 126-142, 1970) and Harberger (Harberger, A. C., *Journal of Political Economy* 70, 215-240, 1962), we consider an economy which consists of two sectors – the corporate sector and the non-corporate sector – and two factors of production, labor and capital, while the corporate wage is indexed to the general price level. Since the corporate wage is assumed not to be market clearing, there is unemployment in equilibrium. The unemployment is thus exclusively a feature of the corporate sector.

We elaborate Miyagiwa's (Miyagiwa, K., *Journal of Public Economics* 37, 103-112, 1988) work in several respects. First, we deal with unemployment benefits indexed to the competitive wage rate. Second, we explicitly consider the government budget constraint in which case unemployment benefits are financed by the corporate income tax. Third, we focus on an issue of balanced-budget incidence analysis.

We derive a counter-intuitive result that unemployment benefits, instead of increasing unemployment, may well decrease unemployment, while we establish Walras' law and the zeroth order homogeneity of the system and also ensure the local stability of the system. This counter-intuitive result regarding the effects of unemployment benefits involves inelasticity in either of the following situations: wages with respect to the 'manufacturing' price or production with respect to factor prices. For instance, as shown by Rao (reprinted in

a Corresponding author. Tel.: +81-134-27-5316; fax: +81-134-27-5213; *E-mail address:* sumino@res.otaru-uc.ac.jp (Ko Sumino)
b Tel.: 217-333-7388; fax: 217-244-6678; *E-mail address:* s-rashid@uiuc.edu (Salim Rashid)

Agarwala, A. N. and Singh, S. P., *The economics of underdevelopment*, New York, Oxford University Press, 1958), Keynesian ideas would not work in India because of the high agricultural component of GNP and the inelasticity of the developing countries (LDCs) supply. These points should take us back to the original debate on the applicability of Keynesian ideas. Our considerations are thus of some intuitive appeal from the real world point of view. This contributes to an older debate on unemployment policy.

**Keywords:** Unemployment benefits; balanced-budget incidence
**JEL Classification:** H22; H53; J64

# 1. INTRODUCTION

A long-lasting issue, that of unemployment, has been a central concern of policy makers and political leaders in both the developed and the developing countries (LDCs). This issue has been discussed in the literatures on international trade and also public finance. Several literatures extended the work of the Harris and Todaro [14] (Henceforth H-T) to various versions.[1] Khan [21] worked with the generalized H-T model and embraced a variety of labor market specifications.[2] Behuria [4], and Imam and Whalley [18] extended the two sector model of tax incidence and considered the issue of unemployment. Following Harberger [13], such these literatures presented a model of incidence analysis by using a general equilibrium framework. Gupta [12], and Gilbert and Wahl [11] studied the effects of alternative subsidy policies on unemployment and welfare of the workers.

Miyagiwa [24] provided a model with sector-specific unemployment as an endogenous variable. In particular, he concluded unemployment benefits cause an increase in unemployment, while considering the incidence of unemployment benefits and its influence upon the rate of unemployment. He also argued a wage indexation function, instead of H-T's fixed wages. Following a based model of Bennasy [5], we can interpret his model from the perspective of a macroeconomic wage indexation mechanism, while recognizing wage rigidities in the result of minimum wage laws or trade unionism. While implicitly assuming Walras' law and local stability, he also analyzed the effects of unemployment benefits on unemployment, in which the government finances unemployment benefits by using a corporate income tax. In this sense the government budget is automatically balanced.

Indeed, much of the literature on public finance has focused on standard devices in a differential incidence analysis. While we argue that nothing fails to have the reliance on these assumptions, nothing is necessarily wrong with the generality of his results. However, his work has several important limitations in the general equilibrium theory of tax incidence. In particular, he did not deal with the issue of balanced-budget incidence analysis. When we examine the effects of unemployment by using the balanced-budget incidence analysis rather than the differential incidence one, we must argue his simplifying assumptions, since it is not obvious

---

[1] Bhagwati and Srinivasan [6] and Basu [3] considered a problem of sector-specific unemployment resulting from the rigidity of the sector-specific real wage. Corden and Findlay [10] and Neary [26] extended models to permit capital mobility between the two sectors in response to any differential in the return on capital.

[2] Stiglitz [27] focused on labor-turnover considerations and Calvo [7] emphasized a trade union operating under one of two behavioral hypotheses.

whether both Walras' law and local stability in this system always hold and whether taxes are associated with offsetting increases in unemployment benefits.

A important feature of the results given in Miyagiwa [24] is that unemployment benefits may well increase unemployment. The main question he addressed is whether the employment effects of unemployment benefits are positive. Such an analysis was offered by Card and Krueger [8] in the course of formalizing theoretical and econometric methods.[3] However, as McCool [23] and Holmlund and Lundborg [15] pointed out, it is not obvious whether the government budget constraint is always balanced, unless we describe a way to finance unemployment benefits in the government.

In this paper we provide a new model and reexamine the effects of unemployment benefits on unemployment by elaborating the work of Miyagiwa. We show some fundamental properties, those are Walras' law, zeroth order homogeneity and local stability of the system. Moreover, we extend the Miyagiwa model in several respects. First, while providing a wage indexation function, we incorporate unemployment benefits indexed to the competitive wage rate. Second, we consider the government budget constraint in which case unemployment benefits are financed by the corporate income tax. Third, we introduce balanced-budget incidence analysis. These properties allow us to define an equilibrium containing possible unemployment and to explore the implications of sector-specific unemployment.

Our main results are that when we analyze the effects of unemployment benefits on unemployment, we derive a counter-intuitive result that unemployment benefits, instead of increasing unemployment, may well decrease unemployment. This counter-intuitive result regarding the effects of unemployment benefits involves inelasticity in either of the following situations: wages with respect to the 'manufacturing' price or production with respect to factor prices. For instance, as shown by Rao ( reprinted in Agarwala and Singh [1] ), Keynesian ideas would not work in India because of the high agricultural component of GNP and the inelasticity of LDC supply. These points should take us back to the original debate on the applicability of Keynesian ideas. Our considerations are thus of some intuitive appeal from the real world point of view. Hopefully, this contributes to an older debate on unemployment policy.

The rest of this paper is organized as follows. In section 2, we present a basic model and discuss some fundamental properties. In section 3, we consider the local stability of simultaneous equilibrium system. In section 4, we examine the effects of unemployment benefits on unemployment. In section 5, we present some concluding remarks. In the appendices, we offer mathematical details and prove both Walras' law and local stability hold in our model.

## 2. THE MODEL

We consider an economy which consists of two sectors, i.e. the corporate sector and the non-corporate sector. Alternatively, following H-T model, we have a division between the manufacturing and the agricultural sectors. There are two factors of production, labor and capital, the total endowments of which are given. The corporate wage is indexed to the general price level, while the non-corporate wage is competitively determined. Since the corporate wage is assumed not to be market clearing, there is unemployment in equilibrium. The unemployment

---

[3] See Compaijen and Vijlbrien [9], and Zavodny [29] for useful surveys.

is thus exclusively a feature of the corporate sector. Following Benassy [5], we explain the sector-specific unemployment in the presence of wage rigidities. An indexation rule is assumed to be the result of minimum wage laws or trade unionism. We also retain all other assumptions of the standard two-sector model: perfect competition, linearly homogeneous, concave production functions, and perfect intersectoral mobility of capital and labor. We use balanced budget incidence analysis based on Holmlund and Lundborg [15], and Miyagiwa [24].[4] We explicitly consider a government budget constraint in which case unemployment benefits are financed by the corporate income tax. We focus on an issue of balanced-budget incidence analysis, while we establish Walras' law and the zeroth order homogeneity of the system and also ensure the local stability of the system.

## 2.1. Fundamental Properties - Walras' Law and Zeroth Order Homogeneity of the System

In this subsection, we present a basic model and discuss some fundamental properties. Following Miyagiwa [24] we consider unemployment benefits indexed to the competitive wage and explore the sector-specific unemployment in the analysis of corporate income tax incidence.

First, let $w_1$ be the corporate wage that is assumed to be indexed to commodity prices, we define the indexation rule:

$$w_1 = F(p_1, p_2),$$

where $p_i$ is the commodity price of the $i$-sector.[5] Note that we can explain the above indexation rule due to the minimum wage legislation or behavior of labor unions. For example, labor unions in practice often pay attention to some set of commodity prices when they decide upon the amount of the corporate wage.

Second, we begin by describing unemployment benefits. We assume that unemployment benefits is indexed to the competitive wage given by $\alpha w_2$, where $w_2$ is the competitive wage of the second sector and $\alpha$ is a fixed constant and $0 < \alpha < 1$. Note that the rate of unemployment benefits is always less than that of the competitive wage and that workers might face a possibility of being unemployed when they want to work in the corporate sector, otherwise they might not have incentives to work.

Third, we define a new migration equilibrating condition. On one hand, both employed and unemployed workers in the corporate sector maximize expected corporate earnings. Note that the expected corporate earnings are given by the corporate wage times the probability of being employed plus unemployed benefits times the probability of being unemployed. On the other hand, the non-corporate sector is run along a competitive line, and provide with full employment. Let $\lambda \equiv (L_1 + L_U)/L_1 \, (>1)$ be the reciprocal number of the rate of corporate sector's

---

[4]We relate our analysis to Harberger [13] and Jones [20] whose works are on the incidence of a sector-specific tax on capital.

[5] In the absence of money illusion the function $F$ is homogeneous of degree one.

employment, where $L_1$ and $L_U$ denote the amounts of labor employed and unemployed in the corporate sector, respectively. Alternatively, $1/\lambda$ denotes the probability of finding a job in the corporate sector. We attaine a migration equilibrating condition by equalizing the expected corporate earnings between the two sectors:

$$w_1/\lambda + (1 - 1/\lambda)\alpha w_2 = w_2,$$

where $w_i$ is the $i$-th sector wage. Taking these properties into account, we can obtain the system in which variables are subject to zeroth order homogeneity of demands and supplies with respect to prices.

Forth, we explicitly pay attention to the government budget constraint. We further assume that unemployment benefits are financed by the corporate income tax. Note that in the usual general equilibrium model without unemployment, we assume that taking Walras' law into account, the government budget constraint is balanced, if both households and producers balance their budget constraints. We regard differential incidence analysis as the incidence of taxes that are isolated from offsetting expenditures. This is a useful device, but it is not clear whether Walras' law holds in the presence of unemployment. When taking the government budget constraint into account, we deal with taxes that are associated with offsetting increases in unemployment benefits, we turn to balanced budget incidence analysis. Following Harberger [13], Homma [16], and Atkinson and Stiglitz [2], we retain other assumptions that taste patterns in the economy are homothetic and neglect any differences between the taste patterns of households, producers and the government. Let $T(= 1 + t)$ be the sum of corporate income tax rate and unity. Let $K_1$ and $r$ be the amount of capital in the corporate sector and the net return to capital, respectively. The government budget constraint takes the form such that $\alpha w_2 L_U = trK_1$. Taking the definitions of $\lambda$ and $T$ into account, we rewrite the government budget constraint:

$$(\lambda - 1)\alpha w_1 c_{L1} x_1 = (T - 1)r c_{K1} x_1,$$

where $x_i$ denotes the $i$-th sector product, and $c_{Lj}$ and $c_{Kj}$ are the marginal labor and capital cost functions which are homogeneous of degree one, respectively. Note that the concept of vertical equity typically has caught hold in the public finance literature,[6] and the government adopts the redistribution policies between capitalists and unemployed workers in the corporate sector. This allows us to interpret the above government budget constraint. Thus, we ensure that Walras' law holds in the presence of the sector-specific unemployment. We are now ready to state the following useful lemma.

*Lemma 1. Suppose that the zeroth order homogeneity of the system holds and that the government budget is balanced. Then Walras' law holds in the presence of the sector-specific unemployment.*

---

[6] For a detailed review of this, see Atkinson and Stiglitz [2].

We prove in Appendix A that Lemma 1 holds. The rest of the analysis proceeds under this lemma of Walras' law.

## 2.2. The Basic Model

In this subsection, we summarize the model. As stated in the previous subsection, Walras' law holds if the government budget is balanced. Taking into account this condition and the zeroth order homogeneity of prices, this allow us that one of the prices is not independent. We choose the price of the second sector as our numeraire, i.e. $p_2 = 1$.

We now fully describe the formal structure containing possible unemployment in the general equilibrium model:

$$w_1 = F(p_1), \tag{1}$$

$$w_1 / \lambda + (1 - 1/\lambda)\alpha w_2 = w_2, \tag{2}$$

$$c_1(w_1, rT) = p_1, \tag{3}$$

$$c_2(w_2, r) = 1, \tag{4}$$

$$\lambda c_{L1} x_1 + c_{L2} x_2 = L_0, \tag{5}$$

$$c_{K1} x_1 + c_{K2} x_2 = K_0, \tag{6}$$

$$x_1 / x_2 = H(p_1), \tag{7}$$

$$(\lambda - 1)\alpha w_2 c_{L1} x_1 = (T - 1) r c_{K1} x_1, \tag{8}$$

where $L_0$ and $K_0$ denote total quantity of available labor and capital, respectively. Equation (1) shows that the first sector wage is indexed to $p_1$, since $p_2$ sets to be one. We define a wage setting function: $w_1 = F(p_1)$, where the wage of the first sector $w_1$ is indexed to $p_1$ and this is linear homogeneous. By equation (1), we assume that $w_1$ is determined in terms of the exogenously given indexation function. From equation (2), the expected wages of the first sector is equal to the competitive wages of the second sector, while $w2$ is competitively determined. In a competitive equilibrium, these unit costs must reflect market prices. Under competitive conditions, the input cost per unit of each commodity is equal to its market price, thus, equations (3) and (4) imply that product prices are equal to average costs in the long run. Equation (5) implies that the total of the employed workers and the unemployed workers is equal to $L_0$. Equation (6) is the capital market clearing condition, while assuming that perfect mobility and full employment of capital. Preferences in the economy are homothetic and neglect any differences between the taste patterns of households, producers and the government, in which case the ratio of quantities demanded depends upon only relative prices. We assume that the relative demand function $H(p_1)$ is homogeneous of degree zero with respect to prices.[7] Taking into account the zeroth order homogeneity of prices and Walras' law, equation (7) is the commodity market equilibrium statement. Equation (8) represents that the government expenditures equalize its revenues under the government budget constraint. Therefore, we can describe the general equilibrium system of our economy which consists of eight equations (1) – (8), with eight endogenous variables, $r, w_1, w_2, p_1, T, \lambda, x_1$ and $x_2$, while $\alpha$ is the only policy parameter. Note that $T$ is the endogenous variable in our model, while focusing on balanced-budget incidence analysis.

# 3. LOCAL STABILITY OF THE GENERAL EQUILIBRIUM SYSTEM

We assume that the equilibrium exists in our model. As long as the government budget constraint is balanced, Walras' law and zeroth order homogeneity of the system hold.[8] We focus on balanced-budget incidence analysis and examine the incidence of unemployment benefits on unemployment. In order to avoid unnecessary complications, we modify the equations with a familiar theoretical apparatus, the so-called *hat-calculus*. Following Harberger [13] and Jones [20], this is customary procedure of tax incidence. Since we can not ensure to hold the local stability condition in the presence of unemployment, we must prove that the equilibrium system is locally stable in our model.[9]

## 3.1. Adjustment Process of Simultaneous Equations

In this subsection, we focus on our attention on the change of the unemployment rate caused by the change of the unemployment benefit and that of the government budget. To begin with, we examine the effect of changes of unemployment benefits in (2) and that of government in (8); later, we analyze the effect on the unemployment rate caused by both above changes. We consider the above two equations of change as the system, rather than each of the equations independently. Differentiating equations (2) and (8) yields:[10]

$$\hat{w}_1 - \hat{w}_2 - (1-\alpha)\lambda / \eta \hat{\lambda} = -(\lambda - 1)\alpha / \eta \hat{\alpha} ,  \tag{2'}$$

$$(\lambda /(\lambda - 1))\hat{\lambda} - S_1 \hat{w}_1 + \hat{w}_2 - (1 - S_1)\hat{r} - (T /(T - 1) - S_1)\hat{T} = -\hat{\alpha} ,  \tag{8'}$$

---

[7] We retain assumptions of Homma [16], and Atkinson and Stiglitz [2].

[8] See Iritani and Sumino [19] for the existence discussion of the solution to the system.

[9] See Atkinson and Stigliz [2], and Neary [25].

[10] In Appendix B, we show the detailed derivation.

where $\eta(\lambda) \equiv (\alpha + \lambda(1-\alpha))$ and $S_i \equiv -(\hat{c}_{Li} - \hat{c}_{Ki})$ for i=1,2. The symbol "^" above variables indicates the rate of change of the variable and $S_i$ $0 \le S_i \le 1$ is the elasticity of substitution between labor and capital on i-th sector.

Totally differentiate equations (1) and (3)-(7) yields:[11]

$$\hat{w}_1 = v_1 \hat{P}_1, \tag{1'}$$

$$a_{1L}\hat{w}_1 + a_{1K}(\hat{r} + \hat{T}) = \hat{p}_1, \tag{3'}$$

$$a_{2L}\hat{w}_2 + a_{2K}\hat{r} = 0, \tag{4'}$$

$$\lambda b_{1L}\hat{\lambda} + \lambda b_{1L}\hat{x}_1 + b_{2L}\hat{x}_2 - g_{L1}\hat{w}_1 - g_{L2}\hat{w}_2 + g_L\hat{r} + g_{L1}\hat{T} = 0, \tag{5'}$$

$$b_{1K}\hat{x}_1 + b_{2K}\hat{x}_2 + g_{K1}\hat{w}_1 + g_{K2}\hat{w}_2 - g_K\hat{r} - g_{K1}\hat{T} = 0, \tag{6'}$$

$$\hat{x}_1 - \hat{x}_2 = -\sigma\hat{p}_1, \tag{7'}$$

where

$$g_{L1} = b_{1L}a_{1K}S_1 \ge 0, \ g_{L2} = b_{2L}a_{2K}S_2 \ge 0 \text{ and } g_L = g_{L1} + g_{L2} \ge 0,$$

$$g_{K1} = b_{1K}a_{1L}S_1 \ge 0, \ g_{K2} = b_{2K}a_{2L}S_2 \ge 0 \text{ and } g_K = g_{K1} + g_{K2} \ge 0.$$

In these equations, $\sigma \equiv -(\hat{x}_1 - \hat{x}_2) \ge 0$ represents the demand elasticity of substitution between commodities and $v_1 \equiv (p_1 / F)/(\partial F / \partial p_1) \ge 0$ represents the elasticity of substitution between the wage indexation function and the price of the first sector, and $a_{ij}$ denotes the gross distributive share of factor j (=K,L) in i-th sector, i.e. $a_{iL} = c_{Li}w_i / c_i$, $a_{iK} = c_{Ki}r_i / c_i$. The usual adding-up properties hold so that $a_{iL} + a_{iK} = 1$, i=1,2, and $b_{ij}$ denotes the fraction of factor j (=K,L) used in i-th sector, i.e. $b_{iL} = c_{Li}x_i / L_0$, $b_{iK} = c_{Ki}x_i / K_0$. The adding-up properties including unemployment hold so that $\lambda b_{1L} + b_{2L} = 1$ and $b_{1K} + b_{2K} = 1$.

Finally, simplifying (2') and (8') and eliminating other variables $\hat{w}_1, \hat{x}_1, \hat{x}_2, \hat{w}_2, \hat{r}, \hat{p}_1$, we derive simultaneous equations system for $(\hat{\lambda}, \hat{T})$ with the parameter $\hat{\alpha}$. Since the calculation procedure is rather complicated, relegating the details of the derivation procedure to Appendix C, we state only the final result:

$$J \cdot \hat{Q} = A \cdot \hat{\alpha}, \tag{9}$$

and let $J$ be the coefficient matrix in (9),12 where

$$\hat{Q} \equiv \begin{bmatrix} \hat{\lambda} & \hat{T} \end{bmatrix}',$$

and

$$A \equiv \begin{bmatrix} -(\lambda-1)\alpha/\eta & -1 \end{bmatrix}'.$$

## 3.2 Local Stability of Simultaneous Equations

In this subsection, before doing a comparative static analysis, we clarify local stability conditions in our system. Because it is ambiguous whether the general equilibrium system is always locally stable in the presence of unemployment, Let $|J|$ be the determinant of the coefficient matrix in (9), i.e.

$$
\begin{aligned}
|J| = & \left( -\left[ \left( \xi + \frac{a_{2K}}{a_{2L}} \right)\left( \frac{\lambda b_{1L}}{R+gB} \right) + \left( \frac{(1-\alpha)\lambda}{\eta} \right) \right] \right) \\
& \times \left[ \left( \frac{(1-\xi)(q_{11}+q_{21})+gB}{R+gB} \right)\left( S_1\xi + \left( \frac{a_{2K}}{a_{2L}} \right) + (1-S_1) \right) - \left( S_1\xi + \left( \frac{T}{T-1} - S_1 \right) \right) \right] \\
& + \left[ \left( \xi + \frac{a_{2K}}{a_{2L}} \right)\left( \frac{(1-\xi)(q_{11}+q_{21})+gB}{R+gB} \right) - \xi \right] \\
& \times \left[ \left( \frac{\lambda}{\lambda-1} \right) + \left( \frac{\lambda b_{1L}}{R+gB} \right)\left( S_1\xi + \left( \frac{a_{2K}}{a_{2L}} \right) + (1-S_1) \right) \right], \quad\quad (10)
\end{aligned}
$$

where

$$R = R_1 + R_2 \geq 0, \ R_1 = (1-\xi)q_{11} + (q_{12}/a_{2L}) \geq 0, \ R_2 = (1-\xi)q_{21} + (q_{22}/a_{2L}) \geq 0,$$

$$q_1 = q_{11} + q_{12} = b_{1K}g_L + b_{1L}g_K \geq 0,$$

$$q_{11} = b_{1K}g_{L1} + b_{1L}g_{K1} \geq 0, \ q_{12} = b_{1K}g_{L2} + b_{1L}g_{K2} \geq 0,$$

$$q_2 = q_{21} + q_{22} = b_{2K}g_L + b_{2L}g_K \geq 0,$$

$$q_{21} = b_{2K}g_{L1} + b_{2L}g_{K1} \geq 0, \ q_{22} = b_{2K}g_{L2} + b_{2L}g_{K2} \geq 0,$$

---

[11] In Appendix B, we show the detailed derivation.

we define that $B \equiv b_{1K}b_{2L} - \lambda b_{1L}b_{2K}$ and $g \equiv \sigma\xi = \sigma v_1 a_{1K}/(1 - v_1 a_{1L}) \geq 0$. Note that the term of B includes the unemployment term $\lambda$, following Miyagiwa [24]. B is positive (resp. negative) if the corporate sector's capital-labor ratio including unemployment is greater (resp. less) than that of the noncorporate sector. In this case, the corporate sector is relatively capital-abundant (resp. labor-abundant). In the presence of unemployment, the condition of local stability, however, requires mathematical manipulations. In order to hold that the equilibrium is stable concerning unemployment, we assume that the term of B is always positive, which implies that there is no factor intensity twist.[13] We establish the following lemma:

> *Lemma 2. Assume that B>0, if |J|>0, then the general equilibrium system is locally stable.*

We prove Lemma 2 in Appendix E. The rest of the analysis proceeds under the condition of local stability.

## 4. BALANCED-BUDGET INCIDENCE ANALYSIS

This section develops the comparative static analysis under the conditions that Walras' law and the zeroth order homogeneity hold in the general equilibrium system, taking the assumption of local stability into account.

### 4.1 Comparative Static Analysis: Case 1

This subsection proceeds by exploring a comparative static analysis under the assumption of local stability. Making use of Cramer's rule to solve the system (9) for $\hat{\lambda}/\hat{\alpha}$:

$$\frac{\hat{\lambda}}{\hat{\alpha}} = |J|^{-1}|J_\alpha|, \tag{11}$$

where

---

12 See Appendix D.

[13] Neary [25] pointed out when factor markets are distorted, the equilibrium is stable if relatively capital (resp. labor) intensive sector in the physical sense is also capital (resp. labor) intensive in the value sense without unemployment.

$$|J_\alpha| = \left( -\frac{(\lambda-1)\alpha}{\eta} \right)$$

$$\times \left[ \left( \frac{(1-\xi)(q_{11}+q_{21})+gB}{R+gB} \right) \left( S_1\xi + \left( \frac{a_{2K}}{a_{2L}} \right) + (1-S_1) \right) - \left( S_1\xi + \left( \frac{T}{T-1} - S_1 \right) \right) \right]$$

$$- \left[ \left( \xi + \frac{a_{2K}}{a_{2L}} \right) \left( \frac{(1-\xi)(q_{11}+q_{21})+gB}{R+gB} \right) - \xi \right],$$

where $|J_\alpha|$ is the determinant with the first column replaced by $\hat{Q}'$.

When we assume that $\xi \to 0 (v_1 \to 0)$, simplifying $|J_\alpha|$ and letting it be $|J_{\alpha\xi}|$, we rewrite the relation (11) such that:

$$\frac{\hat{\lambda}}{\hat{\alpha}} = |J|^{-1} |J_{\alpha\xi}|, \tag{12}$$

where

$$|J_{\alpha\xi}| = -\left( \frac{(\lambda-1)\alpha}{\eta} \right) \left( \frac{1}{Ra_{2L}(T-1)} \right)$$

$$\times \left[ A_1 + a_{2K}(T-1)(q_{11}+q_{21}) + \left( \frac{q_{11}+q_{21}}{R} \right)(1-S_1) + S_1 \right] - \left( \frac{a_{2K}}{a_{2L}} \right) \left( \frac{q_{11}+q_{21}}{R} \right),$$

and

$$A_1 = a_{2L}T\left( \frac{q_{12}+q_{22}}{a_{2L}} - (q_{12}+q_{22}) \right)$$

$$= Ta_{2L}((q_{12}-q_{11})+(q_{22}-q_{21})) + T(q_{12}+q_{22})a_{2K} + (q_{11}+q_{21})a_{2K}(T-1)$$

$$= Ta_{2L}\left( B\left( S_1' - S_2' \right) \right) + T(q_{12}+q_{22})a_{2K} + (q_{11}+q_{21})a_{2K}(T-1).$$

In this equation, we denote $S_1' \equiv a_{1L}S_1$ and $S_2' \equiv a_{2L}S_2$, and assuming that $S_1' > S_2'$, i.e. $A_1 > 0$, we obtain that $|J_{\alpha\xi}| < 0$, along the careful examination of (12). Thus, we have that $\hat{\lambda}/\hat{\alpha} < 0$ as long as the equilibrium system is locally stable, i.e. $|J| > 0$.

We give a formal presentation of our results from interpreting (12). Assuming that the equilibrium of this model is locally stable under the adjustment process. If the following three conditions — (i) $B > 0$, (ii) $\xi \to 0(v_1 \to 0)$ and (iii) $S_1' > S_2'$ — hold, then we have the sign of (12), i.e. $\hat{\lambda}/\hat{\alpha} = |J|^{-1}|J_{\alpha\xi}|$ is negative. This leads us to state:

$$\hat{\lambda}/\hat{\alpha} < 0 \text{ if } B > 0, \ \xi \to 0(v_1 \to 0) \text{ and } S_1' > S_2'.$$

We now give the first proposition:

*Proposition 1. Assume that a general equilibrium system in the presence of unemployment exists and is locally stable under the adjustment process. Assume the following conditions hold: (i) the capital-labor ratio in the first sector including unemployment is greater than that in the second sector, (ii) the price elasticity $v_1$ of the indexed wage is in the neighborhood of zero, and (iii) the elasticity of factor substitution in the first sector is greater than that of the sector two. Then an increase in unemployment benefits reduces an unemployment rate.*

We add some comments on Proposition 1. If $B > 0$, then the first (corporate) sector is relatively more capital-intensive due to Miyagiwa. When $|J| > 0$, taking $B > 0$ into account, we state that the general equilibrium system in the presence of unemployment is locally stable. We assume that the elasticity of the corporate wage with respect to the commodity price produced in the corporate sector is in the neighborhood of zero, i.e. $v_1 \to 0$. Since we can interpret this as the non-food wage component, the wage does not respond to manufactured commodities prices, even though it may do so to agricultural prices. This point is in the original debate on the applicability of Keynesian ideas that would not work in India because of the high agricultural component of GNP. Our considerations are thus of some intuitive appeal from the real world point of view. [14]

This proposition allows us to say counter-intuitive effects of unemployment benefits. Note that we must interpret this proposition with a caution for several reasons. We need to identify some assumptions. First, we assume that the reflection of minimum-wage legislation vanishes, that is, the effects of a rise in unemployment benefits vanish, i.e. $\xi \to 0(v_1 \to 0)$. This result follows from the fact that the combination of (1') and (3') becomes $\hat{w}_1 = \xi(\hat{r} + \hat{T}) = 0$. This indicates a rise in the corporate income tax results in a rise in the first sector wage. In other words, a rise in unemployment benefits results in a rise in the corporate income tax rate via the government budget constraint, focusing on the balanced-budget incidence analysis. This analysis simply looks on the unemployment benefit as a subsidy to unemployed workers which is financed by the corporate income tax. These interpretations allow us to explain that the reflection of minimum-wage legislation vanishes as the result of $\hat{w}_1 = \xi(\hat{r} + \hat{T}) = 0$.

Second, we assume that the elasticity of factor substitution in the first sector is greater than that in the second sector. A rise in unemployment benefits results in a rise in the gross rental rate in the first sector via the government budget constraint when the first sector is relatively more capital-intensive,. The capital demand in the first (resp. second) sector decreases (resp.

---

[14] See Agarwala and Singh [1].

increases) and the labor demand in the first (resp. second) sector increases (resp. decreases). This substitution effect in the first sector is greater than that in the second sector. Thus, the rise in unemployment benefits causes the unemployment rate to decrease.

Third, we assume that $v_1 \rightarrow 0$, which implies that the wage in the corporate sector is not sensitive to a change in the price of the good produced in that sector. Following H-T model, we have a division between the manufacturing and the agricultural sectors rather than the corporate and the non-corporate sectors. Since workers consume essentially agricultural products which are provided by the competitive sector, it is ambiguous who consumes the products of the corporate sector. Next we consider a numerical example in order to answer this question.

## 4.2. Numerical Example: Case 1

This subsection offers a simple numerical example in order to explain the result in the previous subsection. We compute an equilibrium solution for some specific function forms, along the following simple numerical example. First, considering the cost minimization problem and assuming the Cobb-Douglas production function, i.e. $\left(L_i\right)^{1/2}\left(K_i\right)^{1/2}$ for $i=1,2$, we have the demand function for sector $i$:

$$x_i = L_i\left(w_i/r_i\right)^{1/2} = K_i\left(r_i/w_i\right)^{1/2}, \ i=1,2, \tag{13}$$

where $r_1 = rT = r\left(1+t\right)$, $r_2 = r$. Second, considering the utility maximization problem and assuming the Cobb-Douglas utility function, i.e. $U_i\left(x_1, x_2\right) = x_1^{1/2}x_2^{1/2}$ for $i=1,2$, we have the commodity market equilibrium condition from the assumption of the homothetic utility as:

$$x_1/x_2 = p_2/p_1. \tag{14}$$

Taking into account the assumption that the indexation function is homogeneous of degree one, we have the following specific function:

$$w_1 = p_1^\varepsilon, \ 0 \leq \varepsilon \leq 1. \tag{15}$$

We set the net return to capital as our numeraire so that $r = 1$, taking the entire system of equations into account, together with (13), (14) and (15), we derive the quadratic equation of the commodity price of sector 1.[15]

$$f\left(p_1\right) = a_1 p_1^2 + a_2 p_1 + a_3, \tag{16}$$

---

15 See Appendix F.

where $\quad a_1 = \alpha p'\left(1+(1-\alpha)(p')^2\right)$, $\quad a_2 = -2(p')^{-1}$, $\quad a_3 = 2^2(1-\alpha)^2 p'$, $\quad p' = p_2/2$,

$D = (a_2)^2 - 4a_1 a_3$. Taking (16) into account, and assuming that $\varepsilon = 0$, $p_2 = 2^{1/2}$, $\alpha = 1/2$, and $L_0 = K_0 = 1$, we calculate the value of $D$, i.e. $D = 27/4 > 0$. This implies that at least one real number $p_1$, which is an equilibrium price, exists in the above quadratic equation. In this example, assuming the elasticity of factor substitution in sector $i$ is equal to one, i.e. $S_i = 1$ for $i$=1,2. Since the cost function is a continuous function of $S_i$, the above example is still valid, while assuming that there exists an interior solution in the above equilibrium.[16]

## 4.3. Comparative Static Analysis: Case 2

In this subsection, we show another similar result by using other sufficient conditions. When we assume that $S_2 \to 0$, simplifying $|J_\alpha|$ and letting it be $|J_{\alpha S}|$, we rewrite the relation (11) such that:

$$\frac{\hat{\lambda}}{\hat{\alpha}} = |J|^{-1} |J_{\alpha S}|, \tag{17}$$

where

$$|J_{\alpha S}| = -\left[\left(\frac{\lambda}{\eta}\right)A_2 + \left(\frac{1}{T-1}\right)\right],$$

and

$$A_2 = \left(\frac{T'-1}{a_{2L}(T-1)}\right).$$

In this equation we denote $T' \equiv a_{2K}T$, and assuming that $T' > 1$, i.e. $A_2 > 0$, we obtain that $|J_{\alpha S}| < 0$, along the careful examination of (17). Thus, we have that $\hat{\lambda}/\hat{\alpha} < 0$ as long as the equilibrium system is locally stable, i.e. $|J| > 0$.

We give a formal presentation of our results from interpreting (17). Assuming that the equilibrium of the this model is locally stable under the adjustment process. If the following

---

[16] See Varian [28].

three conditions □ (i) $B > 0$, (ii) $S_2 \to 0$ and (iii) $T' > 1$ □ hold, then we have the sign of (17), i.e. $\hat{\lambda}/\hat{\alpha} = |J|^{-1} |J_{\alpha S}|$ is negative. This leads us to state:

$$\hat{\lambda}/\hat{\alpha} < 0 \text{ if } B > 0, \ S_2 \to 0 \text{ and } T' > 1.$$

We give the second proposition:

*Proposition 2. Assume that the general equilibrium system in the presence of unemployment exists and is locally stable under the adjustment process. Assume that the following conditions hold: (i) the capital-labor ratio in the first sector including unemployment is greater than that in the second sector, (ii) the elasticity of factor substitution in the second sector is in the neighborhood of zero, and (iii) the sum of gross corporate income tax is greater than one. Then an increase in unemployment benefits reduces an unemployment rate.*

We add some comments on Proposition 2. We assume that the elasticity of factor substitution in agriculture is in the neighborhood of zero. Assuming that the second sector is the agricultural one, we can recognize a certain capital-labor fixity is plausible. Thus, every farmer must have a plough etc. This is not an exact relationship, but all the result needs is low substitutability. Our considerations are thus of some intuitive appeal from the real world point of view. As shown in Agarwala and Singh [1], Keynesian ideas that would not work in India because of the inelasticity of LDC supply. Note that since this proposition has required some further assumptions, we need to identify some assumptions.

First, the first (corporate) sector is relatively more capital-intensive, i.e. $B > 0$. Second, we assume that the factor substitution effect in the second sector is in the neighborhood of zero. Especially, when the first sector is relatively more capital-intensive and the sum of gross corporate income tax is greater than one, a rise in unemployment benefits results in a rise in the gross rental rate in the first sector via the government budget constraint. The capital demand in the first sector decreases and the labor demand in the first sector increases. In contrast, the factor substitution effect in the second sector vanishes. Thus, the rise in unemployment benefits causes the unemployment rate to decrease. This allows us to present the counter-intuitive conclusion of the standard model of the labor market.

# 5. CONCLUDING REMARKS

In this paper we reexamined the effects of unemployment benefits on unemployment by elaborating the Miyagiwa model. In the first part of this paper we proposed a new model which has established Walras' law and the zeroth order homogeneity of demand and supply functions. We introduced some assumptions that unemployment benefits are indexed to the competitive wage and that the government budget is balanced. In other words, these assumptions allow us to recognize unemployment benefits as endogenous variables in the model. Unemployment emerges as a sector-specific phenomenon in this model. In the second part of this paper we ensured the local stability condition of the system and analyzed the effects of unemployment benefits on unemployment. We focused on the balanced-budget incidence analysis. We derived the counter-intuitive result that unemployment benefits, instead of increasing unemployment, may well decrease unemployment. This result regarding the effects of unemployment benefits involves inelasticity in either of the following situations: wages with respect to the 'manufacturing' price or production with respect to factor prices. As Agarwala and Singh [1] presented, Keynesian ideas would not work in India because of the high agricultural component of GNP and the inelasticity of LDC supply, our considerations are thus of some intuitive appeal from the real world point of view. While applying Keynesian ideas, this contributes to an older debate on unemployment policy.

Our analysis based on several simplifying assumptions such as two competitive sectors, two factors and two commodities, and the specific government balanced budget tax-benefit package. We considered that unemployment benefits are financed by the corporate income tax. Relaxing these assumptions, we may have other possibilities of effects of unemployment benefits on unemployment for the tax incidence analysis. We suggest some extensions for further researches. When we consider that unemployment benefits are financed by borrowing or income tax, our analysis seems to have fairly interesting consequences for issues of unemployment, while assuming that the workings of an informal sector in the H-T type of model rural-urban migration,[17] and that taxes and social premiums levied on both demand and supply sides.[18]

## ACKNOWLEDGEMENTS

We are grateful to Professors A. Wahhab Khandker, Jun Iritani, Tomoichi Shinotsuka for their helpful comments. We have also benefited from the comments of seminar participants at Otaru University of Commerce and Tetsukayama University. We gratefully acknowledge financial supports from Grant-in-Aid for Scientific Research C (2) 15530208 from Japan Society for the Promotion of Science. We retain responsibility for errors and views.

## APPENDIX A

We define the income of an i's household (employed worker) as:

$$p_1 y_{1j} + p_2 y_{2j} = w_j c_{Lj} x_j + r c_{Kj} x_j \, , \text{j=1,2,} \tag{A1}$$

where $y_{ij}$ is the i's demand of a j's household for i=1,2; j=1,2. The household income is equal to the sum of the value of the household wage plus the value of the household's share of capital rental. We define the income of an unemployed worker as :

---

[17] An economy consists of two regions (including three sectors) and is segmented into a rural and an urban region. The urban region is further subdivided into a formal and an informal sector. For instance, Khan [22] and Gupta [12] discuss such a model.

[18] See Compaijen and Vijlbrief [9].

$$p_1 y_{1U} + p_2 y_{2U} = \alpha w_2 L_U = \alpha w_2 (\lambda - 1) c_{L1} x_1, \tag{A2}$$

where $y_{iU}$ is the i's demand of an unemployed worker for i=1,2. Let $HED_i$ be an i's excess demand of each household, we have:

$$HED_i = \left( p_1 y_{1i} + p_2 y_{2i} \right) - \left( w_i c_{Li} x_i + r c_{Ki} x_i \right), \text{ i=1,2} \tag{A3}$$

and let $HED_U$ be an excess demand of unemployed workers, we have:

$$HED_U = \sum_{i=1}^{2} p_{1i} y_{iU} - \alpha w_2 (\lambda - 1) c_{L1} x_1 .$$

Let $AHED$ be an aggregate excess demand of households, taking (A3), (A4) into account, summing up $HED_i$ over all i and adding up $HED_U$, we have:

$$AHED = \sum_{i=1}^{2} HED_i + HED_U ,$$

$$= \sum_{i=1}^{2} \left( \left( p_1 y_{1i} + p_2 y_{2i} \right) - \left( w_i c_{Li} x_i + r c_{Ki} x_i \right) \right) + \left( \sum_{i=1}^{2} p_{1i} y_{iU} - \alpha w_2 (\lambda - 1) c_{L1} x_1 \right).$$

$$= \sum_{i=1}^{2} p_i y_i - \left( \sum_{i=1}^{2} \left( w_i c_{Li} x_i + r c_{Ki} x_i \right) + \alpha w_2 (\lambda - 1) c_{L1} x_1 \right). \tag{A5}$$

where $y_1 = y_{11} + y_{12} + y_{1U}, y_2 = y_{21} + y_{22} + y_{2U}$. Let $PRO_i$ be an i's producer profit, we have:

$$PRO_i = p_i x_i - \left( w_i c_{Li} x_i + r_i c_{Ki} x_i \right), \text{ i=1,2,} \tag{A6}$$

where $T \equiv 1 + t, \ 0 \le t \le 1, \ r_1 = r$ and $r_2 = Tr = (1 + t)r$. Let $APRO$ be an aggregate profit of produces, summing up $PRO_i$ over all i, we have:

$$APRO = \sum_{i=1}^{2} PRO_i$$

$$= \sum_{i=1}^{2} p_i x_i - \sum_{i=1}^{2} \left( w_i c_{Li} x_i + r_i c_{Ki} x_i \right)$$

$$= \sum_{i=1}^{2} p_i x_i - \left( \sum_{i=1}^{2} \left( w_i c_{Li} x_i + r c_{Ki} x_i \right) - (T - 1) r c_{K1} x_1 \right). \tag{A7}$$

Let $AED$ be an aggregate excess demand of an economy, which is equal to the aggregate excess demand of households ( $AHED$ ) minus the aggregate profit of producers ( $APRO$ ), and subtracting (A7) from (A5) yields:

$$AED = AHED - APRO$$

$$= \left( \sum_{i=1}^{2} p_i y_i - \left( \sum_{i=1}^{2} \left( w_i c_{Li} x_i + r c_{Ki} x_i \right) + \alpha w_2 \left( \lambda - 1 \right) c_{L1} x_1 \right) \right)$$

$$- \left( \sum_{i=1}^{2} p_i x_i - \left( \sum_{i=1}^{2} \left( w_i c_{Li} x_i + r c_{Ki} x_i \right) + \left( T - 1 \right) r c_{K1} x_1 \right) \right)$$

$$= \sum_{i=1}^{2} p_i \left( y_i - x_i \right) + \left( T - 1 \right) r c_{K1} x_1 - \alpha w_2 \left( \lambda - 1 \right) c_{L1} x_1$$

$$= \left( T - 1 \right) r c_{K1} x_1 - \alpha w_2 \left( \lambda - 1 \right) c_{L1} x_1 . \qquad (A8)$$

Let $GED$ be an excess demand of the government, we have:

$$GED = \alpha w_2 \left( \lambda - 1 \right) c_{L1} x_1 - \left( T - 1 \right) r c_{K1} x_1 . \qquad (A9)$$

Making use of (A9), taking (A8) into account, we rewrite (A8) such as:

$$AED = \sum_{i=1}^{2} p_i \left( y_i - x_i \right) - GED = 0 . \qquad (A8')$$

We define the government budget such as:

$$\left( \lambda - 1 \right) \alpha w_2 c_{L1} x_1 = \left( T - 1 \right) r c_{K1} x_1 . \qquad (A9)$$

Taking into account the government budget constraint and the zeroth order homogeneity of prices, and together with (A9), this allows us to ensure that Walras' law holds.

## APPENDIX B

Differentiating (1) yields:

$$dw_1 / w_1 = \left( \left( \partial F / \partial p_1 \right) \cdot \left( p_1 / F_1 \right) \right) \cdot \left( dp_1 / p_1 \right), \qquad (B1)$$

making use of $v_1 = \left( \left( \partial F / \partial p_1 \right) \cdot \left( p_1 / F_1 \right) \right)$, we rewrite (B1) such as:

$$\hat{w}_1 = v_1 \hat{p}_1 . \qquad (1')$$

Next, differentiating (2') and taking $\eta(\lambda) \equiv (\alpha + \lambda(1-\alpha))$ into account yield:

$$w_1 \hat{w}_1 - (1-\alpha)\lambda w_2 \hat{\lambda} + (\lambda - 1)\alpha w_2 \hat{\alpha} - \eta w_2 \hat{w}_2 = 0 . \qquad (B2)$$

Dividing (B2) by $w_1 (= \eta w_2)$ yields:

$$\hat{w}_1 - \hat{w}_2 - ((1-\alpha)\lambda / \eta)\hat{\lambda} = -((\lambda - 1)\alpha / \eta)\hat{\alpha} . \qquad (2')$$

Differentiating (3) and (4) and taking into account price normalization $(p_2 = 1)$, we have:

$$a_{1L} \hat{w}_1 + a_{1K} (\hat{r} + \hat{T}) = \hat{p}_1 , \qquad (3')$$

$$a_{2L} \hat{w}_2 + a_{2K} \hat{r} = 0 . \qquad (4')$$

Next, differentiating (5) and (6) yields:

$$\lambda b_{1L} (\hat{\lambda} + \hat{c}_{L1} + \hat{x}_1) + b_{2L} (\hat{c}_{L2} + \hat{x}_2) - \hat{L}_0 = 0 , \qquad (B3)$$

$$b_{1K} (\hat{c}_{K1} + \hat{x}_1) + b_{2K} (\hat{c}_{K2} + x_2) - \hat{K}_0 = 0 . \qquad (B4)$$

Taking cost minimization conditions into account, we have:

$$a_{iL} \hat{c}_{L1} + a_{iK} \hat{c}_{Ki} = 0 , \; i=1, 2. \qquad (B5)$$

We define the elasticity of substitution between labor and capital in $i$-th sector as:

$$S_i \equiv -(d \log(c_{Li} / c_{Ki})) / (d \log(w_i / r_i)) > 0 , \; i=1,2, \qquad (B6)$$

where $r_1 = Tr , r_2 = r$ . Rewriting (B6) yields:

$$S_i \equiv -(\hat{c}_{Li} - \hat{c}_{Ki}) / (\hat{w}_i - \hat{r}_i)(\geq 0), \; i=1, 2. \qquad (B6')$$

In order to solve the above equations for $\hat{c}_{Li}$ and $\hat{c}_{Ki}$ , substituting (B6') into (B5) yields:

$$\hat{c}_{L1} = -a_{1K} S_1 (\hat{w}_1 - (\hat{r} + \hat{T})),$$

$$\hat{c}_{K1} = -a_{1L} S_1 (\hat{w}_1 - (\hat{r} + \hat{T})), \qquad (B7)$$

$$\hat{c}_{L2} = -a_{2K} S_2 (\hat{w}_2 - \hat{r}),$$

$$\hat{c}_{K2} = -a_{2L} S_2 \left( \hat{w}_2 - \hat{r} \right).$$

Substituting (B3) into (B7) yields:

$$\lambda b_{1L} \hat{\lambda} + \lambda b_{1L} \hat{x}_1 + b_{2L} \hat{x}_2 - \lambda b_{1L} a_{1K} S_1 \hat{w}_1 - b_{2L} a_{2K} S_2 \hat{w}_2$$
$$\left( \hat{\lambda} b_{1L} a_{1K} S_1 + b_{2L} a_{2K} S_2 \right) \hat{r} + \lambda b_{1L} a_{1K} S_1 \hat{T} - \hat{L}_0 = 0 , \tag{B8}$$

and setting $\hat{L}_0 = 0$ and rewriting (B8) yield:

$$\lambda b_{1L} \hat{\lambda} + \lambda b_{1L} \hat{x}_1 + b_{2L} \hat{x}_2 - g_{L1} \hat{w}_1 - g_{L2} \hat{w}_2 + g_L \hat{r} + g_{L1} \hat{T} = 0 . \tag{5'}$$

In a similar manner, substituting (B4) into (B7) yields:

$$b_{1K} \hat{x}_1 + b_{2K} \hat{x}_2 + b_{1K} a_{1L} S_1 \hat{w}_1 + b_{2K} a_{2L} S_2 \hat{w}_2$$
$$- \left( b_{1K} a_{1L} S_1 + b_{2K} a_{2L} S_2 \right) \hat{r} + b_{1K} a_{1L} S_1 \hat{T} - \hat{K}_0 = 0 . \tag{B9}$$

and setting $\hat{K}_0 = 0$ and rewriting (B9) yield:

$$b_{1K} \hat{x}_1 + b_{2K} \hat{x}_2 + g_{K1} \hat{w}_1 + g_{K2} \hat{w}_2 - g_K \hat{r} - g_{K1} \hat{T} = 0 . \tag{6'}$$

Differentiating (7) and taking into account the demand elasticity of substitution ($\sigma \equiv -\left[ d \log \left( x_1 / x_2 \right) / d \log p_1 \right] \geq 0$), we have:

$$\hat{x}_1 - \hat{x}_2 = -\sigma \hat{p}_1 . \tag{7'}$$

Differentiating (8) yields:

$$\lambda \alpha w_2 c_{L1} x_1 \hat{\lambda} + \left( 1 - \lambda \right) \alpha w_2 c_{L1} x_1 \left( \hat{\alpha} + \hat{w}_2 + \hat{c}_{L1} + \hat{x}_1 \right),$$
$$- Tr \lambda rc_{K1} x_1 \hat{T} - \left( T - 1 \right) rc_{K1} x_1 \left( \hat{r} + \hat{c}_{K1} + \hat{x}_1 \right) = 0 . \tag{B10}$$

Taking (B7) into account and rewriting (B10) yield:

$$G \left( \lambda / \left( \lambda - 1 \right) \right) \hat{\lambda} + G \hat{w}_2 - G S_1 \hat{w}_1 - G \left( 1 - S_1 \right) \hat{r} - G \left( T / \left( T - 1 \right) - S_1 \right) \hat{T} = -G \hat{\alpha} , \tag{B11}$$

where $G \equiv \left( \lambda - 1 \right) \alpha w_2 c_{L1} x_1 = \left( T - 1 \right) rc_{K1} x_1$. Dividing (B11) by $G$ yields:

$$\left( \lambda / \left( \lambda - 1 \right) \right) \hat{\lambda} + \hat{w}_2 - S_1 \hat{w}_1 - \left( 1 - S_1 \right) \hat{r} - \left( T / \left( T - 1 \right) - S_1 \right) \hat{T} = -\hat{\alpha} . \tag{8'}$$

Note that $\left( T / \left( T - 1 \right) - S_1 \right) > 0$ and $0 \leq S_1 \leq 1$.

# APPENDIX C

Taking (1'), (3') into account and eliminating $\hat{p}_1$ yield :

$$\hat{w}_1 = \xi(\hat{r} + \hat{T}),$$ (C1)

where $\xi \equiv v_1 a_K (1 - v_1 a_{1L})$. Taking (1) into account and substituting (C1) into (7), we have:

$$\hat{x}_1 - \hat{x}_2 = -g(\hat{r} + \hat{T}),$$ (C2)

where $g \equiv \sigma \xi$ . Multiplying (5') by $b_{1K}$ yields:

$$b_{1K}\left(\lambda b_{1L}\hat{\lambda} + \lambda b_{1L}\hat{x}_1 + b_{2L}\hat{x}_2 - g_{L1}\hat{w}_1 - g_{L2}\hat{w}_2 + g_L\hat{r} + g_{L1}\hat{T}\right) = 0 \,,$$ (C3)

and multiplying (6') by $\lambda b_{1L}$ yields:

$$\lambda b_{1L}\left(b_{1K}\hat{x}_1 + b_{2K}\hat{x}_2 + g_{K1}\hat{w}_1 + g_{K2}\hat{w}_2 - g_K\hat{r} - g_{K1}\hat{T}\right) = 0 \,.$$ (C4)

Subtracting (C3) from (C4) to eliminate $\hat{x}_1$, we have:

$$\lambda b_{1L}b_{1K}\hat{\lambda} + \left(b_{1K}b_{2L} - \lambda b_{1L}b_{2K}\right)\hat{x}_2 - \left(b_{1K}g_{L1} + \lambda b_{1L}g_{K1}\right)\hat{w}_1 - \left(b_{1K}g_{L2} + \lambda b_{1L}g_{K2}\right)\hat{w}_2$$
$$+ \left(b_{1K}g_L + \lambda b_{1L}g_K\right)\hat{r} + \left(b_{1K}g_{L1} + \lambda b_{1L}g_{K1}\right)\hat{T} = 0 \,.$$ (C5)

Simplifying(C5) yields:

$$\lambda b_{1L}b_{1K}\hat{\lambda} + B\hat{x}_2 - q_{11}\hat{w}_1 - q_{12}\hat{w}_2 + q_1\hat{r} + q_{11}\hat{T} = 0 \,.$$ (C5')

Multiplying each (5') and (6') by $b_{2K}$ and $b_{2L}$, respectively, and subtracting the former from the latter to eliminate $\hat{x}_2$, we have:

$$-\lambda b_{1L}b_{2K}\hat{\lambda} + \left(b_{1K}b_{2L} - \lambda b_{1L}b_{2K}\right)\hat{x}_1 + \left(b_{2L}g_{K1} + \lambda b_{2K}g_{L1}\right)\hat{w}_1 + \left(b_{2L}g_{K2} + \lambda b_{2K}g_{L2}\right)\hat{w}_2$$
$$-\left(b_{2L}g_K + b_{2K}g_L\right)\hat{r} - \left(b_{2L}g_{K1} + b_{2K}g_{L1}\right)\hat{T} = 0 \,.$$ (C6)

Simplifying (C6) yields:

$$-\lambda b_{1L}b_{2K}\hat{\lambda} + B\hat{x}_1 + q_{21}\hat{w}_1 + q_{22}\hat{w}_2 - q_2\hat{r} - q_{21}\hat{T} = 0 \,.$$ (C6')

Substituting (C1), (4) into (C5'), (C6') to eliminate $\hat{w}_1$ and $\hat{w}_2$, we have:

$$B\hat{x}_2 = -\lambda b_{1L} b_{1K} \hat{\lambda} - R_1 \hat{r} - (1 - \xi) q_{11} \hat{T} , \tag{B5''}$$

$$B\hat{x}_1 = \lambda b_{1L} b_{2K} \hat{\lambda} + R_2 \hat{r} + (1 - \xi) q_{21} \hat{T} . \tag{B6''}$$

Substituting (C5''), (C6'') into multiplying (C2) by $B$ to eliminate $\hat{x}_1$ and $\hat{x}_2$, we have:

$$\hat{r} = -\frac{\lambda b_{1L}}{R + gB} \hat{\lambda} - \frac{(1 - \xi)(q_{11} + q_{21}) + gB}{R + gB} \hat{T} . \tag{C7}$$

Substituting (C1), (4') and (B7) into (2') to eliminate $\hat{w}_1$, $\hat{w}_2$ and $\hat{r}$, we have:

$$-\left[\left(\xi + \frac{a_{2K}}{a_{2L}}\right)\left(\frac{\lambda b_{1L}}{R + gB}\right) + \left(\frac{(1 - \alpha)\lambda}{\eta}\right)\right]\hat{\lambda}$$

$$-\left[\left(\xi + \frac{a_{2K}}{a_{2L}}\right)\left(\frac{(1 - \xi)(q_{11} + q_{21}) + gB}{R + gB}\right) - \xi\right]\hat{T} = -\frac{(\lambda - 1)\alpha}{\eta}\hat{\alpha} \tag{C8}$$

Substituting (C1), (4') and (C7) into (8') to eliminate $\hat{w}_1$, $\hat{w}_2$ and $\hat{r}$, we have:

$$\left[\left(\frac{\lambda}{\lambda - 1}\right) + \left(\frac{\lambda b_{1L}}{R + gB}\right)\left(S_1\xi + \left(\frac{a_{2K}}{a_{2L}}\right) + (1 - S_1)\right)\right]\hat{\lambda}$$

$$+\left[\left(\frac{(1 - \xi)(q_{11} + q_{21}) + gB}{R + gB}\right)\left(S_1\xi + \left(\frac{a_{2K}}{a_{2L}}\right) + (1 - S_1)\right) - \left(S_1\xi + \left(\frac{T}{T - 1} - S_1\right)\right)\right]\hat{T} = -\hat{\alpha} \tag{C9}$$

Taking (C8), (C9) into account, we consider the simultaneous equation system for $(\hat{\lambda}, \hat{T})$ with the parameter $\hat{\alpha}$:

$$J \cdot \hat{Q} = A \cdot \hat{\alpha} . \tag{9}$$

## APPENDIX D

Let $J$ be the coefficient matrix in (9), i.e.

$$J \equiv \begin{bmatrix} J_{11} & J_{12} \\ J_{21} & J_{22} \end{bmatrix}, \tag{D1}$$

where

$$J_{11} = -\left\{ \left( \xi + \frac{a_{2K}}{a_{2L}} \right) \left( \frac{\lambda b_{1L}}{R + gB} \right) + \left( \frac{(1-\alpha)\lambda}{\eta} \right) \right\},$$

$$J_{12} = -\left\{ \left( \xi + \frac{a_{2K}}{a_{2L}} \right) \left( \frac{(1-\xi)(q_{11} + q_{21}) + gB}{R + gB} \right) - \xi \right\},$$

$$J_{21} = \left\{ \left( \frac{\lambda}{\lambda - 1} \right) + \left( \frac{\lambda b_{1L}}{R + gB} \right) \left( S_1 \xi + \left( \frac{a_{2K}}{a_{2L}} \right) + (1 - S_1) \right) \right\},$$

$$J_{22} = \left\{ \left( \frac{(1-\xi)(q_{11} + q_{21}) + gB}{R + gB} \right) \left( S_1 \xi + \left( \frac{a_{2K}}{a_{2L}} \right) + (1 - S_1) \right) - \left( S_1 \xi + \left( \frac{T}{T - 1} - S_1 \right) \right) \right\}.$$

## APPENDIX E

We prove that our general equilibrium system is locally stable where the government budget is balanced. In order to simplify the stability analysis, we assume that the competitive wage of the second sector and the rental rates are adjusted instantly to equate demand and supply for labor including unemployment and capital, respectively. The first sector wage is indexed to commodities prices. We assume that the first sector wage is also adjusted instantly along the path of the wage setting function. Similarly, we assume that the product markets for $x_1$ and $x_2$ are cleared immediately, and that the commodities prices are also adjusted instantly to equate demand and supply for commodities $x_1$ and $x_2$. Since we consider the general equilibrium system of our economy, i.e. (1) - (8) completely, we assume that (1) and (3) - (7) always hold any adjustment path.

We introduce the dynamic adjustment process. Since we focus on (2) and (8) under the above assumptions, we define the following dynamic adjustment process by:

$$\dot{\lambda} = \kappa_1 \{ w_1 - \eta(\lambda) w_1 \}, \tag{E1}$$

$$\dot{T} = \kappa_2 \{ (\lambda - 1)\alpha w_2 c_{L1} - (T - 1) rc_{K1} x_1 \}, \tag{E2}$$

where $\dot{\lambda}$ and $\dot{T}$ denote the time derivative of $\lambda$ and $T$, and $\kappa_i (> 0)$ is the adjustment coefficient.

Next, linearly approximating (E1) and (E2) around the equilibrium. We assume that $\hat{\alpha} = 0$. In order to avoid unnecessary complications, modifying the above system with the theoretical apparatus and making use of equations (1') - (8') and results of Appendix B, we have:

$$\dot{\lambda} = \kappa_1^* \left\{ -\left[ \left( \xi + \frac{a_{2K}}{a_{2L}} \right) \left( \frac{\lambda b_{1L}}{R + gB} \right) + \left( \frac{(1-\alpha)\lambda}{\eta} \right) \right] \left( \frac{\lambda - \lambda^*}{\lambda^*} \right) \right.$$

$$\left. -\left[ \left( \xi + \frac{a_{2K}}{a_{2L}} \right) \left( \frac{(1-\xi)(q_{11} + q_{21}) + gB}{R + gB} \right) - \xi \right] \left( \frac{T - T^*}{T^*} \right) \right\}, \tag{E1'}$$

$$\dot{T} = \kappa_2^* \left\{ \left[ \left( \frac{\lambda}{\lambda - 1} \right) + \left( \frac{\lambda b_{1L}}{R + gB} \right) \left( S_1 \xi + \left( \frac{a_{2K}}{a_{2L}} \right) + (1 - S_1) \right) \right] \left( \frac{\lambda - \lambda^*}{\lambda^*} \right) \right.$$

$$\left. + \left[ \left( \frac{(1-\xi)(q_{11} + q_{21}) + gB}{R + gB} \right) \left( S_1 \xi + \left( \frac{a_{2K}}{a_{2L}} \right) + (1 - S_1) \right) - \left( S_1 \xi + \left( \frac{T}{T - 1} - S_1 \right) \right) \right] \left( \frac{T - T^*}{T} \right) \right\} \tag{E2'}$$

Let $\lambda^*$ and $T^*$ be the equilibrium values of $\lambda$ and $T$. In these equations we denote that $\kappa_1^* = \kappa_1 w_1^* > 0$, $\kappa_2^* = \kappa_2 G^* > 0$, and $G = (\lambda - 1)\alpha w_2 c_{L1} x_1 = (T - 1) r c_{K1} x_1 > 0$.

Observe from these adjustment equations that the equilibrium is locally stable if

$$-\left[ \left( \xi + \frac{a_{2K}}{a_{2L}} \right) \left( \frac{\lambda b_{1L}}{R + gB} \right) + \left( \frac{(1-\alpha)\lambda}{\eta} \right) \right] < 0 \text{ and } |J| > 0, \tag{E3}$$

where $|J|$ is the determinant by $J$ in (9). The first inequality is always satisfied under the assumption $B > 0$. Hence, $|J| > 0$ is sufficient for the local stability of equilibrium, as was to be verified.

Note that we assume that $B > 0$ and $\xi \to 0 (v_1 \to 0)$, we have $|J| > 0$, i.e.

$$|J| = \left( S_1 \xi + \left( \frac{a_{2K}}{a_{2L}} \right) + (1 - S_1) \right) \left( \frac{a_{2K} + \lambda a_{2L}(\lambda(1 + \alpha) + (1 - \alpha))}{a_{2L}(\lambda - 1)} \right) \left( \frac{1}{\alpha + \lambda(1 + \alpha)} \right). \tag{E4}$$

Similarly, we assume that $B > 0$ and $S_2 \to 0$, we have $|J| > 0$, i.e.

$$|J| = \left( \frac{a_{2K}}{a_{2L}} \right) \left( \left( \frac{\lambda}{\eta(\lambda - 1)} \right) + \left( \frac{\lambda a_{2L}}{(1 - \xi)(q_{11} + q_{21}) + gB} \right) (1 - S_1)(1 - \xi) \right)$$

$$+ \left( \frac{1}{T - 1} \right) \left( \left( \xi + \frac{a_{2K}}{a_{2L}} \right) \left( \frac{\lambda a_{2L}}{(1 - \xi)(q_{11} + q_{21}) + gB} \right) + \left( \frac{(1-\alpha)\lambda}{\eta} \right) \right). \tag{E5}$$

We verify $|J| > 0$ under the assumptions that $B > 0$ and i) $\xi \to 0(v_1 \to 0)$ or ii) $S_2 \to 0$. Observe from these adjustment equations that the general equilibrium system is locally stable if $B > 0$ and $|J| > 0$.

## APPENDIX F

We consider the Cobb-Douglas production function such as:

$$(L_i)^{1/2}(K_i)^{1/2}, i=1,2. \tag{F1}$$

Considering the cost minimization problem, we have the demand function for sector $i$ such as:

$$x_i = L_i(w_i/r_i)^{1/2} = K_i(r_i/w_i)^{1/2}, i=1,2. \tag{13}$$

Taking (13) into account and assuming $L_0 = K_0 = 1$, we have the cost functions and the employment conditions for factors for sector $i$ such that:

$$c_i(w_i, r_i) = 2w_i^{1/2}r_i^{1/2} = p_i, i=1,2, \tag{F2}$$

$$\lambda(w_1/r_1)^{-1/2} x_1 + (w_2/r_2)^{-1/2} x_2 = L_0 = 1, \tag{F3}$$

$$(w_1/r_1)^{1/2} x_1 + (w_2/r_2)^{1/2} x_2 = K_0 = 1, \tag{F4}$$

where $r_1 = rT = r(1+t)$ and $r_2 = r$. We have the government budget constraint such as :

$$(\lambda - 1)\alpha w_2(w_1/rT)^{-1/2} = (T-1)r(w_1/rT)^{-1/2}. \tag{F5}$$

Considering the Cobb-Douglas utility function, we have:

$$U_i(x_1, x_2) = x_1^{1/2} x_2^{1/2}, i=1,2. \tag{F6}$$

Considering the utility maximization problem, we have the commodity market equilibrium condition under the assumption of the homothetic utility such as:

$$x_1/x_2 = p_1/p_2. \tag{14}$$

Taking into account the assumption that the function is homogeneous of degree one, we specific the indexation function such as:

$$w_1 = p_1^\varepsilon, \ 0 \leq \varepsilon \leq 1. \tag{15}$$

Considering the migration equilibrium condition, we have:

$$w_1/\lambda + (1 - 1/\lambda)\alpha w_2 = w_2. \tag{2}$$

Let the net return to capital be our numeraire so that $r = 1$. We consider the entire system of equations for the above numerical example, i.e. (F1) – (F6), (2), (13) – (16). Thus, we derive the quadratic equation such as:

$$f(p_1) = \alpha p' \{1 + (1 - \alpha)(p')^2\} p_1^2 - 2(p')^{-1} p_1 + 2^2 (1 - \alpha)^2 p' = 0, \tag{16}$$

where $p' = p_2/2$.

## REFERENCES

Agarwala, A. N. and Singh, S. P., *The economics of underdevelopment*, New York, Oxford University Press (1958).

Atkinson, A. B. and Stiglitz, J. E., *Lectures on public economics*, New York: McGraw-Hill (1980).

Basu, K. C., Optimal policies in dual economies, *Quarterly Journal of Economics* 95 187-196 (1980).

Behuria, S., Taxation and employment in general equilibrium: A two-sector analysis, *Journal of Development Economics* 14, 219-239 (1984).

Benassy, J. P., *Macroeconomics: Non-Walrasian approach*, New York, Academic Press (1986).

Bhagwati, J. N. and Srinivasan, T. N., On reanalyzing the Harris-Todaro model: Policy rankings in the case of sector specific sticky wages, *American Economic Review* 64, 502-508 (1974).

Calvo, G. A. (1978). Urban unemployment and wage determination in LDCs: Trade unions in the Harris-Todaro model, *International Economic Review* 19, 65-81.

Card, D. and Krueger, A. B., *Myth and Measurement: The New Economics of the Minimum Wage*, New Jersey, Princeton University Press (1995).

Compaijen, B. and Vijlbrief, J. A., Benefits and unemployment in an open economy: an equilibrium analysis, *Applied Economics* 26, 765-774 (1994).

Corden, W. M. and Findlay, R., Urban unemployment, intersectoral capital mobility and development policy, *Economica* 42, 59-78 (1975).

Gilbert, J. and Wahl, T., Export restrictions, urban unemployment, and the location of processing activities, *Economics Letters* 71, 105-110 (2001).

Gupta, M. R., Rural-urban migration, informal sector and development policies, *Journal of Development Economics* 41, 137-151 (1993).

Harberger, A. C., The incidence of corporate income tax, *Journal of Political Economy* 70, 215-240 (1962).

Harris, J. R. and Todaro, M. P., Migration unemployment and development: A two-sector analysis, *American Economic Review* 60, 126-142 (1970).

Holmlund, B. and Lundmorg, P., Incidence analysis of financing unemployment benefits in a partially unionized economy, *Economica* 57, 371-382 (1990).

Homma, M., A comparative static analysis of tax incidence, *Journal of Public Economics* 8, 52-65 (1977).

Imam, M.H. and Whalley, J., Incidence analysis of a sector-specific minimum wage in a two-sector Harris-Todaro model, *Quarterly Journal of Economics* 100, 207-224 (1985).

Iritani, J. and Sumino, K., On the existence of unemployment equilibria under wage rigidity, *The Economic Review* 51, Otaru University of Commerce, 271-294 (2001).

Jone, R. W., The structure of simple general equilibrium models, *Journal of Political Economy* 73, 557-572 (1965).

Khan, M. A., The Harris-Todaro hypothesis and the Heckscher-Ohlin-Samuelson trade model: a synthesis, *Journal of International Economics* 10, 527-547 (1980).

Khan, M. A., "Trade and development in the presence of an informal sector: a four-factor model." In Basu, K., M. Majumdar and T. Mitra (Eds), *Capita, Investment and Development*, Oxford, Basil Blackwell (1993).

McCool, T., Wage subsidies and distortionary taxes in a mobile capital Harris-Todaro model, *Economica* 49, 69-79 (1982).

Miyagiwa, K., Corporate income tax incidence in the presence of sector-specific unemployment, *Journal of Public Economics* 37, 103-112 (1988).

Neary, J. P., Dynamic stability and the theory of factor-market distortions, *American Economic Review* 68, 671-682 (1978).

Neary, J. P., On the Harris-Todaro model with intersectoral capital mobility, *Economica* 48, 219-234 (1981).

Stiglitz, J. E., Alternative theories of wage determination and unemployment in LDCs: The labour-turnover model, *Quarterly Journal of Economics* 88, 194-227 (1974).

Varian, H. R., Microeconomic Analysis, third ed, New York, Norton (1992).

Zavodny, M., *Why minimum wage hikes may not reduce employment,* Federal Reserve Bank of Atlanta Economic Review, *18-28 (1998)*.

In: Economics of Unemployment
Editor: Mary I. Marshalle, pp. 109-135
ISBN: 1-60021-138-0

*Chapter 6*

# UNEMPLOYMENT AND UNEMPLOYMENT INSURANCE

## *Dorte Domeland and Norbert Fiess*

World Bank,
1818 H Street, N.W.
Washington , DC 20433
United States

## ABSTRACT

The Brazilian unemployment insurance (UI) system is the largest in Latin America, serving an average of 300,000 to 400,000 beneficiaries each month. According to Law No. 7998 from 1990 the objective of the Brazilian unemployment system is to: (1) provide temporary financial assistance to a worker dismissed without just cause and (2) assist workers in their search for a new job. Concerning the provision of financial assistance to the worker, the law is silent on whether UI benefits are aimed at smoothing consumption or are primarily intended to prevent unemployed workers from falling into poverty.

In this chapter we look not only at unemployment rates, but analyze the determinants of the probability of becoming unemployed, as well as unemployment duration. Separating these two factors is crucial for analyzing the existing UI system. We show that informal sector employees who have neither access to unemployment insurance nor FGTS are most likely to become unemployed in Brazil. Furthermore, the conditional probability of becoming unemployed is highest for minimum wage earners.

The chapter is organized as follows. Section II describes the Brazilian unemployment insurance system and the FGTS. Section III discusses the data used in this analysis and provides some descriptive statistics. Section IV analyzes the evolution of unemployment rates. Estimates of the probability of becoming unemployed and unemployment duration conditional on worker specific characteristics are provided in Section V. Section VI discusses policy implications and concludes

# I. INTRODUCTION

The Brazilian unemployment insurance (UI) system is the largest in Latin America, serving an average of 300,000 to 400,000 beneficiaries each month. According to Law No. 7998 from 1990 the objective of the Brazilian unemployment system is to: (1) provide temporary financial assistance to a worker dismissed without just cause and (2) assist workers in their search for a new job. Concerning the provision of financial assistance to the worker, the law is silent on whether UI benefits are aimed at smoothing consumption or are primarily intended to prevent unemployed workers from falling into poverty.

The main difference between consumption smoothing and safety-net oriented unemployment insurance systems lies in replacement ratio and depth of coverage. Unemployment insurance systems which primarily focus on consumption smoothing generally aim at a high replacement ratio of the previous income. Such systems are often restricted to unemployed workers, who have been employed during a substantial period of time before becoming unemployed. UI programs that emphasize a social net objective generally provide low levels of benefits, but cover a large fraction of the population. The Brazilian UI system is characterized by a low replacement ratio, short benefit duration and the fact that it is restricted to formal sector workers. The latter implies that UI is not accessible to over 50 percent of the workforce. A further inconsistency with the social net objective arrives from the fact that receiving UI is conditional on having access to the severance fund - *Fundo de Garantia do Tempo de Serviço* (FGTS).

The FGTS was created in 1966 (Law No. 5107) by the military regime to serve as an alternative to the job security law prevailing at that time. It is combined with a fine that employers have to pay if they dismiss a worker without just cause. For a long time the FGTS was the only labor market institution that provided income to the workers at the moment they were laid off without just cause. And even nowadays, this aspect of the FGTS is important. UI benefits in Brazil are low and do not exceed two minimum wages. As a consequence, the amount worker receives from their fund at the moment they become unemployed is likely to exceed unemployment benefits by far.

In this chapter we look not only at unemployment rates, but analyze the determinants of the probability of becoming unemployed, as well as unemployment duration. Separating these two factors is crucial for analyzing the existing UI system. We show that informal sector employees who have neither access to unemployment insurance nor FGTS are most likely to become unemployed in Brazil. Furthermore, the conditional probability of becoming unemployed is highest for minimum wage earners.

While formal sector workers are less likely to become unemployed than informal wage earners ceteris paribus, they are more likely to remain unemployed once they have lost their job. Unemployment duration among formal sector workers is higher for those who received FGTS before becoming unemployed. This may hint at the fact that only the "rich" can afford a longer unemployment duration. However, this kind of statement should be treated with care. Formal sector workers may just face a longer unemployment duration as they are more selective when accepting a new job.

We provide evidence on this fact by estimating a competing risk model, which allows to consider not only unemployment duration, but also exit states. Independent of the exit state, formal sector workers are less likely to leave unemployment than informal wage earners. However, this difference turns out to be insignificant when we consider exit to the formal sector.

Among formal sector workers, FGTS (and hence UI) recipients are less likely to exit unemployment. This proves to be independent of the exit state. Thus, at least in terms of the employment sector, the unemployment insurance system seems to fail in its objective to assist workers in their search for new employment. Whether this also holds in terms of wages remains a question to be answered.

The chapter is organized as follows. Section II describes the Brazilian unemployment insurance system and the FGTS. Section III discusses the data used in this analysis and provides some descriptive statistics. Section IV analyzes the evolution of unemployment rates. Estimates of the probability of becoming unemployed and unemployment duration conditional on worker specific characteristics are provided in Section V. Section VI discusses policy implications and concludes.

## II. UNEMPLOYMENT INSURANCE SYSTEM AND THE FGTS

### The Brazilian Unemployment Insurance System

Already in the Constitution of 1946, the Brazilian President Getulio Vargas proposed an unemployment insurance system. However, it was not before 1990 that unemployment insurance became universally accessible. The current Brazilian unemployment system was created in 1986, within the context of the Cruzado Plan. Its success was rather limited due to strict eligibility criteria and severe fiscal limitations. In 1988, the source of funding was changed from general Treasury revenues to the *Fundo de Amparo ao Trabalhador* (FAT).[1] Eligibility criteria were relaxed in 1990 (Law No. 7.998), expanding the base of workers with access to UI benefits. The benefit level was also increased. As a consequence, the number of checks distributed to the unemployed doubled. By 1990, unemployment insurance covered 43 percent of all dismissals from formal employment. In 1994, collection constraints and eligibility criteria were relaxed and potential payments were increased, extending the coverage of the program even further. (Cunningham, 2000)

In order to become eligible for benefits, workers must meet the following criteria:

- **Dismissal without just cause** by the employer or **indirect dismissal**. Indirect dismissal refers to the fact that the employee requests dismissal from his job by court decision, claiming that his employer did not comply with the work contract.
- Employment under a **formal labor contract** for at least six months during the last three years or **legal self-employment** for at least 15 months.
- A **period of unemployment** for at least seven and at most 120 days.[2]
- **Lack of other sources of income** to guarantee own subsistence and that of the family.

---

[1] The FAT is financed by a 0.65 percent tax on revenues of private firms, 1 percent tax on revenues of public firms and a 1 percent of costs in non-profit firms. It then pays UI, the 13th wage (abono salarial), a fiscal stabilization fund, training initiatives from SENAI/SENAC and the National Development Bank (BNDES), which receives 40 percent of the FAT.

[2] For those workers that go to court in order to claim dismissal with just cause or indirect dismissal, this term starts at the end of the court decision or legal ratification of the agreement.

In order to make a claim for unemployment insurance benefits, a worker requires a form from his former employer specifying the time of service as well as earnings received in the three months prior to the dismissal. This form is reviewed by a national clearinghouse, which proves eligibility. Once accepted, the worker receives a proof of eligibility stating the value of benefits and the maximum benefit duration. In order to collect the monthly payment the worker must present this proof together with his signed work-card at a federal bank or employment office. After a successful claim, a worker will not be eligible again for 16 months.

The monthly benefit level (so-called parcela) depends in general on the average wage of the last three months prior to unemployment. It ranges from one minimum wage to approximately twice the minimum wage.[3] The average benefit level in 1998 was about 1.56 minimum salaries. (Thomas, 1999). Benefits do not decrease with unemployment duration. Since 1995, workers with an employment record of 6 to 11 months, 12 to 23 months and more than 24 months within the last three years are eligible to three, four and five parcelas, respectively. The average benefit duration is between 3.5 and 4.5 months (Cunningham, 2000). Neither the benefit level nor the benefit duration is contingent on job search. The payment of unemployment insurance benefit is suspended at the moment the worker finds a new job. If the worker has not used up all parcelas before finding new employment, s/he can accumulate the remaining parcelas for a future incidence of unemployment.

### Box 9.1: Dismissal in the Formal Sector

Formal sector workers who have been formally employed for at least three months have access to their FGTS account if fired without just cause or if they induce indirect dismissal. Latter refers to the fact that the employee requests the dismissal from his job by court decision, claiming that his employer did not comply with the contract.

According to monthly labor surveys in the six largest metropolitan regions (PME) from 1982-1998, 72 percent of workers who reported job separations were in fact fired and 85 percent of fired workers received FGTS.

According to the RAIS 1999, **84.5 percent of formal sector workers** with an employment record of at least six months, who separated from their job, were either fired without just cause or induced indirect dismissal. As receiving FGTS is a precondition for having access to UI, this indicates that the fact that unemployment insurance is related to cause does imply that a substantial fraction of formal sector workers are excluded from access to UI benefits.

**Women are less likely to have access to UI** compared to men. This arises basically from the fact that women are more likely to quit without claiming indirect dismissal. This may be due to the fact that women have to leave their job for specific reasons such as pregnancy or illness of a family member. Furthermore, women are more likely to have a temporary contract.[4]

---

[3] For details of the benefit calculation see http://www.mtb.gov.br/se/fgts/servicos/fgts_idx.htm.

[4] In 1998, the government introduced legislation that allows employers to hire workers on their temporary contracts. (Law No 9601). Under temporary contracts the contribution to the FGTS fund is reduced from 8 to 2 percent and the obligatory fine in case of unjust dismissal is waived.

## The FGTS

In addition to unemployment insurance, dismissed workers receive the Fundo de Garantia do Tempo de Serviço (FGTS). The FGTS is an individualized interest-bearing fund. Each month the employer contributes the equivalent of 8 percent of his employee's current wage to the fund. This implies that the amount accumulated per year in a worker's fund corresponds approximately to one monthly wage. A worker has access to FTGS if dismissed without just cause, upon retirement or death, or as a means of co-financing a private home purchase or high health expenses. The FTGS is transferable between jobs and bears interest if not accessed during a spell of unemployment.

In the case of dismissal without just cause ("sem justa causa"), the worker has not only the right to access his entire fund, including all funds accumulated during previous employment, but also receives a penalty in proportion to the accumulated FGTS in the job he is being dismissed from. This additional compensation amounted to 10 percent of the worker's FGTS balance at the time of dismissal and has been increased to 40 percent of the FGTS balance in 1988 and to 50 percent in 2001.[5]

# III. DATA ISSUES

Our analysis uses data from the *Pesquisa Mensal de Emprego* – PME (Brazilian Monthly Labor Market Survey). The PME is a monthly labor market survey, which provides information on six metropolitan areas in Brazil (Sao Paulo, Rio de Janeiro, Belo Horizonte, Porte Alegre, Recife and Salvador), covering roughly one quarter of Brazil's labor force. The survey is conducted by the Brazilian Census Bureau (IBGE), began in 1980 and after a revision in 1982 remained basically unchanged until to date. The PME provides up to eight interviews for one person. In each year an individual is usually interviewed in four consecutive months. The rotating panel structure of the PME allows to track individual workers for a limited period of time and hence to construct individual work histories.

We also refer to the *Pesquisa Nacional por Amostragem Domiciliar* - PNAD (Brazilian Annual National Household Survey) and the *Relação Anual das Informações Sociais* – RAIS (Brazilian Annual Labor Market Register). The PNAD data is an annual national household survey of approximately 100,000 households, which is performed in the third quarter of each year. It is also conducted by IBGE and began at national level in 1971. Between 1990 and 1992 it underwent a major revision, which makes it difficult to obtain full compatibility of data between the PNAD concept before and after 1992. This is important to keep in mind when comparing data across the last two decades. The survey contains extensive information on personal characteristics, including information on income, labor force participation, and educational attainment and attendance. However as we will discuss below, information provided for the unemployed is rather scarce.

The RAIS is a nationwide register and covers about 90 percent of the formal Brazilian labor force. Employers are required to declare flows and stocks of employees during the course of the year. The RAIS is administrated by the Ministério do Trabalho e Emprego and was first implemented in December 1975.

## IV. UNEMPLOYMENT RATES IN BRAZIL

For Brazil, the beginning of the 1990s seems to mark a pivot point for unemployment. While unemployment was on the decrease through the 1980s, the 1990s showed an increasing trend in unemployment. This change in the trend may have been due to a variety of factors such as the introduction of the Real Plan or the change in the Constitution in 1988. However, rather than investigating the causes of unemployment, we attempt to profile the unemployed in order to evaluate the Brazilian unemployment insurance system.

Figure 9.1 reveals the evolution of different unemployment rates for Brazil. The **official unemployment rate** is measured for workers aged 15 to 65 who are unemployed in the reference period and who have been searching for employment during the last four weeks. This unemployment rate increased from 4 percent in February 1990 to 7 percent in May 1992. The Real Plan brought a short reduction in unemployment, leading to a decline in the official rate to 4 percent in December 1994. After the Asian crisis (October 1997) unemployment rates started to climb again reaching 10 percent in March 2000.

**Unemployment of younger workers** is measured as the official unemployment rate of workers who are between 15 to 24 years old. At the beginning of the 1990s, this unemployment rate was about three times higher than the rate amongst workers older than 25. But this gap increased, such that at the beginning of the new millennium the unemployment rate of younger workers was about five times higher compared to that of older workers. It is important to keep in mind that the unemployment rate of younger workers reflects well the dynamics of the unemployment rate of labor market (re)-entrants, who do not have any access to unemployment insurance.

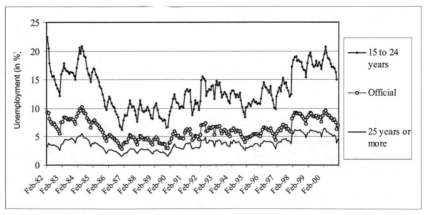

*Source*: PME/IBGE. Elaboration: CPS/IBRE/FGV

---

[5] The FGTS fund is administrated by the government. According to Paes de Barros et al. (1999), inefficiencies in the administration of the FTGS translate in investment returns well below market rates and provide an incentive for workers to seek access to their funds by provoking their dismissal.

Figure 9.1. Different Definitions of Unemployment Rates

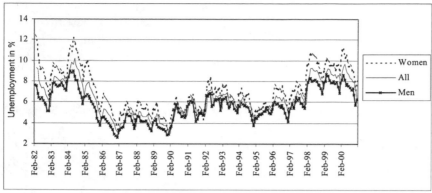

*Source*: PME/IBGE. Elaboration: CPS/IBRE/FGV

Figure 9.2. Unemployment Rates by Gender

**Unemployment by gender** shows that female unemployment is almost 30 percent higher than male unemployment. In May 1998, the female unemployment rate reached its highest peak of the 1990s. From 1991 to May 1998 female unemployment rates faced on average an annual growth rate of 0.33, while the corresponding value for men was 0.002. The sharp increase in female unemployment may be partially explained by an increase in female labor force participation. From 1982 to 2000 the female labor force participation rate rose from 36 percent to 42 percent. Furthermore, the gender gap widened during periods of high unemployment. This may hint at a so-called added worker effect due to women entering the labor force during recessions as other family members especially their spouses become unemployed or face reduction in income, pushing unemployment rates even further up during recessions. On the other hand, it may indicate that women are more likely to be dismissed during recessions as tenure is usually shorter among women and hence the costs of dismissal in terms of the FGTS fine are lower for formal employers. We will provide more evidence on this below.

**Unemployment rates by household status** show that children of the household head face the highest unemployment rate. This is consistent with the above finding that unemployment rates for young workers are relatively high. However, this group faced the lowest increase in the unemployment rate due to the fact that unemployment of sons and daughter had been already at a high level of 9.38 in 1991. The unemployment rate of spouses more than doubled between 1991 and 1998, surpassing the unemployment rate of household heads in 1998.

Table 9.1 provides **unemployment rates by different educational level** and household status. Workers with 9 to 11 years of education (completed secondary education) had the highest unemployment rate in May 1998. This group also faced the highest increase in the unemployment rate from 1991 to May 1998, followed by the lowest education group (primary I education). Hence from Table 9.1, we cannot deduce any clear relation between level of unemployment/change in unemployment and education.

## V. THE PROBABILITY OF BECOMING UNEMPLOYED

The evolution of unemployment rates are determined by the incidence of unemployment and unemployment duration, i.e. unemployment rates may increase because more people become unemployed and/or stay unemployed for a longer time. As separating these two effects is crucial for understanding unemployment and consequently the evaluation of the existing unemployment insurance system, we first analyze the probability of becoming unemployed and then turn to the determinants of unemployment duration.

**Table 9.1. Unemployment Rates by Education and Household Status**

| Characteristic | 1991 | 1994 | May, 1997 | May, 1998 | Change* 91-98 |
|---|---|---|---|---|---|
| By Education |  |  |  |  |  |
| 0- 4 years | 3.88 | 4.03 | 4.41 | 6.66 | 71.65 |
| 5-8 years | 7.03 | 7.03 | 8.41 | 10.10 | 43.67 |
| 9-11 years | 5.37 | 6.00 | 7.39 | 10.28 | 91.43 |
| 12 or more years | 2.59 | 2.41 | 2.66 | 4.10 | 58.30 |
| By Household Status |  |  |  |  |  |
| Head | 3.08 | 3.22 | 3.68 | 5.42 | 75.97 |
| Spouse | 2.59 | 3.11 | 4.42 | 6.43 | 148.26 |
| Son/Daughter | 9.38 | 9.72 | 11.36 | 14.21 | 51.49 |
| Other | 6.16 | 6.68 | 6.93 | 9.55 | 55.03 |

*Change in percent.
*Source:* IPEA/Ministerio do Trabalho (1998). PME (selected years)

## Descriptive Statistics

In our analysis of the probability of becoming unemployed, we use the 12 monthly surveys of the PME 1999. Our sample consists of 421,133 observations on members of the active labor force who are between 15 and 65 years old. As it can be seen in the first column of Table 9.2, less than 5 percent in our sample are unemployed, which is significantly lower than the official Brazilian unemployment rate in 1999 of more than 8 percent. One reason why this is the case is that the mean age in our sample is strikingly high. The unemployment rate of 25 year olds or older workers was 5.8 in February 1999, which is much closer to the statistics provided by the PME.

The PME does not contain directly accessible information on pre-unemployment wages. However, in order to understand the importance of unemployment insurance benefits as a means of providing income support to the unemployed, this information is crucial. As in the PME about 90 percent of the workers are interviewed at least 3 times during the course of a year, we are able to construct individual work histories. In the data we then observe some unemployed workers who had been employed in the previous interview and hence provide information on their pre-unemployment wage. The descriptive statistics of this **sample with wage information** are presented in column 2 of Table 9.2. As all employed workers provide information on their wage, we obtain the sample with wage information by excluding those unemployed individuals for whom we do not observe an employment spell before becoming unemployed. Excluding workers without pre-unemployment wage information hence reduces the proportion of the unemployed and accordingly the proportion of FGTS recipients in the sample even further.

Note that the percentage of unemployed receiving FGTS drops from 45 percent in the unrestricted sample to 33 percent in the sample with wage information. This may be due to the fact that FGTS recipients have a higher unemployment duration and hence we are less likely to observe an employment spell in the data. The statistics of the other variables remain basically unchanged.

The descriptive statistics of the sample of formal sector workers are presented in column 3. We define formal sector workers as a worker with holding a signed labor card or an unemployed person, who had a signed labor card in a previous job. Formal sector workers are more likely to become unemployed. As a consequence, the percentage of unemployed increases to 5.9 percent when we restrict our sample to formal sector workers. Furthermore, the proportion of people employed in the manufacturing sector increases.

## Evolution of the Probability of Becoming Unemployed Conditional on Employment Status

In this section, we analyze the probability of becoming unemployed conditioned on the employment status of a worker *prior* to falling into unemployment. In contrast to the previous section, the term employment status refers here to formal employees, informal employees and self-employed workers.[6] Analyzing the probability of becoming unemployed conditional on the employment status is motivated by the fact that the informal sector is very large in Brazil. In our unrestricted sample (column 1 in Table 9.2) nearly 50 percent of the respondents are either informal wage earners or self-employed. We differentiate among self-employed and informal employees, as their economic behavior is different.

As can be seen in Figure 9.3, the probability of becoming unemployed increased from 1986 onwards for all workers independent of their employment status. After the Real Plan of 1994, the probability of becoming unemployed stabilized for a while, but has been growing strongly after 1997. Self-employed were least likely to become unemployed while informal sector workers suffered the highest probabilities of loosing their job during the 1990s.

The evolution of the unemployment probabilities seems to be closely tied to the underlying labor market functioning as argued by Fiess, Fugazza and Maloney in Chapter 2. It seems therefore not surprising that we find an increase in the unemployment probabilities (most pronounced for informal employees) after the Collor plan failed and the economy was on a recessive path with increasing fear of a rapid and incisive opening of the economy. The return of hyperinflation without perfect indexation of wages allowed firms to adjust mainly through prices rather than quantities in 1993 and in the first half of 1994. This corresponds to falling unemployment probabilities (again most pronounced for informal employees) and lower and relatively stable unemployment probabilities during the economic recovery in the aftermath of the Real Plan. The Asian crisis then again brought increasing unemployment probabilities which

---

[6] We exclude employers as the number of employers who lost their job is very low in our data set.

is in line with the findings of Fiess, Fugazza and Maloney that the labor market adjusted during this crises predominantly through quantities.

## Table 9.2. Descriptive Statistics

| Variable | All | Wage Information | Formal Sector |
|---|---|---|---|
| Age | 41.9 | 41.0 | 39.3 |
| Yes | 2.2 | 0.5 | 5.0 |
| No | 97.8 | 99.5 | 95.0 |
| Employed | 95.1 | 98.5 | 94.1 |
| Unemployed | 4.9 | 1.5 | 5.9 |
| Female | 18.3 | 18.1 | 17.5 |
| Male | 81.7 | 81.9 | 82.5 |
| Formal Employee | 44.2 | 43.7 | 100 |
| Informal Employee | 21.2 | 21.0 | 0 |
| Self-employed | 28.3 | 28.82 | 0 |
| Employer | 6.3 | 6.5 | 0 |
| Manufacturing | 16.8 | 16.6 | 26.1 |
| Construction | 11.1 | 10.9 | 7.0 |
| Commerce | 14.0 | 14.0 | 12.1 |
| Service | 49.4 | 49.6 | 51.6 |
| Other Sectors | 8.7 | 8.9 | 3.2 |
| No education | 22.6 | 22.6 | 21.1 |
| Primary | 26.1 | 25.9 | 25.9 |
| Lower Secondary | 17.0 | 16.9 | 18.5 |
| Secondary | 22.3 | 22.4 | 23.9 |
| Tertiary | 12.0 | 12.2 | 10.6 |
| Rio de Janeiro | 17.8 | 18.0 | 16.9 |
| Sao Paulo | 20.9 | 20.9 | 21.7 |
| Rio Grande do Sul | 17.5 | 17.5 | 18.1 |
| Minas Gerais | 18.3 | 18.4 | 18.7 |
| Bahia | 13.1 | 12.9 | 13.7 |
| Pernambuco | 12.4 | 12.4 | 10.8 |
| # of observations | 241,133 | 213,065 | 106,590 |

*Source:* PME 1999– Authors' own calculations.

It has been claimed that the increase in the FGTS fine in 1988 from 10 to 40 percent has motivated formal workers to induce their dismissal. The drop in unemployment probabilities across the board during 1988 and 1989 provides little evidence for this hypothesis. In fact the general comovement of unemployment probabilities for different working classes appears to be more driven by the prevailing macroeconomic environment and the degree of labor market segmentation and less by specific changes in the labor market legislation.[7]

---

[7] This finding is also supported by Ramos and Carneiro (2003). They find no econometric evidence that the change in the level of turnover rates observed at the end of the 1980s was associated with a change in legislation. De Barros

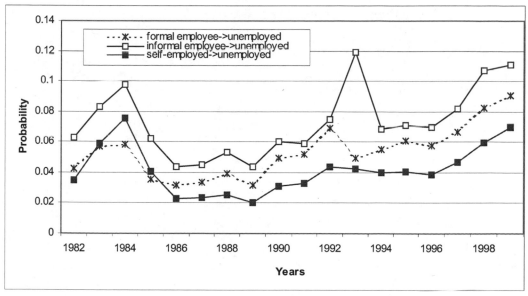

*Source:* PME – Authors' own calculations.

Figure 9.3. Unemployment Entrance Probability Conditional on Employment Status

## Probability of Becoming Unemployed Conditioned on Individual Characteristics

In the previous section, we showed that informal sector workers are most likely to become unemployed, followed by formal sector workers. Here, we determine the probability of becoming unemployed conditional on different individual characteristics. The estimation method is a probit analysis, where the dependent variables is a dummy that assumes value 1 if a person is unemployed and 0 otherwise.

In Table 9.3, we present the results of four different sample specifications. Specification 1 includes all workers. Specification 2 is restricted to formal sector workers. Specification 3 includes only workers who provide information on their job prior to becoming unemployed. Specification 4 restricts specification 3 to formal sector workers. The different specifications are not only estimated for different groups of workers, they also include different sets of explanatory variables as we only have information about pre-unemployment wages for the workers in specification 3 and 4.

As already mentioned, neither PME nor PNAD contain directly accessible information on the wage and the tenure a worker had obtained before becoming unemployed. However, in order to understand the importance of unemployment insurance benefits as a means of providing income support to the unemployed, this information is crucial.

---

et al. (1999) find some evidence that the 1988 constitution by increasing firing costs lowered separation rates and increased employment spells. However, they also acknowledge the difficulty to isolate the impact of the 1988 constitutional changes from the impact of the large macroeconomic changes at the end of the 1980s and beginning of the 1990s.

## Table 9.3. Probability of Becoming Unemployed

| | All | | Formal | | Wage Information | | Formal and Wage Information | |
|---|---|---|---|---|---|---|---|---|
| | Coef. | Z | Coef. | Z | Coef. | z | Coef. | z |
| Age: 25-44 | -0.141 | -7.17 | -0.060 | -2.13 | -0.071 | -2.25 | -0.026 | -0.535 |
| Age: >45 | -0.219 | -10.66 | -0.089 | -2.97 | -0.161 | -4.83 | -0.062 | -1.182 |
| Female | 0.161 | 13.99 | 0.131 | 8.01 | -0.092 | -4.35 | -0.138 | -4.086 |
| Working Class: | | | | | | | | |
| Formal employee | -0.113 | -10.14 | | | -0.161 | -8.77 | | |
| Self-employed | -0.447 | -33.32 | | | -0.364 | -17.64 | | |
| Employer | -0.781 | -24.23 | | | -0.693 | -12.08 | | |
| Sector: | | | | | | | | |
| Construction | 0.246 | 15.28 | 0.306 | 13.01 | 0.298 | 11.85 | 0.347 | 8.882 |
| Commerce | -0.069 | -4.25 | 0.029 | 1.35 | -0.089 | -3.23 | 0.034 | 0.876 |
| Service | -0.140 | -11.23 | -0.084 | -5.47 | -0.101 | -4.73 | -0.041 | -1.461 |
| Other | -0.429 | -19.15 | -0.541 | -10.36 | -0.369 | -9.91 | -0.392 | -4.188 |
| Education : | | | | | | | | |
| Primary | 0.029 | 2.38 | 0.049 | 2.71 | 0.033 | 1.69 | 0.060 | 1.908 |
| Lower Sec. | 0.018 | 1.27 | 0.071 | 3.61 | 0.027 | 1.20 | 0.101 | 2.905 |
| Secondary | -0.064 | -4.68 | -0.026 | -1.39 | -0.076 | -3.21 | 0.025 | 0.712 |
| Tertiary | -0.331 | -16.72 | -0.288 | -10.42 | -0.284 | -7.46 | -0.167 | -2.890 |
| Wage: | | | | | | | | |
| 1-2 SM | | | | | -0.332 | -16.24 | - | - |
| 3-5 SM | | | | | -0.515 | -19.40 | -0.217 | -6.767 |
| 5-20 SM | | | | | -0.620 | -19.49 | -0.341 | -8.246 |
| >20 SM | | | | | -0.770 | -7.89 | -0.375 | -3.241 |
| Region: | | | | | | | | |
| Rio de Janeiro | -0.191 | -12.16 | -0.158 | -7.26 | 0.172 | 5.49 | 0.023 | 0.544 |
| Minas Gerais | -0.052 | -3.63 | -0.059 | -2.97 | 0.397 | 12.96 | 0.145 | 3.672 |
| Rio Grande do Sul | -0.020 | -1.42 | 0.005 | 0.25 | 0.373 | 14.14 | 0.122 | 3.189 |
| Pernambuco | 0.172 | 11.67 | 0.159 | 7.73 | 0.614 | 22.83 | 0.043 | 9.942 |
| Bahia | 0.045 | 2.84 | 0.010 | 0.42 | 0.393 | 13.78 | 0.361 | 0.978 |
| Constant | -1.222 | -48.77 | -1.491 | -44.38 | -1.860 | -45.46 | -2.221 | -37.223 |
| # of observations | 241,133 | | 106,590 | | 213,065 | | 92,690 | |
| Log Likelihood | -45,200.6 | | -23,352.5 | | -15,306.4 | | -6,470.3 | |

Source: PME 1999.Authors' own calculations.

As in the PME about 90 percent of the workers are interviewed at least 3 times during the course of a year, we are able to construct individual work histories. We then obtain wage information for workers who had been employed during one interview and unemployed in the preceding interview. Using this restricted sample, we are able to provide evidence on how the previous wage affects the probability of becoming unemployed. Wages are deflated using monthly INPC data to ensure comparability over time.

Explanatory variables in specification 1 and 2 include age, gender, education levels, sector of employment, employment status as well as regional dummies. By employment status, we refer to self-employed, employer, formal or informal wage earner. The baseline dummy for this group refers to informal wage earners, which implies that the coefficients of the other employment status dummies have to be interpreted relative to this group. The baseline dummy for the regional dummies is Sao Paolo.

The coefficients of specification 1 in Table 9.3 show that men are less likely to become unemployed and that the probability of becoming unemployed decreases with age. Consistent with the unconditional probabilities, informal sector wage earners face the highest conditional probability of becoming unemployed, followed by formal sector workers. Being formal (self-employed) reduces the probability of becoming unemployment relative to informal workers. Relative to the industrial sector, working in construction increases the probability of becoming unemployed, while for the service sector the opposite is the case. Workers in Rio de Janeiro and Minas Gerais are less likely to become unemployed respective to workers in Sao Paulo, while workers in the Northeast of Brazil (Pernambuco and Bahia) are more likely to fall into unemployment.

Regarding education, we find that individuals with primary or secondary education are more likely to become unemployed than non-educated workers. However, this difference is not always significant.

This changes when we restrict our sample to formal wage earners (specification 2). We now find that workers with primary and secondary education are significantly more likely to become unemployed than non-educated formal sector workers. This may indicate a sorting effect in the sense that only highly motivated or able non-educated workers achieve formal sector status. Higher educated individuals, on the other hand, are less likely to become unemployed.

Specification 3 and 4 control for wages. Both specifications clearly show that the probability of becoming unemployed decreases with wages.[8]

Note however, that we are only able to deduce wage information for short-term unemployed. If workers who earn very low wages have a relatively short unemployment duration, then we are likely to overestimate the probability of becoming unemployed for this wage group. The following analysis on unemployment duration will shed more light on this issue. Moreover, we have shown above that women are more likely to become long-term unemployed. The fact that we eliminate the long-term unemployed through our sample selection criteria is likely to produce the observed change in the sign of the female dummy coefficient. Additionally, in the unrestricted sample women are more likely to become unemployed as they belong usually to the group with the lowest earnings.

---

[8] As formal sector workers cannot be paid legally below the minimum wage, we use the wage bracket between one and two minimum wages as the base line dummy in specification 4. We find that about 0.35 percent of formal employees report salaries below one minimum wage. These workers were dropped from the sample in specification 4.

Low open unemployment rates in developing countries are commonly attributed to the hypothesis that unemployment is a luxury that the poor – especially household heads – simply cannot afford. Unemployment is then a phenomenon afflicting the relatively young, secondary earners in households, or the better educated. Our findings from the probit analysis do not support this point of view. It is the low-income, less educated households who are most likely to become unemployed.

# VI. UNEMPLOYMENT DURATION

Unemployment rates are determined by the *incidence* and *duration* of unemployment. A distinguishing feature of duration data is that it is censored. Censoring is caused by the fact that we do not observe a complete unemployment spell for individuals who are still unemployed at the time of their last interview. As estimates that ignore censoring actually underestimate unemployment duration, we account for censoring, by identifying complete and uncomplete unemployment spells from individual work histories.

## Data and Descriptive Statistics

The samples used for the duration analysis are described in Table 9.4. The **basic sample** consists of unemployed individuals, who are between 15 to 65 years old and who are at most 48 weeks without employment. Dropping the unemployed who have been without work for more than 48 weeks does not change the characteristics of our sample as it can be seen by comparing column 1 (*All*) and column 2 (*Basic*) of Table 9.4.[9]

### Table 9.4. Descriptive Statistics of Duration Data

| Variable | (Mean Values) | | | |
|---|---|---|---|---|
|  | All | Basic | Formal | Wage |
| Age | 38.63 | 38.4 | 38.0 | 38.2 |
| FGTS |  |  |  |  |
| Yes | 42.2 | 41.0 | 84.2 | 34.9 |
| No | 57.8 | 59.0 | 15.8 | 65.1 |
| Gender |  |  |  |  |
| Female | 22.4 | 22.0 | 19.0 | 16.1 |
| Male | 77.6 | 78.0 | 81.0 | 83.9 |
| Former Employment Status |  |  |  |  |
| Formal Employee | 50.0 | 49.0 | 100 | 44.0 |
| Informal Employee | 30.0 | 30.5 | 0 | 31.8 |
| Self-employed | 18.8 | 19.2 | 0 | 23.2 |
| Employer | 1.2 | 1.3 | 0 | 1.0 |
| Former Sector of Employment |  |  |  |  |
| Manufacturing | 18.6 | 17.8 | 25.6 | 16.1 |

---

[9] Unfortunately We Are Not Able To Differentiate In The Data Whether A Person Was Four Weeks Or One Month Without Employment. We Thus Assume That Each Month Corresponds To Four Weeks. This Implies That We Are Actually Underestimating Unemployment Duration.

## Table 9.4. Descriptive Statistics of Duration Data (Continued)

(Mean Values)

| Variable | All | Basic | Formal | Wage |
|---|---|---|---|---|
| Construction | 19.4 | 20.4 | 13.9 | 25.8 |
| Commerce | 12.9 | 12.8 | 13.8 | 11.8 |
| Service | 43.3 | 43.3 | 45.2 | 41.8 |
| Other Sectors | 5.8 | 5.7 | 0.5 | 4.5 |
| Education | | | | |
| No education | 27.6 | 28.0 | 24.3 | 31.4 |
| Primary | 29.9 | 30.1 | 28.4 | 30.3 |
| Lower Secondary | 19.1 | 19.2 | 21.5 | 19.4 |
| Secondary | 18.8 | 18.3 | 21.0 | 15.7 |
| Tertiary | 4.6 | 4.4 | 4.8 | 3.1 |
| Duration | | | | |
| Duration in weeks | 20.8 | 15.2 | 17.3 | 11.0 |
| Censored | 36.8 | 36.3 | 34.1 | 33.2 |
| Former Wage | | | | |
| Wage | 350.5 | 351.55 | 408.2 | 351.55 |
| # of observations | 8167 | 7549 | 3674 | 2350 |

*All* includes all unemployed who are between 15 to 65 years old. *Basic, Formal* and *Wage* are restricted to unemployed, who are between 15 to 65 years old and at most 48 weeks without employment. *Formal* refers to unemployed who had a signed work card before becoming unemployed. *Wage* consists of those unemployed who provide information on pre-unemployment wages.
*Source:* PME 1999. Authors' own calculations.

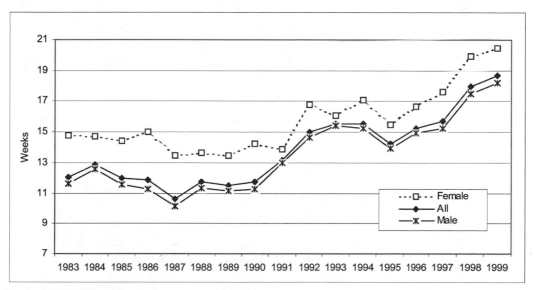

*Source:* PME 1983-1999. Authors own calculations.

Figure 9.4. Mean Unemployment Duration by Gender

Sample characteristics change when we eliminate informal sector workers from our sample. In the **formal sample**, the percentage of men and former manufacturing workers increases relative to the basic sample, which is similar to our findings in Table 9.1. Mean wages as well as unemployment duration are significantly higher in the formal sector. As only formal sector workers have access to FGTS, the proportion of workers who received FGTS before becoming unemployed increases.

The **wage sample** restricts the basic sample to workers for whom we can deduce pre-unemployment wages. Relative to the basic sample, the percentage of formal sector workers and hence the proportion of manufacturing workers, FGTS recipients and workers with higher education decreases. We underestimate the proportion of formal sector workers in the wage sample due to the fact that in order to obtain the wage information, we required that the worker had been employed during at least one interview before becoming unemployed. As the mean unemployment duration is longer for formal sector workers, we are less likely to observe a pre-unemployment employment spell for a formal worker.

## Evolution of Unemployment Duration

The **duration of unemployment** spells is significantly higher today than in the mid1980s. As it can be seen from Figure 9.4, after the introduction of the new constitution in 1988, unemployment spells rose by about 50 percent. Similarly, to unemployment rates, this trend came to a halt between mid 1994 and mid 1997. After the Asian crisis, unemployment duration increased again.

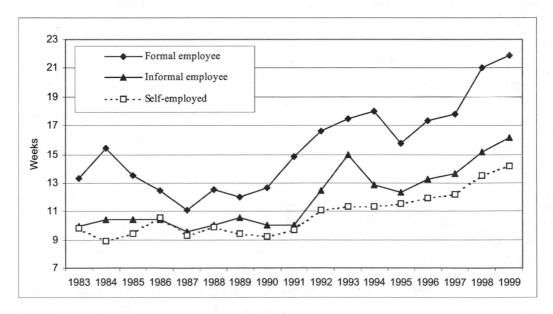

*Source:* PME 1983 -1999. Authors own calculations.

Figure 9.5. Mean Duration by Working Class

Looking at **unemployment duration by gender**, it can be seen that male unemployment duration traces the mean unemployment duration closely. During the 1990s male unemployment duration increased from 13 weeks in 1990 to more than 15 weeks in 1997. Similarly, female unemployment duration has become longer and exceeds male unemployment duration on average by 20 percent. The gap between male and female unemployment duration seems to have narrowed at the end of the 1980s, but started to widen again after the Asian crisis.

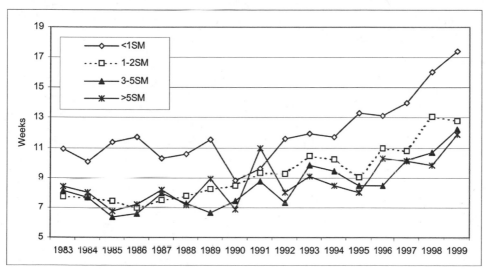

*Source:* PME 1983 -1999. Authors own calculations.

Figure 9.6. Unemployment Duration by Wage Groups

The evolution of **unemployment duration by working class** is displayed in Figure 9.5. Unemployment duration of the self-employed grew since 1990 without interruption, but formal sector workers faced the highest increase in unemployment duration during the 1990s. From 1990 to 1997 their unemployment duration increased by 73 percent. The corresponding increases for informal wage earners and self-employed amount to 61 and 53 percent, respectively. Note that only formal sector workers may have access to their FGTS account. Hence, the mean duration of workers who received FGTS traces that of formal sector workers closely.

Figure 9.6 provides a breakdown of **unemployment duration by wage groups.** Unemployment duration increased for all wage groups, however most dramatically for those earning less than a minimum wage. From 1990 to 1999 the unemployment duration of this wage group nearly doubled. Strikingly enough, the group with the second highest increase in unemployment duration during this period consists of the highest wage earners (73 percent), followed by workers who earned three to five minimum wages (64 percent) and one to two minimum wages (51 percent).

## Kaplan Meier Estimates

In order to provide some first evidence on unemployment duration, we present the Kaplan Meier estimators of the survivor function.[10] From Figure 9.7, it can be seen that the probability of facing an unemployment spell of $t$ weeks is higher for women than for men at all times. The difference between the respective fraction of **men and women** increases with unemployment duration, indicating that it becomes more difficult for women than men to find a job as unemployed duration increases. The probability of facing an unemployment spell of at least 48 weeks is above 0.5 for women, but only 0.25 for men.

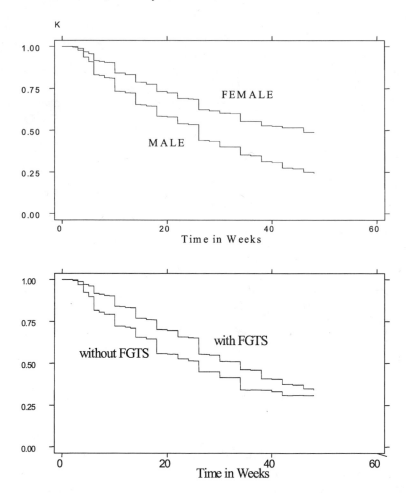

Figure 9.7. Estimated Kaplan Meier Survivor Function by Gender and FGTS

Figure 9.7 shows the Kaplan Meier Survivor function for the **formal sector**, stratified by FGTS recipients and those who do not receive FGTS. Recall that receiving FGTS is a precondition for receiving unemployment benefits. As it can be seen, the probability of an

---

[10] The Kaplan Meier estimator is a strictly empirical approach to estimating survival functions and hence does not rely on distributional assumptions. This makes it an interesting starting point for the analysis of duration data. The survivor function indicates the probability that the unemployment spell is at least of length $t$ or put differently, it indicates the fraction of unemployed who are at least $t$ weeks without employment and plots this fraction against $t$.

unemployment spell lasting at least $t$ periods is higher for FGTS recipients as compared to formal sector workers who did not receive FGTS before becoming unemployed. The difference in this probability between FGTS and non FGTS recipients increases first and reaches its maximum after 28 weeks. (Unemployment benefits are available for 12 to 20 weeks). The probability of an unemployment spell in excess of 48 months is again very similar for the two subgroups: 0.34 for FGTS recipients and 0.31 for non recipients.[11]

## Conditional Unemployment Duration

Above, we presented evidence on unemployment duration for different groups of workers. Here, we apply a regression analysis to the sample of observed unemployment spells in order to characterize expected duration conditional on a set of covariates. These covariates include age, gender, education and regions, as well as pre-unemployment working class, sector and wage. Again, we proxy duration of unemployment spells by the number of weeks spent searching for a job for those currently unemployed.

Table 9.5 presents the estimation results of the Cox Proportional Hazard (Cox PH) model. The Cox PH model allows to derive the effects of the covariates on the hazard from unemployment to work without placing any restrictions at all on the shape of the baseline hazard.[12] The negative coefficients on the female dummy indicate that women have lower hazard rates ceteris paribus than men, i.e. a lower conditional rate of leaving unemployment and hence longer survival times. At each survival time, the hazard rate for **women** is less than 60 percent of the male hazard rate. Similarly, older workers are less likely to leave unemployment.

Former self-employed workers hence face the highest conditional probability of leaving unemployment. The hazard rate of **formal sector workers** is about 68 percent of the hazard rate of former informal employees, while the hazard rate of self-employed is nearly 30 percent higher. The coefficients on the **education** dummies are negative, hinting at the fact that the probability of leaving unemployment actually decreases with education. Concerning the **sector** of employment, we have seen above, that construction workers are more likely to lose their job. But as it can be seen in Table 9.5 they also have less difficulties in finding a ne job than former manufacturing workers. The **regional dummies** reveal that in Sao Paulo the unemployed are least and in Minas Gerais most likely to exit unemployment.

The results for former formal sector workers are displayed in column 2 of Table 9.5. The coefficient on **FGTS** indicates that at each survival time, the hazard rate of those who receive FGTS is only 66 percent of the hazard of those who did not receive FGTS. Note that receiving FGTS is a condition for having access to unemployment benefits. This may hint at some kind of moral hazard issue, where those who receive unemployment benefits reduce their search effort. Or it may indicate that FGTS recipients are more selective when accepting a new job offer as

---

[11] We use a log-rank test in order to test for the equality of the survivor functions of men and women and FGTS and non FGTS recipients. The respective chi square statistics are 126.97 and 26.97, we therefore reject the null hypothesis of no subgroup difference in the survivor function for both groupings.

[12] In order to account for the fact that our data is continuous rather than discrete, we also estimate a discrete complementary log-log (proportional hazard) model with a log time baseline hazard for the entire sample and the formal sector. There exists no significant difference among the coefficients of the two models. The log time coefficient indicates the hazard is increasing over time, but at a decreasing rate.

compared to non FGTS recipients and only accept "good" matches. The latter would be in line with the objective of the UI system to assist workers in their search for a new job.

## Table 9.5. Cox Proportional Hazard Model

| | Basic | | Formal | | Wage | |
|---|---|---|---|---|---|---|
| | Coefficient | Z | Coefficient | z | Coefficient | z |
| Age | -0.017 | -9.078 | -0.021 | -6.827 | -0.009 | -2.399 |
| Female | -0.550 | -9.629 | -0.439 | -5.069 | -0.393 | -3.216 |
| FGTS | | | -0.431 | -5.618 | | |
| Working Class: | | | | | | |
| Formal employee | -0.376 | -8.201 | | | -0.418 | -4.768 |
| Self-employed | 0.270 | 4.860 | | | 0.159 | 1.621 |
| Employer | -0.230 | -1.314 | | | -0.274 | -0.731 |
| Sector: | | | | | | |
| Construction | 0.302 | 4.802 | 0.233 | 2.514 | 0.258 | 2.136 |
| Commerce | -0.039 | -0.812 | 0.069 | 0.717 | -0.080 | -0.561 |
| Service | -0.05 | -0.094 | -0.024 | -0.327 | 0.025 | 0.218 |
| Other | 0.008 | 0.007 | -0.394 | -1.224 | -0.068 | -0.309 |
| Education : | | | | | | |
| Primary | -0.084 | -1.717 | -0.107 | -1.393 | 0.012 | 0.131 |
| Lower Sec. | -0.088 | -1.553 | -0.056 | -0.672 | -0.080 | 0.744 |
| Secondary | -0.361 | -5.757 | -0.305 | -3.366 | -0.237 | -1.783 |
| Tertiary | -0.370 | -3.471 | -0.247 | -1.665 | -0.065 | -0.277 |
| Wage: | | | | | | |
| 1-2 minimum wage | | | | | 0.229 | 2.163 |
| 3-5 MW | | | | | 0.355 | 2.672 |
| 5-20 MW | | | | | 0.287 | 1.731 |
| >20 MW | | | | | -0.670 | -1.110 |
| Region: | | | | | | |
| Rio de Janeiro | 0.212 | 2.880 | 0.334 | 3.190 | 0.413 | 3.29 |
| Minas Gerais | 0.436 | 7.048 | 0.508 | 5.454 | 0.496 | 4.491 |
| Rio Grande do Sul | 0.195 | 3.013 | 0.198 | 2.057 | 0.296 | 3.003 |
| Pernambuco | 0.100 | 1.424 | 0.066 | 0.585 | 0.280 | 2.540 |
| Bahia | 0.051 | 1.107 | 0.170 | 1.837 | 0.029 | 0.732 |
| # of observations | 7549 | | 3674 | | 2350 | |
| Log Likelihood | -21,829.6 | | -9,140.0 | | -5,249.56 | |

*Basic, Formal* and *Wage* are restricted to unemployed, who are between 15 to 65 years old and less than one year without employment. *Formal* refers to unemployed who had a signed work card before becoming unemployed. *Wage* consists of those unemployed who provide information on pre-unemployment wages. *Source:* PME 1999 – Authors' own calculations.

Evidence on the effect of **wages** on the hazard rate is provided in column 3. Minimum wage earners are less likely to leave unemployment compared to workers who earn less than 20 minimum wages, which is consistent with Figure 9.6. However, the Cox PH model reveals that the hazard rate of the highest wage group is ceteris paribus lower than the hazard rate of the lowest wage group. The coefficient for the highest wage group however is not statistically significant due to the few number of observations in the sample. The results furthermore may be due to outliers and hence should be interpreted with care.

## Conditional Unemployment Duration and Exit States

So far, we have only looked at the time until exit from unemployment and ignored the question whether an unemployed worker exits to a formal or informal sector job. To overcome this issue, we estimate an independent competing risks model, which allows us to differentiate among two or more independent exit destinations.[13] In our model these destinations are either formal or informal sector, or formal wage earner, informal wage earner and self-employed. The results we present below are estimated using a discrete complementary log-log (proportional hazard) model with flexible baseline hazard. The model assumes that for each time interval, there exists an interval-specific parameter that is constant over this interval. Due to zero observations, we choose two weeks as the relevant time interval.[14]

We are not the first to apply a competing risk model to the analysis of unemployment duration in the Brazilian labor market. Cunningham (2000) uses this methodology and PNAD data to analyze the impact of the 1994 increase in UI benefits on unemployment duration. Cunningham's approach differs from ours in the sense that she is able to identify the effect of unemployment insurance on unemployment duration and exit states. Our approach is not able to provide evidence on the causal effects of unemployment insurance, as it is more descriptive in nature.

The first column of Table 9.6 presents the effects of the covariates on the hazard from unemployment to formal sector employment. In the second column we present the estimates which refer to exit to the informal sector. This subsumes informal wage earners, self-employed and employers. In the last column we provide the results on exit to self-employment. Independent of the exit destination, **age** has a significant negative impact. The negative age effect is lower for exit to the informal sector as compared to the formal sector and lowest for exit to self-employment. This indicates that older workers are less likely to exit to a formal sector job, once unemployed. Women are less likely to exit to formal employment. The female hazard rate to formal employment is less than 40 percent of the hazard rate of men. The gender differential in the hazard rate decreases when we consider exit to informal employment.

Regarding **working class**, we see that previous informal wage earners have the highest hazard rate to the formal and to the informal sector. The hazard rate to formal employment for former formal sector workers is about 87 percent of the hazard rate of informal wage earners. This indicates that former informal wage earners are actually not deprived from finding a job in the formal sector and contradicts the conventional dualistic perception of the Brazilian labor market. Furthermore, it shows that former formal sector workers are in general less likely to exit unemployment than self-employed, but that they are more likely to exit unemployment to the formal sector. Concerning the hazard rate to informal employment, we find that former formal sector workers face a hazard which is about 52 percent of the hazard rate of informal wage earners. The respective relative hazard rate of self-employed is 71 percent. Considering exit to self-employment, the hazard rate to self-employment for previously self-employed is 85 percent higher than the respective hazard rate of previously informal wage earners and 260 percent

---

[13] The competing risks model is based on the assumption that an individual actually enters the destination which corresponds to the minimum of the latent survival times.

[14] We use a flexible baseline hazard as this procedure provides more robust results than parametric approaches. We do not allow for unobserved individual heterogeneity. According to recent research this does not seriously bias our results given a fully flexible baseline hazard specification (see for example, Han and Hausman 1990, Meyer 1990).

higher than the respective hazard rate of previously formal sector workers. Former self-employed are hence again most likely to exit to self-employment. The pre-unemployment working class is, hence, an important determinant of exit to a specific destination.

### Table 9.6. Competing Risk - Basic Sample

| | Unemployment spell ends with move to: | | | | | |
|---|---|---|---|---|---|---|
| | Formal Sector | | Informal Sector | | Self-employed | |
| | Coefficient | Z | Coefficient | z | Coefficient | z |
| Age | -0.060 | -17.559 | -0.041 | -16.435 | -0.027 | -14.440 |
| Female | -0.955 | -7.454 | -0.463 | -5.622 | -0.820 | -10.292 |
| **Working Class:** | | | | | | |
| Formal employee | -0.140 | -1.505 | -0.682 | -9.949 | -0.667 | -10.920 |
| Self-employed | -0.660 | -3.792 | -0.337 | -3.357 | 0.615 | 9.164 |
| Employer | -0.539 | -1.055 | -0.546 | -1.606 | -0.256 | -0.937 |
| **Sector:** | | | | | | |
| Construction | 0.026 | 0.192 | 0.080 | 0.781 | 0.326 | 4.194 |
| Commerce | -0.142 | -1.006 | -0.039 | -0.361 | -0.197 | -2.075 |
| Service | -0.101 | -0.985 | 0.012 | 0.014 | -0.159 | -2.236 |
| Other | -0.352 | -1.238 | -0.009 | -0.048 | -0.037 | -0.283 |
| **Education :** | | | | | | |
| Primary | -0.285 | -2.596 | -0.150 | -1.901 | -0.315 | -5.280 |
| Lower Sec. | -0.225 | -1.913 | -0.148 | -1.685 | -0.439 | -5.954 |
| Secondary | -0.149 | -1.246 | -0.415 | -4.257 | -0.865 | -10.153 |
| Tertiary | -0.074 | -0.345 | -0.436 | -2.453 | -1.003 | -6.092 |
| **Region:** | | | | | | |
| Rio de Janeiro | 0.166 | 1.039 | -0.184 | -1.558 | 0.381 | 3.996 |
| Minas Gerais | 0.682 | 2.738 | 0.270 | 2.840 | 0.559 | 6.849 |
| Rio Grande do Sul | 0.352 | 5.263 | -0.456 | -1.483 | 0.159 | 1.873 |
| Pernambuco | -0.189 | -1.141 | -0.133 | -1.290 | 0.309 | 3.618 |
| Bahia | 0.107 | 0.857 | -0.495 | -5.094 | 0.189 | 2.542 |
| # of observations | 143,648 | | 140,378 | | 144,246 | |
| Log Likelihood | -3,387.96 | | -5,493.45 | | -7,500.81 | |

Note: The Basic Sample is restricted to the unemployed, who are between 15 to 65 years old and less than one year without employment. All estimations include biweekly spell dummies. Source: PME 1999 – Authors' own calculations.

## Table 9.7. Competing Risk - Formal Sample

| | Unemployment spell ends with move to: | | | | | |
|---|---|---|---|---|---|---|
| | Formal Sector | | Informal Sector | | Self-employed | |
| | Coefficient | z | Coefficient | Z | Coefficient | Z |
| Age | -0.061 | -14.182 | -0.049 | -12.835 | -0.041 | -12.807 |
| Female | -0.794 | -4.910 | -0.258 | 2.102 | -0.729 | -5.547 |
| FGTS | -0.586 | -4.837 | -0.706 | -6.697 | -0.526 | -5.549 |
| **Sector:** | | | | | | |
| Construction | 0.187 | 1.121 | 0.115 | 0.734 | 0.400 | 3.250 |
| Commerce | -0.032 | -0.199 | -0.009 | -0.064 | -0.132 | -0.947 |
| Service | -0.079 | -0.657 | -0.067 | -0.612 | -0.079 | -0.817 |
| Other | -- | -- | 0.051 | -0.112 | -0.329 | -0.724 |
| **Education:** | | | | | | |
| Primary | -0.076 | -0.563 | -0.294 | -2.444 | 0.296 | -2.950 |
| Lower Sec. | -0.173 | -1.178 | -0.144 | -1.169 | -0.463 | -4.051 |
| Secondary | -0.039 | -0.264 | -0.527 | -3.711 | -0.755 | -5.397 |
| Tertiary | 0.106 | 0.040 | -0.700 | -2.461 | -0.583 | -2.549 |
| **Region:** | | | | | | |
| Rio de Janeiro | 0.444 | 2.428 | 0.616 | 0.616 | 0.549 | 3.754 |
| Minas Gerais | 0.698 | 4.411 | -0.189 | -1.886 | 0.636 | 4.790 |
| Rio Grande do Sul | 0.236 | 1.506 | 2.592 | 2.592 | 0.087 | 0.659 |
| Pernambuco | -0.164 | -0.768 | -0.098 | -0.098 | 0.240 | 1.589 |
| Bahia | 0.105 | 0.682 | -3.267 | -3.267 | 0.355 | 3.009 |
| # of observations | 82,131 | | 79,477 | | 83,481 | |
| Log Likelihood | -2,255.57 | | -2,664 | | -3,143.72 | |

*Note:* The *Formal* Sample is restricted to the unemployed, who are between 15 to 65 years old, less than one year without employment and had a signed work card in the pre-unemployment job. *All* estimations include biweekly spell dummies. *Source:* PME 1999 – Authors' own calculations.

Our estimates reveal that individuals without **education** face the highest probability ceteris paribus of exiting to the formal and to the informal sector. However, the difference in the hazard rate to formal employment decreases with education, indicating that those with more education leave unemployment to the formal sector at a faster rate than those with some education. This result is reversed when we consider exit to the informal sector. It becomes even stronger when we look explicitly at exit to self-employment. The hazard rate to self-employment with respect to individuals with no education is 73 percent education for those with primary education, but only 37 percent for individuals with tertiary education. This indicates that primarily workers with low education exit from unemployment to self-employment.

In order to analyze the effect of **FGTS**, we re-estimate the above described model for the formal sector and present the estimated coefficients in Table 9.7. The effect of FGTS on the exit from unemployment is negative and independent of the destination. The hazard rate to the formal sector of FGTS recipients is 56 percent of the respective hazard rate of those who have not received FGTS. Of particular interest is the role of FGTS for the exit to self-employment. Cunningham (2000) finds that an increase in unemployment insurance leads to an increase in self-employment for those with longer recent experience in the formal sector. She argues that one possible interpretation may be that, given credit constraints, unemployment insurance provides a means of start-up capital and hence may provide a perverse incentive to increase the informal sector even further. The coefficient on the FGTS indicates that FGTS recipients are less likely to exit to self-employment than non recipients. But the differential in the hazard rate among FGTS recipients and non-recipients is lowest when considering exit to self-employment, which supports Cunningham's findings.

## VII. POLICY IMPLICATIONS AND CONCLUDING REMARKS

When most of the features of the Brazilian UI system were implemented at the beginning of the 1990s, this benefit was claimed to (1) provide temporary financial assistance to unemployed worker and (2) assist workers in their search for a new job. As UI benefits are only available to formal sector workers, the present system covers only about 50% of the total workforce. Further, according to the evidence provided above, unemployed workers who receive FGTS and hence UI are less likely to exit unemployment, even to the formal sector. This hints at the fact that unemployment insurance does not help workers to re-enter formal wage employment, however it may ease the transition to (informal) self-employment.

According to Barros et al. (2001) there exist two theoretical justifications for limiting UI benefits to the formal sector:

- First, if formal sector workers have a higher share in the aggregate demand function, limiting UI programs to the formal sector could be justified from a macro-stabilization point of view. The Brazilian UI system does not mention macro-stabilization as an explicit target. Further, as the formal sector in Brazil has been declining throughout the 1990s, any potential basis for formal sector based macro-stabilization potential is increasingly eroded. Unless the trend into informality is reversed, limiting UI benefits to the formal sector cannot be justified by macro-stabilization or consumption smoothing arguments.
- Second, if the human capital of formal sector workers has a higher social value, then formal sector workers should be protected during spells of unemployment so as to avoid that they are rationed into the informal sector, where their human capital is depleted at a faster rate.

However, unemployment insurance may induce longer unemployment spells. As such, UI may actually contribute to a depletion of human capital. We find that unemployment duration is longer for worker who receive FGTS. However, we are not able to determine if UI actually *causes* longer unemployment. Furthermore, we are not able to discriminated between the impact of FGTS and UI.

While low level and duration of Brazilian unemployment benefits *per se* is unlikely to induce longer unemployment duration, there are arguments that UI should be combined with search conditions and with training opportunities for young workers.

Barros et al. (2001) hypotheses are based on the assumption that productivity is highest in the formal sector. This corresponds to the traditional, dualistic labor market view that informal sector jobs are of lower quality than protected formal sector jobs. Newer theories argue that this is not necessarily the case. The informal sector and especially self-employment may be preferable for certain individuals as they are not subject to the constraints imposed in the formal sector and can choose their level of earnings, benefits and labor protection optimally (Maloney 1999, Carneiro and Henley 2002).

## Unemployment Insurance and Informality

Cunningham (2000), Mazza (2001), Barros et al. (2001) point out that the Brazilian unemployment insurance system contributes to increasing informality. A possible explanation is that employers may enter in agreement with formal employees to fire and then to rehire them under an informal contract.

It is appears difficult to separate the discussion of unemployment insurance from a wider discussion of the causes of informality. If informality were purely the outcome of tax avoidance, than ensuring tax compliance would be sufficient to reduce informality. As a consequence, the tax base would be increased and the extension of UI coverage to a wider basis would be implied. However, if informality and in particular informal self-employment is partly the outcome of a rational decision of workers linked to the fact that benefits and costs of being formal are misaligned, then, forcing informal workers to comply with existing formal regulation can be counter-productive.

Cunningham (2000) points to another channel why UI might increase informality. She finds that the increase in UI benefits in 1994 led to an increase in self-employment for workers with a substantial experience in the formal sector. One possible interpretation may be that, given credit constraints, unemployment insurance provides a means of start-up capital. If workers use their financial assistance as a start-up capital for new firms, this hints at the need of improved access to finance through e.g. micro-credit schemes.

## FGTS, UI and Unemployment

In Brazil, workers who are laid off do not only receive unemployment insurance but also FGTS. The FGTS fine is especially difficult to handle for informal firms, as they are small in size, more likely to be credit constraint and have a more volatile production (Levenson and Maloney, 1998). High dismissal costs, hence, increase the premium for small firms to stay informal. But, most of the jobs during the 90's were created in small firms implying an increase in the number of workers not protected by labor legislation.

Macedo (1985) and Amadeo and Camargo (1996) document that the FGTS system and in particular the FGTS fine provide significant incentives for workers to induce their own dismissal. Two main incentives are highlighted: First, FGTS funds are poorly managed and provide negative returns or returns well below market rates. Secondly, short-sightedness or credit constraints might lead workers to heavily discount the future (see Barros et al .2001). However, these claims should be treated with care.

A reform of the administration of FGTS funds aimed at increasing returns and removing inefficiencies in the administration seems therefore strongly indicated. Also, the FGTS and the UI represent two instruments for the same purpose. It is questionable if this duplication is efficient. Under the present system, if a worker has been working for a few years, it is likely that his/her FGTS account will exceed any UI benefit. As Barros et al. (1999) point out, it seems worthwhile to consider UI insurance as complementary for workers who have not been able to accumulate sufficient funds in their FGTS to insure against unemployment.

Further, it might be worthwhile to delink access to FGTS funds from the cause of dismissal. FGTS funds are individualized accounts and act as a compensation fund. As firms can discount their FGTS contributions through lower wages, the FGTS account represents forced savings for formal sector workers. If workers had access to their FGTS account independently of the cause of dismissal, this would ensure that workers fired with just cause have access to UI and FGTS, while workers fired without just cause had access to their FGTS accounts.

The FGTS fine on the other hand is distortionary. It should be reduced and/or offered by firms on a voluntary basis. Under the present system, Brazilian employers do not contribute to the UI system. If employers were to be co-opted in the financing of the UI system, employer's contribution to the UI system could replace the function of the FGTS fine as a dismissal fine.

Finally, while many incentives for workers to induce their own dismissal can be established from a theoretical point of view, it should however be kept in mind that the empirical support is very modest.

## Human Capital and UI

Further, during the 1990s the unemployment rate of young workers increased. At the beginning of the new millennium the unemployment rate of workers aged 15 to 25 was about five times higher compared to workers older than 25. Mazza (2001) shows that workers under 30 years of age use increasingly the UI insurance system. This is consistent with the high increase in the unemployment rate of young workers. High unemployment rates among young workers may have high costs for the society as a whole, such as loss of human capital, crime or drug abuse. Special youth training programs might aid the job search of young workers.

Our findings show that education alone does not necessarily protect against unemployment. The high rates of unemployment among job-seekers with primary and secondary education may indicate a mismatch between schooling and skills required by firms. As such job intermediation services should be improved and public training programs should be more targeted to employment opportunities.

## Special Support for Poor Workers

The probability of becoming unemployed decreases with wage, indicating that workers who earn below the minimum wage face the highest probability of becoming unemployed. At the same time, apart from the highest wage earners, they are least likely to exit unemployment. Paes de Barros, Corseuil and Foguel (2001) find that 32% of the poor and only 7% of the extremely poor receive UI benefits and conclude that the majority of UI beneficiaries are from non-poor families. Further, the poor also receive lower average benefits. Average monthly UI benefit for the poor is R$ 135 compared to R$ 215 for the non-poor. As unemployment insurance is not available for informal sector workers and as a disproportionally large number of low income workers are represented in the informal sector, this further undermines the ability of the Brazilian unemployment insurance system to serve as a social safety net.

# REFERENCES

Amadeo, E.; Camargo, J.M. (1996), *Instituições e o mercado de trabalho brasilerio*, in: Camargo, J.M. (ed.): Felxibilidade do mercado de trabalho no Brasil, Rio de Janeiro. FGV.

Carneiro, Francisco and Andrew Henley (2002), *Earnings and Choice of Formal versus Informal Employment in a Developing Economy Labour Market: Evidence for Brazil*, University of Wales at Aberystwyth Working Paper, UK.

Cunningham, Wendy (2000), Unemployment Insurance in Brazil: Unemployment Duration, Wages and Sectoral Choice, World Bank.

Han, A. and J. Hausman (1990): Flexible Parametric Estimation of Duration and Compcting Risks Models. *Journal of Applied Econometrics*, 5. pp.1-28.

Levenson, A. and W.F. Maloney (1988), *The Informal Sector, Firm Dynamics and Institutional Participation*. IBRD Working Paper 1941, Latin America and the Caribbean Region, Poverty Reduction and Economic Management Unit, World Bank, Washington, D.C. Processed.

Macedo, R.B.M. (1985): Diferenciais de salários entre empresas privadas e estatais no Brasil, *Revista Brasileira de Economia*, 39, 4, 448-473.

Mazza, Jacqueline (2001): Unemployment Insurance: Case Studies and Lessons for Latin America and the Caribbean. Research Department Working Paper #411, Inter-American Development Bank, Washington, D.C.

Meyer, B., D. (1990): Unemployment insurance and unemployment spells, *Econometrica*, 58 (4), pp. 757-782.

Paes de Barros, Ricardo, Carlos Corseuil and Monica Bahia (1999), Labor Market Regulations and the Duration of Employment in Brazil. Texto para Discussao, No. 676. IPEA, Rio de Janeiro.

Paes de Barros, Ricardo, Carlos Corseuil and M. Foguel (2001), Incentivos Adversos e a Focalizacao dos Programas de Protecao ao Trabalhador no Brazil, Texto para Discussao No. 784., IPEA, Rio de Janeiro.

Ramos, Carlos (1999), Impacto Distributivo dos Gastos Sociais no Mercado de Trábalho, in Gasto Social: O IPEA Debate, IPEA, Ministry of Planning and Budget, Brazil.

Ramos, Carlos and Francisco Carneiro (2002), Os Determinantes da Rotatividade do Trabalho no Brasil: Instituições x Ciclos Econômicos, *Nova Economia*, 12:31-56.

Thomas, Mark (1999): Unemployment Insurance in Brazil, World Bank Working Paper.

In: Economics of Unemployment
Editor: Mary I. Marshalle, pp. 137-152

ISBN: 1-60021-138-0
© 2006 Nova Science Publishers, Inc.

*Chapter 7*

# EMPLOYMENT-RELATED ISSUES IN BANKRUPTCY

### *Robin Jeweler*
Legislative Attorney American Law Division

## ABSTRACT

This report provides an overview of the status of employee wages and benefits, including retiree benefits, when an employer files in bankruptcy, and the amendments made to the U.S. Bankruptcy Code by the Bankruptcy Abuse Prevention and Consumer Protection Act. Private pensions, regulated by the Employee Retirement Income Security Act, are generally protected, although defined benefit pension plan payments may be substantially reduced. Health and life insurance benefits, which are not required by federal law, are vulnerable to an employer's bankruptcy-driven modification or termination. This report examines those provisions in the U.S. Bankruptcy Code which govern the priority of employee wage and benefit claims, including severance payments; procedures for a chapter 11 debtor to modify benefits under a collective bargaining agreement; and procedures for a chapter 11 debtor to modify retiree life and health insurance benefits. It examines the role of employees on creditor committees and procedures in bankruptcy that facilitate lawsuits that may be directed at an employer/debtor. Finally, it considers the treatment accorded some aspects of managerial compensation, such as retention bonuses.

## INTRODUCTION

This report provides an overview of employment related issues when a business files in bankruptcy under the U.S. Bankruptcy Code, 11 U.S.C. § 101 *et seq.,* as amended by the Bankruptcy Abuse Prevention and Consumer Protection Act (BAPCPA).[1] A business employer will generally file under one of two of the operative chapters of the Code. It may seek to cease operation and liquidate under chapter 7, or to continue in business and reorganize under chapter 11. The status of basic benefits, such as wages, pensions, and health care for active and retired

---

[1] P.L. 109-8 (2005).

employees, which have to date been the subject of greatest concern to employees of a company in bankruptcy are examined.

The behavior and compensation of a debtor's executives have become more controversial in recent years, corresponding to many high-profile bankruptcies, for example, those of Enron and Worldcom, that were caused, in part if not solely, by managerial malfeasance as opposed to external economic factors. This report considers compensation of debtor's management as well.

## EMPLOYEE BENEFITS

Many employees, especially retirees, fear loss of all employment benefits upon learning that their employer has filed in bankruptcy. Fortunately, this is not necessarily the case, although some benefits may be subject to modification or termination. It is important to know that employee benefits, including retiree benefits, have no universal legal referent; they may be covered by a wide variety of federal and state laws. More important though is the fact that specific employee welfare benefit plans are governed by contract terms which vary from plan to plan. And, each bankruptcy – and the consequences for each of the debtor's creditors, including its employees – is highly case specific. Unique to bankruptcy, however, is the demarcation between prepetition (pre-filing) and postpetition (post-filing) claims. Because the entire bankruptcy process is concerned with debt forgiveness of pre-bankruptcy indebtedness, the classification of a claim as pre- or postpetition is of great consequence. Determining whether a claim accrues pre- or postpetition is not always clear cut.

### Active Employees of an Employer in a Chapter 11 Reorganization.

Typically, a chapter 11 debtor will get an order from the bankruptcy court permitting it to continue business and to compensate its employees just as it had prior to filing. Postpetition operating expenses are considered to be high priority administrative expenses, i.e., "the actual, necessary costs and expenses of preserving the estate, including wages, salaries, and commissions for services rendered after the commencement of the case."[2] Thus, in many instances, employees of a chapter 11 debtor will realize no change in the terms and conditions of their employment. The BAPCPA amended the Code to also include back pay (i.e., prepetition wages) due to employees as a consequence of illegal behavior by the debtor as an administrative expense. The bankruptcy court must determine that the inclusion of back pay will not substantially increase the probability of layoff or termination of current employees.[3]

In traditional employment-at-will situations, a debtor/employer may lay off employees or attempt to renegotiate the terms of employment, just as the employee is free to accept a different compensation structure or terminate the employment relationship. These contingencies may occur in connection with the debtor/employer's bankruptcy. But there are special requirements for a chapter 11 debtor seeking to renegotiate collective bargaining agreements with union employees.

---

[2] 11 U.S.C. § 503(b).

[3] *Id.* at § 503(b)(1)(ii).

## Rejection of Collective Bargaining Agreements.

In 1984, the U.S. Supreme Court held that a collective bargaining agreement (CBA) could be rejected, i.e., terminated, by a debtor.[4] In response to the Court's interpretation, Congress enacted a statute which prescribes the procedures that a debtor in chapter 11 must take before it may alter the terms of or terminate a collective bargaining agreement.[5]

After a petition is filed, if the debtor wishes to alter or terminate the collective bargaining agreement, it must supply the authorized representative of the employees complete and reliable information to demonstrate the need, in order to facilitate a reorganization, for the modifications to the employees' benefits and protections. The employees and debtor are required to engage in "good faith" negotiations with respect to proposals for alteration or termination of such agreements.

If the debtor files an application to reject a CBA, the court is directed to schedule a hearing for not later than fourteen days after the filing. All interested parties may attend and participate in the hearing and the court should rule on the application within thirty days after the beginning of the hearing.

The court may approve the application for rejection only if it finds (i) that the debtor, prior to the hearing, provided the authorized representative of the employees with the necessary information; (ii) the authorized representative has refused to accept the proposal without good cause; and, (iii) the balance of the equities clearly favors rejection.

In addition the court may, after a hearing, authorize interim changes in the terms, conditions, wages, benefits or work rules provided by a collective bargaining agreement, when it is still in effect, if it is essential to the continuation of the debtor's business or is necessary to avoid irreparable damage to the estate. The implementation of interim changes does not, however, moot the procedures and requirements for an application for rejection.

## Active Employees of an Employer in Liquidation.

If an employer must shut down, it is likely to file under chapter 7. In this chapter, the court appoints a trustee who oversees the debtor's liquidation. The debtor's assets are reduced to cash and distributed among creditors. Although chapter 7 traditionally governs liquidation, a debtor may also liquidate its business under chapter 11. When a business closes, health and life insurance benefits are terminated because, unlike pensions, they are not pre-funded. Pension assets, for the reasons discussed below, are generally held in trust for the employee and are not available to the debtor's creditors.

A common scenario in bankruptcy involves an employer who, at the time of filing, is in arrears in the payment of wages or contributions to employee benefit plans that require continuous funding. Employees who have a contractual claim to payment are considered "unsecured" creditors.

---

[4] National Labor Relations Board v. Bildisco & Bildisco, 465 U.S. 513 (1984), holding that collective bargaining agreements are "executory contracts" under 11 U.S.C. § 365 and may be rejected by a debtor unilaterally if the debtor can show that the agreement burdens the estate and that the equities balance in favor of rejection.

[5] 11 U.S.C. § 1113.

The Code establishes priorities for the payment of unsecured claims.[6] With the exception of administrative expenses, discussed above, priority claims generally cover prepetition debts. Because priority unsecured claims are paid before nonpriority claims there is a much greater chance for a creditor to realize payment for those having priority status. As amended by the BAPCPA, fourth priority is designated for unsecured claims for wages, salaries, or commissions, but only to the extent of $10,000 for each individual, including vacation, severance and sick leave pay earned by an individual or corporation within 180 days before the date of filing or the date of the cessation of the debtor's business, whichever occurs first; or, for sales commissions earned by an individual or by a corporation with only one employee acting as an independent contractor in the sale of goods or services for the debtor.[7]

Fifth priority is similar to the fourth but governs unsecured claims for contributions to an employee benefit plan arising from services rendered within 180 days before the filing or cessation of the debtor's business, but only to the extent of the number of employees covered by each such plan multiplied by $10,000 less (1) the aggregate amount paid to such employees under the fourth priority and (2) the aggregate amount paid by the estate on behalf of such employees to any other employee benefit plan. Hence, the fourth and fifth employee priorities together have an aggregated cap of $10,000 per employee. Creditors covered by this priority may include, in addition to the employees themselves, entities that administer employee benefits, such as health or worker's compensation insurers.[8]

## Severance Benefits

The bankruptcy priority for prepetition employee wages and benefits, including severance pay, is an important benchmark. In a liquidation scenario, it means that each employee with a claim in this category will be near the head of the line for distribution of the priority amount. Nonpriority unsecured claims will be distributed pro rata among unsecured creditors, including employees.

The priority is significant in a reorganization as well. The priority amount must be paid through the reorganization plan in order for it to be confirmed by the court. As noted above, the priority is conferred on claims accruing prior to the bankruptcy filing. Severance earned postpetition, however, may qualify for an administrative expense priority.[9] Claims for severance, particularly those asserting priority as postpetition administrative expenses, will be evaluated according to several factors and decided under the law of the federal circuit. The court will consider the terms of the agreement establishing severance, including whether it is payable in a lump sum or is based on length of service, and when it was agreed to. A determination of when

---

[6] 11 U.S.C. § 507.

[7] This amount will be adjusted at three-year intervals to reflect changes to the Consumer Price Index. 11 U.S.C. § 104.

[8] *See* In re J.G. Furniture Group, Incorp., 405 F.3d 191 (4th Cir.), *cert. denied sub nom.* Ivey v. Great-West Life & Annuity Ins. Co., 2005 WL 2414231 (Oct. 3, 2005); Howard Delivery Service, Inc. v. Zurich American Ins. Co., 403 F.3d 228 (4th Cir. 2005).

[9] *See* In re AcoustiSeal, Inc., 290 B.R. 354 (Bankr.W.D.Mo. 2003)(employees that debtor had terminated postpetition would be allowed administrative priority for the pro rata share of severance pay actually earned postpetition; and severance pay claims asserted by nonexecutive employees were in part prepetition claims entitled to priority to the extent that they were earned within 90 days of filing, and in part postpetition claims entitled to priority as administrative expenses to the extent they accrued postpetition.)

the benefit accrues – pre- or postpetition – is not always readily apparent and rules governing it may also vary among the circuits.

Prior to the BAPCPA, the priority amount for prepetition employee benefits, including severance, was capped at $4,925 earned within 90 days of the bankruptcy filing. Nevertheless, at least one court took advantage of the flexibility inherent in the bankruptcy process to enlarge the amount allocated to employee severance pay. Invoking the court's equitable authority,[10] the U.S. Bankruptcy Court for the Southern District of New York permitted an increased allowance for prepetition employee severance payments in both the Enron and WorldCom bankruptcies. The Enron decision implemented a settlement of litigation brought by former employees of Enron.[11] The court also allowed creditor committees to bring avoidance actions to recover certain prepetition lump sum payments made to selected employees labeled as "90-day retention bonuses" to help fund the severance claims. Parties agreeing to the settlement received a maximum allowance of $13,500 per employee.

In the WorldCom bankruptcy, the debtor requested – and the court granted – permission to pay prepetition severance pay due to terminated employees over the amount set by statute.[12] The debtor justified its request by asserting that adverse publicity from the terminated employees could negatively impact WorldCom's relationship with its current employees. The payments were necessary to restore the confidence of current employees, whose cooperation and loyalty were essential to the reorganization effort.

## Pension Benefits

Federal law does *not* require an employer to provide health insurance or pensions to employees. Although the tax laws are designed to *encourage* employers to provide these benefits, they may be altered or terminated within or outside of bankruptcy.

The creation and administration of private sector pension plans are governed exclusively by the Employee Retirement Income Security Act (ERISA).[13] In 1974, Congress enacted ERISA to protect the interests of private sector participants and beneficiaries in a wide variety of employee welfare benefit and pension plans. A prime underlying policy of the act, articulated by the Supreme Court, is the congressional guarantee that "'if a worker has been promised a defined pension benefit upon retirement – and if he has fulfilled whatever conditions are required to obtain

---

[10] 11 U.S.C. § 105.

[11] In re Enron Corp., Case Nos. 01-16034, *Order of Final Approval, under 11 U.S.C. §§ 105(a), 363(b), 1103 (c) (5) and 1109(b) and Fed. R. Bankr. P. 9019, Approving Settlement of Severance Claims of Similarly-Situated Claimants and Authorizing the Official Employment-R elated Issues Committee to Commence Certain Avoidance Actions on Behalf of Estates*, Aug. 28, 2002 at [http://www.elaw4enron.com/default.asp].

[12] In re WorldCom, Inc., Case Nos. 02-13533, *Order Authorizing the Payment of Severance Benefits and Related Obligations to Terminated Employees and Rejection of Certain Severance Agreements*, Oct. 1, 2002 at [http://www.elaw4enron.com/ WorldComdefault. asp].

[13] 29 U.S.C. § 1001 *et seq*. Pension benefit plans generally fall into one of two broad categories, namely, defined contribution plans or defined benefit plans. The former is a plan in which contributions are fixed, but not benefits, e.g., a fixed amount or percentage of compensation is invested in the plan and comprises the basis for accruing plan benefits. The latter, a defined benefit plan, is a pension plan that specifies the benefits or method of determining the benefits, but not the contribution. The sponsor of the defined benefit plan bears the risk of investment performance and must compensate for any discrepancies between the amounts invested and the amounts promised to be paid as benefits. ERISA regulates private sector defined benefit and defined contribution plans. *See* CRS Report 95-926 EPW, *Regulating Private Pensions: A Brief Summary of ER ISA*, by Patrick Purcell.

a vested benefit – he will actually receive it.'"[14] Because of ERISA's comprehensive regulatory scheme, pension benefits are the *least* likely of employee benefits to be affected by bankruptcy, although they may be diminished or reduced in several situations. Thus, employees in many of the defined benefit "legacy" industries, such as steel, airlines, and, more recently, automobile parts manufacturers, have experienced substantial reductions in their pensions as a result of bankruptcy-related distress terminations.

There are a wide variety of tax-qualified employee pension programs. Among the most common are defined contribution and defined benefit plans. In the former which includes 401(k) plans, the employee, and perhaps the employer, makes contributions to the retirement account on behalf of the employee. The fund, though managed by an employer in accordance with requirements of ERISA and the U.S. Tax Code, is property of the employee. In the event of the employer's bankruptcy, defined contribution trust funds are *not* assets available to the debtor's creditors. Under a defined benefit plan, an employee is promised a set payment, typically one based upon salary and years of service. According to the Pension Benefit Guaranty Corporation (PBGC), there is a significant trend away from traditional defined benefit plans, discussed below, to new "hybrid" pension plans, such as cash balance plans, which are a form of defined benefit plan insured by the PBGC.[15]

Defined benefit pension plans may be terminated voluntarily by an employer or involuntarily by the PBGC. An employer may terminate a plan voluntarily in one of two ways. It may proceed with a standard termination only if it has sufficient assets to pay all benefit commitments. A standard termination does not, therefore, implicate PBGC insurance responsibilities.

If an employer wishes to terminate a plan whose assets are insufficient to pay all benefits, the employer must demonstrate that it is in financial distress as defined by ERISA. The concern connected with a distress termination is the adequacy of the plan's funding. That is, is there enough money to support payment of the pension commitment? This is where the PBGC's pension insurance program, which is funded by employer paid premiums, is implicated.[16] If an under-funded corporate pension plan is terminated, the PBGC insurance program guarantees some payment to covered employees. The PBGC then seeks recovery of the deficiency from the employer, asserting a lien therefor, if necessary. Although the PBGC guaranty program is designed to minimize the impact of corporate bankruptcy on the debtor's retirees, when an under-funded pension plan is terminated, the PBGC imposes a statutory ceiling on guaranteed payments. Thus, beneficiaries of an under-funded terminated plan may receive payments that are substantially less than promised.

Neither a standard nor a distress termination by the employer is permitted if termination would violate the terms of an existing collective-bargaining agreement. But negotiations in bankruptcy are influenced by the prospect of the debtor's possible liquidation. The PBGC may, nonetheless, terminate a plan involuntarily, notwithstanding the existence of a collective-bargaining agreement. Likewise, termination can be undone and restoration ordered by PBGC.

---

[14] Connolly v. Pension Benefit Guaranty Corp., 475 U.S. 211, 214 (1986), quoting Pension Benefit Guaranty Corp. v. R.A. Gray & Co., 467 U.S. 717, 720 (1984).

[15] PBGC, *A Predictable, Secure Pension For Life: Defined Benefit Plans* 6 at [http://www.pbgc.gov/publications/defined_benefit_pens.htm]. *See* CRS Report RL30196, *Pension Issues: Cash-Balance Plans,* by Patrick Purcell.

[16] Under ERISA pension regulation, participation, vesting, and funding standards are administered by the Internal Revenue Service; fiduciary standards and reporting and disclosure requirements are regulated by the Department of Labor; benefit insurance provisions are regulated by the Pension Benefit Guaranty Corporation.

When a plan is restored, full benefits are reinstated and the employer, rather than the PBGC, is again responsible for the plan's unfunded liabilities.

The largest pension default in U.S. history occurred with the termination – and transfer to the PBGC – of four defined benefit plans administered by United Airlines.[17] Over the strenuous objection of its union employees, United Airlines, in reorganization under chapter 11 of the Code, entered into negotiations with the PBGC, which agreed to assume them, invoking its involuntary termination authority. The plans, covering pilots, ground employees, flight attendants, and others, were collectively underfunded by $9.8 billion, of which $6.6 billion is guaranteed. The courts have, to date, upheld the plans' termination and transfer to the PBGC despite challenges by the Union of Flight Attendants.[18]

## Retiree Benefits

*Pensions.* As discussed above, retiree pension benefits are held in trust for the retiree and are regulated by ERISA.

*Health and Life Insurance Benefits.* Many employers reserve a right to modify or terminate employee welfare benefit plans and do so outside of bankruptcy.[19] Courts reviewing plan alteration or termination generally base their decisions on the specific terms of a plan's documents or associated collective bargaining agreement. In bankruptcy, the status of retiree life and health insurance benefits is largely determined by the nature of the action – chapter 11 reorganization versus liquidation under chapter 7 or chapter 11.

The reorganization of the LTV Corp. proved to be a prime force behind clarification of the Bankruptcy Code's treatment of retirees' health and life insurance benefits *during* reorganization. On the same day it filed in bankruptcy in 1986, LTV Corp. notified more than 66,000 retirees of its intention to terminate health and life insurance coverage under the company's employee benefit plan. Acting swiftly to express its disapproval of LTV's interpretation of the Bankruptcy Code's requirements, Congress enacted legislation blocking LTV's cessation of insurance payments on the retirees behalf.[20] Then, in 1988, Congress amended the Code by adding new 11 U.S.C. § 1114 entitled "Payment of insurance benefits to retired employees." The procedures for a debtor's termination of retiree insurance benefits are modeled after those for termination of collective-bargaining agreements in chapter 11.

In summary, § 1114 provides that a debtor in reorganization may *not* terminate health and life insurance payment programs maintained for retirees and their spouses and dependents *without first negotiating proposed modifications* in benefit payments with representatives of the retirees, and second, *seeking and receiving court approval* to make the modifications. If the debtor and the retirees cannot agree upon modifications, and the debtor believes them to be necessary to permit reorganization, the court may permit modifications, subject to statutory guidelines. The debtor must

---

[17] *Judge Afirms Pension Default Pact Between United Airlines and PBGC,* 17 BN A  BA N K R . L. J. 659 (U.S. District Court for the Northern District of Illinois affirms decision of bankruptcy court).( July 28, 2005).

[18] *See* Assoc. of Flight Attendants-C WA v. PBGC, 372 F. Supp.2d 91 (D.D.C. 2005); In re UAL Corp., 2005 WL 1154264 (Bankr.N.D.Ill. 2005), *af'd,*      F.3d      , 2005 WL 2848938 (7th Cir., Nov. 1, 2005).

[19] *See* U.S. Dept. of Labor, *Can the Retiree Health Benefits Provided By Your Employer Be Cut?,* at [*http://www.dol.gov/dol/pwba/public/pubs/brief1.htm*]. For general background, see CRS Report RL3 2944, *Health Insurance Coverage for Retirees* by Hinda Ripps Chaikind and Fran Larkins.

[20] P.L. 99-591, § 608 (1986); P.L. 99-656 (1986); P.L. 100-41 (1987).

have negotiated with the representative of the retirees in good faith, and the court, after a hearing in which all parties have had an opportunity to be heard, must find that the proposed modification is *necessary* to permit the reorganization of the debtor and assures that all creditors, the debtor, and all of the affected parties are treated fairly and equitably. Thus, in the course of a chapter 11 reorganization in which the debtor continues to operate the business, it *must* continue to pay retiree health and life insurance benefits unless it has negotiated necessary modifications – or termination of payments – with the representatives of the affected group, or has received the bankruptcy court's permission to do so. Payments made are accorded high priority "administrative expense" status.

The BAPCPA amended § 1114 to add a "look back" provision for eve-of-filing modification of retiree insurance benefits. If the debtor, while insolvent, modifies retiree benefits within 180 days of filing, the court may reinstate the benefits unless the balance of equities supports modification.[21]

If a corporate debtor's reorganization is unsuccessful, it may liquidate. In a liquidation, the retirees' claims for lost insurance benefits would be unsecured claims. The fourth and fifth priorities for employee benefits apply only to payments on behalf of present employees, not retirees. When Congress passed § 1114 ensuring the continuation of payments of retiree health and life insurance benefits throughout a reorganization if the debtor could afford to pay them, it did not appear to address the status of these claims in liquidation. Nor did it amend § 507 of the Code, which creates high priority unsecured claims. Obviously, when a company ceases operation, it cannot continue to incur business-related operating expenses. Retirees with insurance claims would be unsecured creditors of the debtor, and any amount they might recover would depend upon the nature and amount of claims outstanding relative to the funds available to satisfy them.[22]

## COBRA Continuation Coverage

Under the provisions of Title X of the Consolidated Omnibus Budget Reconciliation Act of 1985 (COBRA),[23] as amended, employers are required to permit employees or family members to continue their group health insurance coverage at their own expense, but at group rates, if they lose coverage because of designated work or family-related events.[24] Among the "qualifying events" which trigger COBRA's continuation coverage is an employer's filing a case under the Bankruptcy Code (on or after July 1, 1986) *with respect to a covered employee who has retired.*[25] "To lose coverage" for COBRA purposes includes a substantial elimination of coverage that

---

[21] 11 U.S.C. § 1114(l).

[22] At least one court has held that § 1114 does not apply if the case is converted to chapter 7. Retiree benefit payments have administrative expense status only while a debtor operates under chapter 11. In re Ionosphere Clubs, Inc., 134 B.R. 515 (Bankr. S.D.N.Y. 1991) .

[23] P.L. 99-272 (April 7, 1986).

[24] *See* U.S. Dept. of Labor, *Health Benefits Under the Consolidated Omnibus Budget Reconciliation Act, COBRA* at [*http://www.dol.gov/dol/pwba/public/pubs/COBRA/cobra99* .pdf] and CRS Report RL3 0626, *Health Insurance Continuation Coverage under COBRA,* by Heidi Yacker.

[25] 29 U.S.C. § 1163.

occurs within twelve months before or after the date on which the bankruptcy proceeding begins.[26]

In general, a "covered employee" is an individual who is provided coverage by virtue of employment (or previous employment) with the employer. Hence, the definition includes retirees who receive health coverage in addition to their pension. In the case of a retiree of a bankrupt employer, the continuation coverage must be available until the death of the covered employee or the qualified beneficiary. In this situation, a "qualified beneficiary" includes a covered employee who has retired on or before the date on which coverage was eliminated, and any other individual who, on the day before the bankruptcy proceedings, was a beneficiary under the plan, either as the spouse, dependent child, or surviving spouse of the covered employee. For the surviving spouse or dependent children of the covered employee, the period of coverage is limited to 36 months after the death of the covered employee.

Although COBRA provides retirees' lifetime coverage, it is contingent upon the employer's maintaining the plan for current employees. Continuation coverage for all qualified beneficiaries terminates on the date when the employer ceases to provide any group health plan to *any* employee, i.e., when the plan ends.

COBRA may be a useful safety net if an employer in bankruptcy terminates a retiree health plan but continues to offer health benefits to current employees. In that event, retirees would be entitled to continuation coverage under the employer's ongoing plan. But COBRA works in conjunction with ERISA and the Bankruptcy Code; it *does not* require an employer to fund independent health insurance for retirees or to maintain the plan on behalf of current employees notwithstanding other permissible termination provisions of ERISA or the Code.

## EMPLOYEE PARTICIPATION IN BANKRUPTCY PROCEEDINGS

### Employee Representation on Creditor Committees

Viewed broadly, a chapter 11 reorganization contemplates a negotiated settlement of claims by the debtor with its creditors under the supervision of the court and within the strictures of the Code. Creditors actively participate in the development of a reorganization plan, and ultimately vote to accept or reject it. Employees may have a limited voice or a more active role in reorganization negotiations.

Rules of bankruptcy practice expressly grant a labor union, an employees' association, or a representative of employees a right to address the court "to be heard on the economic soundness of a plan affecting employees' interests."[27] The right is limited, however, because the employee representative does not generally have standing to appeal any of the bankruptcy court's rulings.

A more active role in the reorganization planning is reserved to creditor committees. Shortly after the bankruptcy petition is filed, the U.S. trustee will appoint an official committee of creditors holding unsecured claims.[28] In complex cases, the court may create additional committees if necessary to ensure adequate representation of creditors. The unsecured creditors'

---

[26] 64 Federal Register 5165 (Feb. 3, 1999).

[27] Fed. Rules of Bankr. Procedure, Rule 2018.

[28] 11 U.S.C. § 1102.

committee is generally comprised of persons willing to serve who hold the seven largest claims of the types represented by the committee. Among the committee's powers and duties is the authority:

- to consult with the trustee or debtor concerning the administration of the case;
- to investigate the acts, conduct, assets, liabilities, and financial condition of the debtor, the operation of the debtor's business and the desirability of the continuing it;
- to participate in the formulation of a plan, to advise those represented by the committee of any committee determinations and/or any plan formulated; and
- to generally represent the interests of creditors who are represented.[29]

Every bankruptcy is intensely fact-specific with specific creditor claims dictating the composition of the creditor committee(s). When employees are unsecured creditors, they may be represented on creditor committees.[30] If and when appropriate, the court may allow the creation of official or unofficial committees composed solely of employee representatives. For example, in the Enron bankruptcy, the court appointed a committee "for the purpose of investigating the issues relating to: (1) the continuation of health or other benefits for former employees of the Debtors; (2) the investigation of claims uniquely held by employees, as such, against the Debtors; (3) the treatment of employees' claims under any plan(s) of reorganization or liquidation; (4) possible Warn Act violations by the Debtors in discharging employees; (5) possible violation by the Debtors of state labor laws and certain provisions of ERISA; and (6) dissemination of non-confidential information relating to items (1) through (5) hereof to employees[.]"[31] Unofficial committees comprised of self-selected members may be free of the fiduciary responsibilities required of an official committee.

Section 1114 expressly provides for the appointment of committees of retired employees when a debtor seeks to modify or terminate retiree benefits. The U.S. Trustee appoints members to act as "authorized representatives" for retirees. Ordinarily, retirees whose benefits are covered by collective bargaining agreements are represented by the labor organization. Recognizing that there can be internal conflicts between the interests of active employees and retirees covered by a CBA and their interests in the bankruptcy case, the labor organization may elect not to serve as authorized representative. In that case, a committee may be comprised of other retirees found by the court to be appropriate.

---

[29] 11 U.S.C. § 1103.

[30] *See, e.g.,* In re Altair Airlines, Inc., 727 F.2d 88 (3rd Cir. 1984)(Pilots' association, which was the exclusive bargaining agent for pilots holding claims for unpaid wages which amounted to the second largest unsecured claim against the debtor, was entitled to appointment to the unsecured creditors' committee.); In re Salant Corp., 53 B.R. 158 (Bankr.S.D.N.Y. 1985)(When the creditor committee was made up of seventeen members, including one representative of managerial employees, the court was willing to grant a union's motion to add an additional three members to represent non-managerial employees.)

[31] In re Enron, *Amended Appointment of Employment-Related Issues Committee,* (Bankr.S.D.N.Y. 2002), at 2002 Extra LEXIS 537.

## Employee Litigation-Based Claims Against an Employer

The bankruptcies of Enron and other companies, such as Polaroid, Global Crossing, and WorldCom, raised new concerns about corporate responsibility for harm employees experience as a result of illegal stock manipulation and other forms of corporate malfeasance. For example, employees' defined contribution pension funds, when comprised of their employer's stock, can be devastated by employer mismanagement. Discussed below is the process a bankruptcy court may use to consider a civil claim for damages that has not been reduced to judgment prior to the bankruptcy filing.

History teaches that the U.S. Bankruptcy Code is not an efficient vehicle to protect the funding and management of employment benefits.[32] By the time an employer is in bankruptcy, if the system has already failed, it is generally too late to impose new management, auditing, fiduciary, or funding safeguards to restore benefits. Other laws, such as ERISA, the Tax Code, and COBRA, address these employment benefit programs prospectively. Nevertheless, employees who are victims of wrongdoing may wonder if they can assert those claims in the bankruptcy and increase their distributive share of the debtor's assets.

It is frequently said that a debtor in bankruptcy "cannot be sued." While it is correct that bankruptcy's automatic stay stops the continuation of a judicial process to collect a money judgment,[33] it does not mean that a debtor corporation is immune from claims that have *not yet* been reduced to judgment. If employees want to sue their employer/debtor, they may still have a "claim" in bankruptcy, even if it has not been reduced to judgment.[34]

When a claim that must be established through a lawsuit is stayed, the bankruptcy court is permitted to estimate "any contingent or unliquidated claim, the fixing or liquidation of which, as the case may be, would unduly delay the administration of the case[.]"[35] The court may also estimate any right to payment "arising from a right to an equitable remedy for breach of performance."[36] This occurs pursuant to the bankruptcy court's mandate to allow or disallow claims against the estate. Estimating claims for the purpose of confirming a plan under chapter 11 is expressly cited as a core proceeding within a bankruptcy court's jurisdiction.[37]

Hence, the chapter 11 filing triggers a series of decisions by the court evaluating the stayed litigation. Do the best interests of the parties and the bankruptcy estate require the estimation of outstanding claims or should they be reduced to a sum certain, i.e., fixed by litigation authorized

---

[32] After the LTV Corp. filed under chapter 11 in 1986, the debtor and the PBGC engaged in a great deal of litigation concerning payment of arrearages as a result of underfunding of the debtor's pension plans. Although the PBGC was initially unsuccessful in asserting administrative and unsecured priority claims for underfunding arrearages, it ultimately succeeded in ordering restoration of the terminated plans. *See* In re Chateaugay Corp., 115 B.R. 760 (Bankr.S.D.N.Y. 1990), *order vacated and withdrawn,* 17 Employee Benefits Cas. 1102 (S.D.N.Y. 1993). *See also* PBGC v. LTV Corp., 496 U.S. 633 (1990).

[33] 11 U.S.C. § 362.

[34] A "claim" in bankruptcy is defined broadly at 11 U.S.C. § 10 1(5) to mean "(A) right to payment, whether or not such right is reduced to judgment, liquidated, unliquidated, fixed, contingent, matured, unmatured, disputed, undisputed, legal, equitable, secured, or unsecured; or (B) right to an equitable remedy for breach of performance if such breach gives rise to a right to payment, whether or not such right to an equitable remedy is reduced to judgment, fixed, contingent, matured, unmatured, disputed, undisputed, secured, or unsecured."

[35] 11 U.S.C. § 502(c)(1). *See* In the Matter of Interco Incorp., 137 B.R. 993 (Bankr.E.D. Mo. 1992)(Claims of a multiemployer pension fund against a debtor may be estimated).

[36] *Id.*

[37] 28 U.S.C. § 1 57(b)(2)(B). A bankruptcy court may not, however, liquidate or estimate personal injury tort or wrongful death claims.

by the court? Agreeing on appropriate methodology to estimate a claim is in itself a complicated issue.

The courts have discretion to consider the most appropriate manner to handle an unliquidated, contingent claim – whether it should be estimated or whether the stay should be lifted. The goal of the bankruptcy process is to fix an amount, i.e., assign a value for a claim in order to expedite reorganization; to determine whether reorganization itself is feasible; and, to assist the parties in fashioning a plan. It is also necessary to create a yardstick to enable the court to apply the "best interests of the creditor" test for a chapter 11 debtor. The court cannot confirm a chapter 11 reorganization plan unless creditors will receive more under the plan than if the debtor were liquidated.[38]

And, of course, creditors are constrained by practical strategic considerations. Litigation is an expensive proposition and it may not be worthwhile in the face of a looming prospect of the debtor's having inadequate assets to satisfy the claim. Simply put, does the potential distribution warrant the costs of litigation? Some portion or all of the creditors' damages may be discharged in the bankruptcy and any recovery will be reduced by distributions among all unsecured creditors.

Employees whose pensions have suffered under the fiduciary mismanagement of corporate debtors face many difficult decisions. Claims against their employers may be based on many legal theories grounded in many different laws. Claims may be directed at different parties within and without bankruptcy and this may also affect decisions regarding litigation. The bankruptcy process, however, does allow claims that have not been finalized to be considered. And, as in all bankruptcies, the outcome is dependent upon the unique situation of each debtor and its creditors.

The Enron bankruptcy is a case study. Numerous suits have been filed against the debtor by or on behalf of employees, and although few went to trial, several settlements have been announced. In December of 2001, a federal district court consolidated all of the ERISA claims brought in the Southern District of Texas under the caption, *Tittle v. Enron Corp.*[39] In June of 2005, the court approved a proposed settlement between former Enron employees and insurers for numerous pension plan fiduciaries that would give a judgment reduction credit of $85 million, representing the policy limits on two fiduciary liability policies.[40] Basically, in return for releasing defendants from further claims for indemnity or contribution arising from ERISA-based claims, the plaintiffs will collect insurance proceeds. The district court judge is quoted as explaining:

> Without question this settlement is driven by the need to preserve for the plaintiff class the insurance policy proceeds, which otherwise are likely to be consumed by litigation defense costs. This factor works to justify a settlement for less than what Plaintiffs might obtain if they continued to prosecute their claims through trial, only to find that the actual recovery has gone up in smoke[.][41]

In another proceeding, the U.S. Dept. of Labor announced an agreement that would give participants in an Enron retirement plan a general unsecured bankruptcy claim of $356.25

---

[38] 11 U.S.C. § 1129(a)(7).

[39] For background on the litigation, see CRS Report RL3 1282, *Tittle v. Enron Corp. and Fiduciary Duties under ERISA* by Jon Shimabukuro.

[40] *Court Approves Partial Settlement in Enron Fiduciary Breach Litigation,* 17 BNA BANKR. L. REPTR. 488 (June 2, 2005).

[41] *Id.*

million.[42] The announcement notes that the final distribution that plan participants receive will depend upon the total amount of assets available. Earlier in the bankruptcy, the PBGC announced an agreement it reached with Enron requiring it to place $321 million in escrow to fund a standard termination of its defined benefit pension plan[43]

A major bankruptcy may involve a great deal of litigation, much of which is designed to assess and/or settle claims both against and on behalf of the debtor. Just discussed are examples of employee and federal agency claims against Enron. Likewise, suits brought by Enron against others have been settled.[44] Claims settled in Enron's favor bring assets into the bankruptcy estate for ultimate distribution to creditors. Thus, the bankruptcy process does, to some extent, encompass procedures for addressing debtor wrongdoing. There are strong incentives for creditors and the debtor to attempt to evaluate and settle civil claims in order to reorganize.

## MANAGERIAL COMPENSATION IN BANKRUPTCY

The substantial amounts that many attorneys and professionals earn as fees for work performed in a major bankruptcy case has been, and continues for many to be a subject of widespread interest. So too, more recently, has the amount of executive compensation earned by debtor's management on the eve of or in the course of the bankruptcy. In many cases, debtor companies retain "turn around" experts or bring in new executives to guide the company through the restructuring and bankruptcy process. Executive compensation, like other employee benefits, comes in many forms and is contract specific. Although a trustee is always appointed in chapter 7, chapter 11 is premised on the supposition that a reorganization is most likely to be successful and creditors and the public are most likely to benefit from continued operation of the business by existing management.[45] Under chapter 11, management may be removed "for cause, including fraud, dishonesty, incompetence, or gross mismanagement[.]"[46]

In the ordinary course of a bankruptcy, certain claims are "disallowed. This means that even though a creditor may have a perfectly legal claim, bankruptcy law declines to permit, or allow it – generally for the purpose of maximizing the debtor's estate for distribution to all creditors. One example of such are claims by an employee whose employment contract is terminated for damages that exceed more than one year's compensation under the contract.[47]

Like all bankruptcy claims, the disposition of executive compensation may depend upon when it was earned and/or paid, that is, before or after the bankruptcy filing. Postpetition

---

[42] *Labor Department Announces Agreement Giving Enron Participants Unsecured Claim,* 17 BNA BANKR. L. REPTR. 611 (July 14, 2005).

[43] *Enron Agrees to Pay $321 Million To Preserve Plans' Defined Benefits,* 16 BNA BANKR. L. REPTR. 817 (Sept. 16, 2004).

[44] *See JPMorgan Chase Settles With Enron; Will Pay $350 Million in Bankruptcy Case,* 17 BNA BANKR. L. REPTR. 742 (August 25, 2005).

[45] H.Rept. 95-595, 95th Cong., 1st Sess. 233 (1977), comprising part of the legislative history of the 1978 bankruptcy law. "Moreover, the need for reorganization of a public company today often results from simple business reverses, not from any fraud, dishonesty, or gross mismanagement of the part of the debtor's management."

[46] 11 U.S.C. § 1104. Pursuant to amendment by the BAPCPA, the U.S. Trustee shall seek appointment of a trustee if "there are reasonable grounds to suspect that current members of the governing body of the debtor...participated in fraud, dishonesty, or criminal conduct in the management of the debtor or the debtor's public financial reporting." § 1104(e).

[47] 11 U.S.C. § 502(b)(7).

payments are generally subject to court approval, and prepetition payments, to a more limited extent, may be subject to avoidance. Generally, the debtor must assume the employment contract, that is reaffirm it after the bankruptcy filing, in order for an executive to lay claim to payments thereunder as an administrative priority.[48]

Nevertheless, retention bonuses and similar compensation for executives are commonly sought and approved by the courts.[49] But they may be challenged by parties to the bankruptcy proceeding and denied in whole or part. In a pre-BAPCPA decision in the U.S. Airways bankruptcy, the court considered proposed severance and retention plans for its officer and non-officer managerial employees.[50] The proposed plan, called a Key Employee Retention Plan or KERP, affected executives and over 1,800 management employees and was formulated in contemplation of a merger of the debtor with another airline. The motion to approve the plan was supported by the Official Committee of Unsecured Creditors, which had negotiated a number of changes to the original proposal, and was opposed by the U.S. Trustee and by the unions representing the debtor's pilots, flight attendants, mechanics, and reservation agents. Explaining its rationale, the court observed:

> The Bankruptcy Code does not specifically address so-called Key Employee Retention Plans, or KERPs, whether adopted before the filing of a bankruptcy petition or after. It is common, however, for bankruptcy courts to approve the adoption of post-petition KERPs, or the assumption of pre-petition KERPs, if the debtor has used "proper business judgment" in adopting the plan, and the plan is "fair and reasonable." In re Aerovox, Inc., 269 B.R. 74, 80 (Bankr.D.Mass.2001). Nevertheless KERPs have something of a shady reputation. All too often they have been used to lavishly reward– at the expense of the creditor body– the very executives whose bad decisions or lack of foresight were responsible for the debtor's financial plight. But even where external circumstances rather than the executives are to blame, there is something inherently unseemly in the effort to insulate the executives from the financial risks all other stakeholders face in the bankruptcy process. Congressional concern over KERP excesses is clearly reflected in changes to the Bankruptcy Code that will become effective for cases filed after October 17, 2005. Bankruptcy Abuse Prevention and Consumer Protection Act of 2005, Pub.L. No. 109-8, § 331, 119 Stat. 23, 102-03 (April 20, 2005). Those changes will severely limit both the circumstances under which severance and retention payments may be made to insiders as well as the amount of such payments, which will be limited to 10 times the average amount of severance or retention payments for non-management employees during the same calendar year.[51]

---

[48] *See, e.g.,* In re FBI Distribution Corp., 330 F.3d 36 (1st Cir. 2003)(Executive who was terminated by chapter 11 debtor after rendering postpetition services was not entitled to administrative priority claim for employment and retention benefits under prepetition employment agreement that was rejected by the debtor. The executive was entitled to the reasonable value of her postpetition services that benefitted the estate.).

[49] *See, e.g.,* In re Pacific Gas and Electric Co., 2001 WL 34133840 (Bankr.N.D.Ca. 2001)(Court approves management retention program supported by Official Committee of Unsecured Creditors over objections of U.S. Trustee.); In re American West Airlines, Inc., 171 B.R. 674 (Bankr.D. Ariz. 1 994)(Court approves "success" bonus for chief executive officer and others who successfully downsized airline and settled substantial administrative claims despite seven hundred letters to the court from rank and file employees objecting to management bonuses. The court found that the executives had accomplished a "maj or feat" and were essential to the reorganization process.); In re Interco Incorp., 128 B.R. 229 (Bankr.E.D.Mo. 1991)(Court approves performance-based executive retention program to ensure that critical executives remained with debtors throughout reorganization.).

[50] In re U.S. Airways, 329 B.R. 793 (Bankr.E.D.Va. 2005).

[51] *Id.* at 797-798.

In support of their objections, the U.S. Trustee and the unions argued that the plan was overly broad and would undercut employee morale by sparing management from financial sacrifices that the unionized workforce had to bear.

First, the court considered whether the debtor made a threshold showing that it used sound business judgment in adopting the plan. It concluded that "[t]here can be little doubt, based on the evidence, that the plan is in response to a serious retention problem," because there were 340 unfilled open positions. The court ultimately approved a modified KERP that applied to management employees below the officer level upon approval, but deferred applicability to senior level officers until plan confirmation.

> Of the objections to the program, surely the most compelling, from a purely human point of view, is that it represents a betrayal of the principle of "shared sacrifice" that was championed by the company in the litigation and negotiations that resulted in over $900 million of wage and other concessions by its unionized workforce. While management employees took some pay cuts and benefit reductions, the plain truth is that those cuts were significantly less than the cuts experienced by the non-management employees. It is hardly any wonder, therefore, that the rank and file employees have reacted to the proposal with considerable outrage, as evidenced, for example, by the petition that was admitted at the hearing signed by 2,209 members of the Communications Workers of America denouncing the proposed severance plan and urging this court not to approve it.
>
> The court is certainly sensitive to what one witness described as the "uproar in the workplace" after the company announced it would seek approval of the severance plan. At the same time, the court cannot ignore the fact that the landscape has significantly changed. At the time the labor concessions were negotiated, the company was headed along a particular path, that of transformation. Now it is headed on a different path, that of merger. Under a transformation plan, employees--whether management or rank and file--were equally likely to keep their jobs (if the company successfully emerged from chapter 11 as a viable airline) or to lose them (if the company had to liquidate). Under the proposed merger, by contrast, few of the unionized employees are likely to face the loss of their jobs, since there is little overlap in the route structure of the two airlines. However, somewhere between one-third and one-half of the management employees are expected ultimately to lose their jobs. The problem the company faces is that those management employees will be needed up until the day their employment is terminated, perhaps two years from now. If they leave too soon, the merger itself (and with it, the jobs of the rank and file employees) will be threatened.
>
> The argument that the program is too broad and that any retention benefits should be narrowly targeted to "critical" or "key" employees likewise misses the mark. The evidence at the hearing convincingly established that the headquarters organization cannot afford further attrition without effectively eliminating its ability to carry the company through the merger. Put another way, once a football team has been reduced to 11 players, every one of them is "critical," since you cannot field a team with fewer.[52]

Although postpetition retention and severance payments are substantially modified by the BAPCPA, the foregoing illustrates how a bankruptcy court attempts to balance economic and non-economic competing interests and claims in the reorganization process.

The court has less control over prepetition payments, although they can be avoided in some circumstances, such as when they are found to be fraudulent, as discussed above in the Enron

---

[52] *Id.* at 799-800.

bankruptcy. Nevertheless, there is an inherent tension in the policy decision to allow existing management to steer a prospective debtor through reorganization when self-policing is also an issue. The implicit conflict of interest that can arise between a chapter 11 debtor company, its management and its creditors is acknowledged by the courts. A U.S. Court of Appeals considered whether a bankruptcy court can authorize a creditors' committee to sue derivatively on behalf of the trustee to recover alleged fraudulent conveyances made by management.[53] It concluded that a court-approved derivative suit for the benefit of the debtor's estate was permissible under the Bankruptcy Code.

As a component of its analysis, the court observed that avoiding a fraudulent conveyance could be a particularly "vexing" problem in a chapter 11 context:

> This situation immediately gives rise to the proverbial problem of the fox guarding the henhouse. If no trustee is appointed, the debtor--really, the debtor's management--bears a fiduciary duty to avoid fraudulent transfers that it itself made. One suspects that if managers can devise any opportunity to avoid bringing a claim that would amount to reputational self-immolation, they will seize it. For that reason, courts and commentators have acknowledged that the debtor-in-possession "often acts under the influence of conflicts of interest." These conflicts of interest can arise even in situations where there is no concern that a debtor's management is trying to save its own skin. For example, a debtor may be unwilling to pursue claims against individuals or businesses, such as critical suppliers, with whom it has an ongoing relationship that it fears damaging. Finally, even if a bankrupt debtor is willing to bring an avoidance action, it might be too financially weakened to advocate vigorously for itself. In any of these situations, the real losers are the unsecured creditors whose interests avoidance actions are designed to protect.[54]

In conclusion, although the Bankruptcy Code presumes that a debtor company's management is best qualified to lead the debtor through the reorganization process, there are equitable and statutory mechanisms to address intentional wrongdoing and less damaging departures from sound business judgment. And, while there is substantial flexibility in the reorganization process and employees are provided some level of protection, there is no question that the reorganization process is used strategically by business debtors to shed what are perceived to be onerous employee benefit programs.

---

[53] Official Committee of Unsecured Creditors of Cybergenics Corp. v. Chinery, 330 F.3d 548 (3d Cir.), *cert. denied*, 540 U.S. 1001, 1002 (2003).

[54] *Id.* at 573. (Citations omitted).

In: Economics of Unemployment
Editor: Mary I. Marshalle, pp. 153-185

ISBN: 1-60021-138-0
© 2006 Nova Science Publishers, Inc.

*Chapter 8*

# THE ROLE OF PUBLIC BENEFITS: A CASE STUDY FOR SEVEN EUROPEAN COUNTRIES

## *Hans Hansen*

Danish National Institute of Social Research
Herluf Trolles Gade 1, DK-1052 Copenhagen, Denmark

## ABSTRACT

Non-voluntary unemployment is a risk outside the control of the individual. By selecting certain occupations the individual knows that he or she may be exposed to a higher risk of unemployment than in other occupations, e.g. workers in the construction and building industry are exposed to unemployment due to the weather to a higher degree than employees in the IT industry.

Such varying risks of unemployment may be reflected in the pay agreements of different industries, but exactly who may be unemployed and for how long, is still beyond the control of the individual. Unemployment insurance benefits are designed to help coping with the financial situation as unemployed, they secure the financial basis for existence in this situation, and enables the unemployed to have time to look for a new relevant job. The primary aim of unemployment insurance benefits is to provide security, the main hypothesis being that human beings perform better when they feel financially secure.

Future ageing problems and early retirement from the labour market is a bad mixture. Early retirement is very popular in many countries and there are several roads leading to this situation, in some countries also via public schemes, which almost guide to early retirement. Early retirement may be interpreted as a kind of voluntary unemployment. The incentives to join and to stay in such schemes will be studied.

The schemes for sickness and disability are different from those for unemployment and early retirement because they are health related. Compensation for sickness often results in high replacement rates, which could be an invitation to short term leaves.

# INTRODUCTION

Non-voluntary unemployment is a risk outside the control of the individual. By selecting certain occupations the individual knows that he or she may be exposed to a higher risk of unemployment than in other occupations, e.g. workers in the construction and building industry are exposed to unemployment due to the weather to a higher degree than employees in the IT industry.

Such varying risks of unemployment may be reflected in the pay agreements of different industries, but exactly who may be unemployed and for how long, is still beyond the control of the individual. Unemployment insurance benefits are designed to help coping with the financial situation as unemployed, they secure the financial basis for existence in this situation, and enables the unemployed to have time to look for a new relevant job. The primary aim of unemployment insurance benefits is to provide security, the main hypothesis being that human beings perform better when they feel financially secure.

It is widely discussed 'how' secure people should be and for how long. If the benefits are too generous and the benefit period too long, the situation as unemployed may tend to become permanent. The financial incentives to look for a job may disappear or become very small. In this situation the society is losing production and the public expenditures will be higher than necessary.

The challenge is to design the unemployment insurance schemes in such a way that they strike a good balance between social security as unemployed and good incentives to look for a relevant job. There may even exist a theoretical optimal unemployment insurance scheme. This challenge has to some extend been blurred by the implementation of active labour market measures for unemployed over the last couple of decades. One argument runs as follows: Generous benefits is not a problem when all unemployed are participating in activation, they are 'forced' to look for jobs and to participate in educational and training programs etc. Even as a participant in active labour market measures it is evident that the intensity in applying for a 'real' job increases when the benefits decrease. There are many good arguments for active labour market measures, but one of them is not that they replace good incentives for work in the benefit schemes. The ideal is to construct active labour market measures and benefit schemes in such a way that they both support the return of the unemployed to a relevant job. It is not the return to any job, implying any bad job, which is the aim. The objective of the active measures is to keep up or improve the employability of the unemployed, implying the return to as 'good' a job or even a better job than the previous one. This is not an easy task, and as will become evident in the following, countries use very different designs to obtain this goal.

Unemployment insurance benefit schemes are not the only relevant ones in this context. Many countries have unemployment assistance schemes as follow-on schemes to insurance benefits, other countries have social assistance schemes to fulfil this role. These schemes will also be studied, but they are not the only ones.

In most West European countries there are hundreds of thousands (many millions in the large countries) outside the labour force even if they are in the 'working ages'. Some persons are long term ill or disabled, other persons have retired early. Illness and disability are usually caused by health problems and cannot be directly compared with unemployment. Never the less, financial incentives to apply for these schemes as well as to stay in them will be studied. Several countries, e.g. the Netherlands who has particularly many disability pensioners, have tightened the access criteria, reduced benefits and introduced more frequent control to ensure continued eligibility for benefits. Other countries, e.g. Denmark, have turned the medical criteria 'up side down', the focus is now on what the disabled can do, not on how disabled in general terms he or she is. The potential gains from avoiding people to enter these schemes 'incorrectly' are very substantial.

Future ageing problems and early retirement from the labour market is a bad mixture. Early retirement is very popular in many countries and there are several roads leading to this situation, in some countries also via public schemes, which almost guide to early retirement. Early retirement may be interpreted as a kind of voluntary unemployment. The incentives to join and to stay in such schemes will be studied.

## UNEMPLOYMENT INSURANCE BENEFIT SCHEMES

The countries included in this study, Denmark, Finland, Great Britain, Italy, the Netherlands, Spain and Sweden all have unemployment insurance schemes. Denmark, Finland and Sweden have voluntary schemes or components of schemes, which are voluntary. The schemes of the other countries are mandatory.

The access conditions to benefits and the entitlements from these schemes will be described very shortly for each country based on 2000 rules, with significant later changes up to 2004 also being mentioned. The sequence of the countries listed above will be changed in the following to be more in accordance with the established categorization of welfare state regimes. The Nordic countries will be first, followed by the Netherlands, then Italy and Spain and finally Great Britain.

Besides the unemployment insurance schemes the countries also have 'follow-on' schemes or alternatives to the insurance schemes. These will also be described, but the insurance schemes will be first.

## Denmark

*Main characteristics:* Completely voluntary, income related scheme with a low cap and a high floor, long benefit period.

*Access conditions for benefits:* Membership of the voluntary scheme for 1 year, shorter for newcomers, and work for 1 year within the last 3 years before the unemployment spell. Only work periods after joining the scheme count.

*Entitlements:* The general rule is compensation of 90 percent of the lost income up to a cap, which is approximately 65 percent of the full time average wage for an industrial worker equivalent to OECD's average production worker, the APW. If the unemployed person has a work record of 3 years (full time work) there is a minimum benefit, which is 82 percent of the maximum benefit. The floor is reached at approx. 55 percent of the APW income level. The benefit period is maximum 4 years, in the last 3 of which the unemployed participates in active labour market measures. Lower rates for some groups of young unemployed exist, but are not applied in this study.

*Recent developments:* The described structure has not been changed in recent years.

## Finland

*Main characteristics:* Voluntary income related component, a relatively low floor and no ceiling, a relatively short benefit period.

*Access conditions for benefits:* The voluntary earnings related component requires 10 months membership of the insurance scheme. Both components, the basic and the voluntary, require a work period of at least 43 weeks (minimum 18 hours a week) within the last 24 months before the unemployment spell. Only work after joining the voluntary component counts.

*Entitlements:* The benefit in the basic component is a pure flat rate. This benefit also constitutes the minimum benefit in the voluntary component. Lost income (95 percent) above the level of the minimum benefit is compensated by 42 percent up to a monthly income of 90 times the daily minimum benefit. 95 percent of the lost income about that level is compensated by 20 percent. There is no maximum for the benefit, the minimum benefit is reached at approx. 21 percent of the APW level. The scheme includes additional benefits for children. This benefit can be received for a maximum of 500 days, 100 weeks for both components. There is a waiting period of 7 days.

*Recent developments:* the 42 percent was increased to 45 percent. A compensation of 55 percent (instead of 45 percent) in 150 days was also introduced in case of lay offs and a membership period of at least 5 years. The work requirement of 43 weeks is now within the last 28 months.

## Sweden

*Main characteristics:* Voluntary income related component, a relatively high cap and a relatively low floor. Until recently there were no effective time limitations on the benefit period.

*Access conditions for benefits:* A 12 months membership period is required in the voluntary income related insurance scheme. For both the basic and the voluntary component there are specific work requirements (a certain amount of hours within 6 months), which have to be met in order to be eligible for benefits. Only work periods after joining the voluntary scheme count.

*Entitlements:* The benefit in the basic scheme is a flat rate, which is also the minimum benefit in the voluntary component, just as in Finland. The compensation in the voluntary scheme is 80 percent of the lost income up to a cap of approx. 85 percent of the APW income level. The floor is at approx. 35 percent of the APW income level. The span of income, where the scheme is income related (80 percent of lost income) is much wider than in the Danish scheme. The benefit period is 300 days (5 days a week) with a waiting period of 5 days. Until recently the benefit period could be renewed repeatedly by participation in active labour market measures, there was in practise no time limitation.

*Recent developments:* The possibility of repeated renewal of the rights to benefits through participation in active labour market measures no longer exists. An 'activity guarantee' has been introduced and the benefit period can only be renewed once, but there are no time limitations on the 'stay' in the 'activity guarantee'. The cap in the voluntary component has been increased in both 2001 and 2002 for the first 100 days of unemployment and is now approx. equivalent to 100 percent APW income level. The minimum benefit (the flat rate in the basic scheme) was also increased considerably in both 2001 and 2002. The higher cap for the first 100 days of unemployment is similar to the higher compensation rate in the Finnish scheme for the first 150 days in case of lay-offs.


## The Netherlands

*Main characteristics:* Mandatory scheme, composite working requirement, duration of benefit period depends on length of working period and age, high cap and a relatively low floor.

*Access conditions for benefits:* The scheme is mandatory. Access to income related benefits depends on the length of the work period. There are two components in the requirement, one is work for at least 26 weeks out of the last 39 weeks before the unemployment spell, and another is work for at least 52 days in each of 4 years out of the last 5. If only the first component is met, the benefit will be a flat rate.

*Entitlements:* The compensation percentage is 70 in the income related scheme with a cap of approx. 1.4 APW income level. The floor is at approx. 50 percent of the APW income level. The flat rate benefit is related to the minimum legal wage, for a single it is 70 percent of that wage. The benefit period varies with the length of the working period and the age of the recipient, the variation is from 6 to 60 months. After the ordinary benefit period has expired it is possible to receive the minimum benefit for up to 2 years.

*Recent developments:* The described structure has not been changed in recent years.


## Italy

*Main characteristics:* Mandatory scheme, several components with varying benefit levels and duration of benefit periods.

*Access conditions for benefits:* General unemployment scheme: Benefits are paid to dismissed workers who have paid contributions for at least 52 weeks in the last 2 years before the unemployment spell and have been registered on the placement lists for at least 2 years (an indication that you belong to the work force). The scheme is mandatory and available for unemployed who have been laid off individually or collectively and who are not eligible for the mobility benefit. First time job seekers are not eligible for benefits from the scheme.

Mobility scheme: the benefit is paid to workers who have been laid off from firms eligible for the 'Wage Supplementation Funds', primarily large firms. 6 months of work is required.

*Entitlements:* General scheme: Compensation is 30 percent of the former wage up to a cap. The benefit period is up to 6 months.

Mobility scheme: Compensation is 64 percent of the former wage up to the same maximum as for the general scheme resulting in a much lower cap, because the compensation percentage is much higher. The benefit period can be up to 4 years.

There are several variants of both schemes, the descriptions here cover the mainstream variants.

*Recent developments:* The compensation was increased to 40 percent in the general scheme and the benefit period is now 9 months for unemployed over 50 years.

## Spain

*Main characteristics:* Mandatory scheme, variable benefit period, minimum and maximum benefits depend on number of family members.

*Access conditions for benefits:* This mandatory scheme requires contributions for a minimum of 360 days within the last 6 years for benefit eligibility.

*Entitlements:* Compensation is 70 percent of the former income for the first 180 days, thereafter 60 percent. The minimum benefit is equivalent to the official minimum wage, the maximum is 1.7 times the minimum wage, all for a single. The minimum and maximum benefits are higher for families with children. The benefit period is as a minimum 120 days. Depending on the former work record it can be up to 2 years.

*Recent developments:* The described structure has not been changed in recent years.

## Great Britain

*Main characteristics:* mandatory scheme, pure flat rate benefits, short benefit period, same basic benefit level for follow-on scheme.

*Access conditions for benefits:* The Jobseekers Allowance, JSA, scheme is for people who are unemployed and who are seeking for a job. The contribution based component JSA ( c ), requires a former work record, a specific contribution record to be precise, within the last two tax years before the unemployment spell. The income based component, JSA ( ib ), is for unemployed who are seeking for a job, but who do not meet the contribution requirement for the JSA ( c ) scheme or who have been 'out-insured', i.e. have exhausted their benefit rights from the JSA ( c ) component.

*Entitlements:* The benefit level depends on age, for those aged over 25 years it was 52.20 GBP/week in 2000 (highest rate) . The basic benefit level is the same in the JSA ( c ) and the JSA ( ib) components, but in the last mentioned it is means tested against other income and net wealth. The JSA ( ib ) scheme contains benefit supplements for dependent spouses and for children. These supplements are also available for recipients from the JSA ( c ) scheme. There is a waiting period of 3 days. The benefit period in the JSA ( c) component is 6 months. There are no time limitations for the JSA ( ib ) scheme.

*Recent developments:* The supplements for children in the JSA ( ib ) component will be replaced by tax credits from the Child Tax Credit and Work Tax Credit schemes from April 2004.

## NET REPLACEMENT RATES AS UNEMPLOYED

What is the outcome of being unemployed according to the just described insurance rules of the seven countries? The result is contained in table 1 for a single person without children. It is assumed, that the housing costs constitute 20 percent of the gross wage of the average worker (OECD concept, here referred to as the 100 percent APW), both when he or she works and when he or she is unemployed, the person stays where he or she lived when in work. The income after tax, social contributions (paid by the APW) and housing costs (reduced by housing benefits received) in unemployment is related to the corresponding amount when in work, the result is the net replacement rate. The wage income varies around the average for industrial workers, more precisely around the gross wage of OECD's average production worker, the APW.

The calculations of net replacement rates have been performed by national teams doing 'their own' countries according to a common framework agreed upon by all the teams.

**Table 1. Net replacement rates for a single in unemployment (insured), 2000.**

| APW inc | DK | FIN | S | NL | IT | ES | GB |
|---|---|---|---|---|---|---|---|
| 0.67 | 74 | 55 | 68 | 82 | 31 | 53 | 49 |
| 0.80 | 57 | 50 | 71 | 64 | 31 | 60 | 38 |
| 1.00 | 46 | 44 | 55 | 60 | 33 | 63 | 29 |
| 1.25 | 36 | 37 | 42 | 62 | 33 | 51 | 22 |
| 1.50 | 30 | 34 | 35 | 66 | 33 | 41 | 18 |

Source: '7 country study'.
Note: DK: Denmark, FIN: Finland, S: Sweden, NL: the Netherlands, IT: Italy, ES: Spain, GB: Great Britain.

**Table 2. Net replacement rates for sole provider (one child) in unemployment (insured), 2000.**

| APW inc. | DK | FIN | S | NL | IT | ES | GB |
|---|---|---|---|---|---|---|---|
| 0.67 | 89 | 83 | 87 | 83 | 50 | 55 | 50 |
| 0.80 | 79 | 82 | 86 | 77 | 50 | 54 | 46 |
| 1.00 | 69 | 70 | 74 | 65 | 53 | 61 | 41 |
| 1.25 | 57 | 58 | 60 | 50 | 51 | 61 | 33 |
| 1.50 | 49 | 52 | 51 | 42 | 50 | 50 | 27 |

Source: '7 country study'.

Two countries, Denmark and Great Britain have flat rate unemployment benefits and the replacement rates decrease accordingly over the entire income interval. The profile is, however, not solely determined by unemployment benefits but also by taxation and housing benefits. The profile for Sweden also shows decreasing replacement rates after the 1.00 APW income level. Italy has almost constant net replacement rates, the cap for the ordinary unemployment benefit, used here, is quite high. The Netherlands also has an almost constant profile after the lowest income level where the income as unemployed is 'topped-up' by social assistance benefits. Finland's stepwise scheme results in a more gradual decrease of the replacement rates than is the case for Denmark and Great Britain. The profile for Spain is an inverted 'U', mainly caused by taxation. Taxation is also the reason behind the increase for Sweden from the first to the second income level. Only the Netherlands , Denmark and Sweden reach replacement rates above 70 percent, there are no serious incentives problems in relation to work for this case except for the Netherlands at the lowest income level.

The sole provider for children is often regarded as belonging to a socially 'exposed' group. The sole provider will be our next family type, it could be interpreted as an extended single family type, children are 'added'. What are the consequences of adding a child? The result is contained in table 2.

The sole provider is assumed to be young, 22 years of age. The first to notice is that almost all replacement rates are considerably higher than for the single person, cf. table 1. The reason is that some of the U.B. schemes contain supplements for children, e.g. those for Finland and Great Britain, but also that most housing benefit schemes favour families with children, and that housing benefits in general are higher in unemployment than in work. Finally, sole providers usually receive more in child benefits than married couples and the same amount disregarding income. This also helps to increase the net replacement rate for the sole provider in unemployment. The profile for the Netherlands is now one of decreasing replacement rates, the young mother will only receive the income related benefit for a short period, increasing with age, the rest of the time a flat rate benefit is received.

Serious incentives problems in relation to work are now evident at the two lowest income levels in all three Nordic countries and the Netherlands. Taking the possibility that return to work may be at a lower wage than received before the unemployment into consideration, the incentives to work are even more problematic at low income levels in the four mentioned countries. The high net replacement rates have here been used to indicate serious incentives problems, the argument can also be turned around, and then high replacement rates indicate a good protection against drastic reductions in income, when unemployment occurs.

A third variation is to augment the single family with one adult, a spouse, who can work or not. We start with a situation where the spouse is not working, it is the 'classical' one-earner couple. This case may not be so interesting any more, because the two-earner couple is gradually replacing the classical family type. However, there is still a considerable variation in women's labour market participation across Europe, and in the Nordic countries, where women's labour market participation is high, there are many immigrant families with one breadwinner. The case therefore has some relevance and from a system approach, it is also of interest to see what happens, when an adult is 'added' to the single family type.

The replacement rates for the one-earner couple are higher than for the single, except for Spain where they are slightly lower. This is due to supplements for the dependent spouse, 'topping-up' to a minimum income for this family type or to taxation of a couple, where unused tax allowances for the non working spouse can be transferred to the other spouse. Housing benefits might also have an impact.

Compared to the sole provider especially Finland, the Netherlands and Great Britain have higher replacement rates for the one-earner couple than for the sole provider. Finland 'sticks' out with replacement rates in the 90'es up to the 1.00 APW income level, the Netherlands up to the 0.80 level.

Finally we look at the two-earner couple with children. It is assumed that one spouse always has 50 percent of the income of the other. Table 4 contains the results from the cases where the high income spouse becomes unemployed while the lower income spouse continues to work and visa versa. The housing cost assumption is now 30 percent of the gross wage of the 1.00 APW.

Before interpreting the net replacement rates it should be noted that the income of the working spouse is included in both the nominator and the denominator when the replacement rate is calculated. It should also be noted that the income of the high income spouse constitutes 2/3 of the gross wage income of the couple, leaving 1/3 to the low income spouse.

One feature to be noted is that the difference between corresponding replacement rates from the two cases often is surprisingly small, some times down to less than 5 percentage points. Another is that losing 2/3 of the couple's wage income has a very small effect on disposable income, less than 10 percent at the lowest income levels in Denmark and Sweden.

**Table 3. Net replacement rates for one-earner couple (no children) in unemployment (insured), 2000.**

| APW inc. | DK | FIN | S | NL | IT | ES | GB |
|----------|-----|-----|-----|-----|-----|-----|-----|
| 0.67 | 78 | 96 | 68 | 99 | 45 | 50 | 73 |
| 0.80 | 62 | 95 | 71 | 92 | 44 | 55 | 62 |
| 1.00 | 50 | 95 | 55 | 74 | 45 | 61 | 46 |
| 1.25 | 39 | 78 | 42 | 67 | 42 | 50 | 35 |
| 1.50 | 34 | 65 | 35 | 70 | 41 | 41 | 28 |

Source: '7 country study'.

**Table 4. Net replacement rates for a two-earner couple (2 children) when one of the spouses is unemployed (insured), while the other works. 2000.**

| APW inc. | DK | FIN | S | NL | IT | ES | GB |
|----------|-------|-------|-------|-------|-------|-------|-------|
| 1.00 | 96/99 | 74/80 | 90/94 | 74/86 | 57/74 | 67/84 | 84/85 |
| 1.20 | 90/97 | 71/77 | 90/93 | 76/86 | 57/73 | 73/87 | 72/74 |
| 1.50 | 72/90 | 62/77 | 78/91 | 77/86 | 56/72 | 76/86 | 56/60 |
| 1.88 | 63/85 | 57/78 | 67/92 | 78/88 | 54/71 | 77/85 | 39/57 |
| 2.25 | 58/81 | 57/78 | 62/92 | 80/88 | 54/72 | 72/83 | 34/57 |

Source: '7 country study'.

In the Netherlands the effect is a reduction of between 1/5 and ¼ of the disposable income when in work over the entire income span.

When the low income spouse loses her or his income, it is hardly visible at the two lowest income levels in Denmark, slightly more visible in Sweden, where the reduction is 7 percent. The loss of 1/3 of the wage income in the Netherlands and Spain implies a loss of approximately 1/6 of the net income of the couple in work over the entire income span.

There are some very serious incentives problems in relation to work in two of the Nordic countries, Denmark and Sweden, at the two lowest income levels, the two countries in the world having the highest labour market participation among women also implying the highest proportion of two-earner couples among married or cohabiting couples.

In most of the countries in this study the unemployed has to participate in active labour market measures during the benefit period or immediately after. The persons are then typically not registered as unemployed any longer but they receive a benefit, which in most countries is equivalent to unemployment benefits. Spain has no activation programme for unemployed and for the other countries it is only in Italy and the Netherlands that participation in active labour market measures implies a higher benefit than ordinary unemployment benefits. In most of the countries there are no financial incentives to participate in activation, it is a compulsory activity when unemployed.

## Benefit Duration

Before the results are summarized below it is important to emphasize the duration of the benefit periods in the countries included in the study, because potential incentives problems are more severe if they can last for a long time. Denmark has a benefit period with a fixed duration of 4 years, for Finland the fixed duration benefit period is almost 2 years. Sweden has a benefit period of 1 year and 2 months but participation in the 'Activity Guarantee' is without time limitations. In the Netherlands the length of the benefit period varies with the previous work record and age, it is from ½ to 5 years. The ordinary unemployment insurance scheme in Italy has a benefit period of 6 months, for the Mobility Benefit it is up to 4 years in special cases, usually it is 1 year. In Spain the length of the benefit period depends on the former work record, it varies from less than ½ year to 2 years. In Great Britain the JSA ( c ) scheme has a fixed benefit period of ½ year.

The span presented her is from less than ½ year (Spain) to 5 years (the Netherlands) and for Sweden the benefit period combined with participation in the 'Activity Guarantee' is without time limitations.

## Main Results

For the single person there are no serious incentives problems in any of the countries except in the Netherlands at the lowest income level. For the young single provider the Netherlands and the Nordic countries have serious incentives problems at the two lowest income levels. This is also the case for the one-earner couple in the Netherlands and in Finland, in Finland it is for the first three income levels. For the two-earner couple it is especially in Denmark and Sweden that the net replacement rates are very high at the two lowest income levels. The difference between the results when it is the spouse with the high income who is unemployed and the spouse with the low income who works and the reversed situation is often surprisingly small.

## FOLLOW-ON/ALTERNATIVE SCHEMES FOR UNEMPLOYED

As just mentioned, the variation in the duration of the benefit period for unemployment insurance benefits in the seven countries is very considerable. In the case of Sweden there was (and probably still is) no effective time limitation, in the Netherlands the duration is up to 5 years, in Denmark it is 4 years and in e.g. Italy, Spain and Great Britain it is ½ year. It is therefore of great importance to include follow-on schemes or 'exit' schemes from unemployment insurance benefit schemes to assess the financial situation for long term unemployed. One set of such schemes is social assistance or unemployment assistance another set is early retirement schemes. We start with social assistance and unemployment assistance schemes.

The follow-on or alternative schemes of the countries studied here will be presented in a very compact form.

## Denmark

*Main characteristics*: Social assistance is 'follow-on' as well as alternative scheme for unemployment insurance, no automatic 'topping-up', no time limitations.

*Access conditions for benefits*: Social assistance is a 'last resort' scheme for which you are eligible in case of a social event, i.e. unemployment, sickness, divorce, and when there are no other possibilities for financial support for you and your family. Recipients are obliged to participate in active labour market measures.

*Entitlements*: The benefit is related to the maximum unemployment benefits, approx. 60 percent of this if the claimant is a non-provider in relation to children, 80 percent if he or she is a provider in relation to children. In a couple each spouse receives the benefit, and both spouses may receive social assistance even if only one of them has experienced a social event. There is also an allowance for housing costs, it is coordinated with ordinary housing benefits. There are no time limitations for the benefit period.

*Recent developments:* It has always been the aim, that social assistance benefits should not be higher than unemployment insurance benefits. This has been difficult to obtain the way social assistance is allocated to couples. Reductions have therefore been implemented for social assistance for couples and ordinary housing benefits have also been included in the limits for total support.

## Finland

*Main characteristics:* Labour market support is a follow-on scheme to unemployment insurance and an alternative scheme, when the access conditions to the insurance scheme are not met.

*Access conditions for benefits:* Labour market support is payable when the rights to benefits from the insurance scheme have expired or when the membership requirements (income related scheme) and work requirements for the insurance scheme (both components) are not met.

*Entitlements:* The benefit level is the same as for the basic component in the insurance scheme. It is, however, tapered when other income, also that of a spouse, exceeds a certain ceiling. There are also additional benefits for children, but rates are lower than those in the insurance scheme. There are no time limitations for the benefit period.

*Recent developments:* The described structure has not been changed in recent years.

## Sweden

*Main characteristics:* Swedish social assistance is, as in other countries, a last resort scheme and only available if there is no other way of earning a livelihood. It sets a minimum standard, but there is no automatic topping-up to this standard if other income, e.g. unemployment benefits from the insurance scheme, is below the social assistance level. It is an alternative scheme.

*Access conditions for benefits:* The scheme is, as already mentioned, a last resort scheme, which is available when there are no other possible ways of earning a livelihood. The recipient has, if he or she is able to work, an obligation to apply for jobs, to participate in active labour market measures and/or participate in educational programmes to improve the chances for getting back to work.

*Entitlements:* The level of social assistance is determined by the size and composition of the family. There are specific rates for adults, cohabiting adults and children, differentiated according to age. Even if the Swedish social assistance constitutes minimum income levels, there is no automatic topping-up to these levels if other income is lower.

*Recent developments:* The described structure has not been changed in recent years.

## The Netherlands

*Main characteristics:* Guaranteed minimum standard, to which other income below this standard is 'topped-up'.

*Access conditions for benefits:* Dutch citizens and foreigners living legally in the Netherlands and without sufficient means for a living, are granted social assistance also as a 'top-up' of other income sources, if their combined level is below the minimum standard. There are no specific labour market obligations attached to the scheme.

*Entitlements:* Dutch social assistance rates are related to the legal minimum wage. The rates are defined as varying proportions of the legal minimum wage according to family size and composition. There are special additions to cover housing costs, maximum 20% of the legal minimum wage. There are no time limitations for the benefit period.

*Recent developments:* The described structure has not been changed in recent years.

## Italy

*Main characteristics:* Pilot program with the aim of providing a guaranteed minimum standard. The scheme is also an alternative for the unemployment insurance scheme, which has limitations in the access for benefits.

*Access conditions for benefits:* Italian citizens with a low income and lack of sufficient means for a living are granted social assistance, also as a 'top-up' of other income. EU citizens have to stay 1 year, other nationalities 3 years, in Italy to become eligible for social assistance. Recipients are obliged to look for jobs and to participate in active labour market measures.

*Entitlements:* The scheme consists of flat rate benefits according to family size and composition. There is 'topping-up' of other income sources to the minimum standard. There are disregards for income from work with the aim of encouraging recipients of social assistance to take paid work. There are no time limitations for the benefit period.

*Recent developments:* The pilot program was terminated in 2001 and replaced by a 'minimum income support' scheme from 2002. The new scheme is administered at local level. Its characteristics are not very well defined.

## Spain

*Main characteristics:* The scheme applied here is a follow-on scheme to the unemployment insurance scheme, it is time limited for most recipients.

*Access conditions for benefits:* Only those for whom the rights for the unemployment insurance scheme have expired, are eligible for benefits.

*Entitlements:* The scheme has flat rate benefits related to the legal minimum wage, the rate is 75 percent of the minimum wage. The scheme is time limited typically with a maximum benefit period of 21-30 months, depending on age and family size. For unemployed, who are more than 52 years of age, there are no time limitations for the benefit period.

*Recent developments:* The described structure has not been changed in recent years.

## Great Britain

*Main characteristics:* JSA (ib) is a follow-on or an alternative scheme to JSA ( c ) . The basic benefit level is the same in the two schemes.

*Access conditions for benefits:* JSA (ib) is for unemployed looking for a job and who do not meet the contribution requirements for the JSA ( c ) scheme or who are 'out-insured' from that scheme.

*Entitlements:* The basic benefit level is the same as in the JSA ( c ) scheme, cf. the description of unemployment insurance schemes, and there are also benefits for a dependent spouse and for children. All benefits are means tested. There are no time limitations for the benefit period.

*Recent developments:* The benefits for children in the JSA (ib) scheme will be replaced by tax credits from the Child Tax Credit and the Work Tax Credit schemes from April 2004.

## NET REPLACEMENT RATES AS UNEMPLOYED, INSURED/FOLLOW-ON OR ALTERNATIVE SCHEMES

**Table 5. Net replacement rates for a single in unemployment, first insured, then follow-on scheme, 2000.**

| APW inc. | DK | FIN | S | NL | IT | ES | GB |
|---|---|---|---|---|---|---|---|
| 0.67 | 74/60 | 55/32 | 68/73 | 82/88 | 31/33 | 53/13 | 49/49 |
| 0.80 | 57/46 | 50/25 | 71/57 | 64/70 | 31/27 | 60/11 | 38/38 |
| 1.00 | 46/37 | 44/20 | 55/41 | 60/52 | 33/21 | 63/9 | 29/29 |
| 1.25 | 36/29 | 37/15 | 42/32 | 62/40 | 33/16 | 51/7 | 22/22 |
| 1.50 | 30/24 | 34/13 | 35/27 | 66/33 | 33/14 | 41/6 | 18/18 |

Source: '7 country study'.

The effect of moving from unemployment insurance to a follow-on scheme (for Sweden to apply an alternative scheme) for a single unemployed is contained in table 5.

The replacement rates in front of the / are identical to those in table 1. At the lowest income level the replacement rates of the follow-on schemes are higher than those for the insurance scheme in the Netherlands, Sweden and Italy, this is also the case for the next income level in the Netherlands, which seems to have an incentives problem at least at the lowest income level also for social assistance. For Great Britain the replacement rates for the two schemes are identical at all income levels, JSA ( c ) and JSA ( ib ) have the same basic rate. At all other income levels the follow-on scheme results in a lower compensation than the insurance scheme for all countries except Great Britain.

**Table 6. Net replacement rates for sole provider (two children) in unemployment, first insured, then follow-on scheme, 2000.**

| APW inc. | DK | FIN | S | NL | IT | ES | GB |
|----------|-------|-------|-------|-------|-------|-------|-------|
| 0.67 | 89/82 | 87/67 | 90/58 | 84/84 | 53/56 | 59/22 | 65/65 |
| 0.80 | 82/75 | 85/63 | 89/55 | 76/78 | 51/47 | 61/17 | 60/60 |
| 1.00 | 72/66 | 83/59 | 79/46 | 71/67 | 54/42 | 59/13 | 55/55 |
| 1.25 | 63/58 | 71/49 | 67/42 | 62/53 | 52/35 | 65/10 | 46/46 |
| 1.50 | 55/51 | 64/43 | 59/36 | 64/45 | 50/30 | 58/9 | 38/38 |

Source: '7 country study'.

In some of the countries i.e. Spain, Finland and Italy the follow-on replacement rates are very low at least at middle to higher income levels. It should be noted that for Sweden social assistance is not a follow-on scheme but an alternative, so the interpretation for that country is not a sequence where one scheme follows after the other, but more of two parallel schemes, you are either in one or the other all the time.

The next family type is the single provider. This time it is not the young mother with one child but the 40 years old mother with two children who experiences the transition from the insurance scheme to the follow-on scheme. The results are contained in table 6.

**Table 7. Net replacement rates for one-earner couple (no children) in unemployment, first insured, then follow-on scheme, 2000.**

| APW inc. | DK | FIN | S | NL | IT | ES | GB |
|----------|-------|-------|--------|-------|-------|-------|-------|
| 0.67 | 78/60 | 96/96 | 68/114 | 99/98 | 45/42 | 50/13 | 73/73 |
| 0.80 | 62/47 | 95/95 | 71/88 | 92/92 | 44/35 | 55/10 | 62/62 |
| 1.00 | 50/38 | 95/95 | 55/64 | 74/77 | 45/33 | 61/8 | 46/46 |
| 1.25 | 39/30 | 78/78 | 42/50 | 67/62 | 42/28 | 50/6 | 35/35 |
| 1.50 | 34/26 | 65/65 | 35/41 | 70/52 | 41/24 | 41/5 | 28/28 |

Source: '7 country study'

For most of the countries the replacement rates for the follow-on schemes are higher than for the single at almost all income levels, Sweden being the exception. The reasons are the same as mentioned for the insured unemployed single provider, cf. table 2. The Netherlands and Denmark have high to very high replacement rates for the follow-on schemes at the two lowest income levels. In Spain and to some extend also in Italy the drop in disposable income from the insurance scheme to the follow-on scheme is quite dramatic. This is also the case for Sweden, but here you do not move from scheme to scheme.

Now follows the situation for the classical one-earner couple when the breadwinner moves from the insurance to the follow-on scheme. Table 7 contains the results.

**Table 8. Net replacement rates for two-earner couple (2 children) when the 'high wage' spouse is unemployed, first insured, then follow-on scheme, while the other works, 2000.**

| APW inc. | DK | FIN | S | NL | IT | ES | GB |
|---|---|---|---|---|---|---|---|
| 1.00 | 96/98 | 74/62 | 90/83 | 74/50 | 57/72 | 67/43 | 84/84 |
| 1.20 | 90/84 | 71/56 | 90/72 | 76/40 | 57/61 | 73/42 | 72/72 |
| 1.50 | 72/67 | 62/49 | 78/57 | 77/31 | 56/53 | 76/41 | 56/56 |
| 1.88 | 63/58 | 57/41 | 67/45 | 78/24 | 54/32 | 77/41 | 39/39 |
| 2.25 | 58/48 | 57/35 | 62/38 | 80/26 | 54/33 | 72/41 | 34/34 |

Source: '7 country study'.

Here we see some very high replacement rates at the lower income levels in Sweden, the Netherlands and Finland for the follow-on schemes (parallel scheme for Sweden). They are close to 100 percent or even over 100 percent. If the non working spouse in the Danish couple is willing to work the replacement rate would be significantly higher both for the insurance scheme (topping-up by social assistance) and the follow-on scheme, at the lowest income level the replacement rates would be 105/109. In contrast there is a dramatic drop in compensation in Spain when moving from one scheme to the next.

**Table 9. Net replacement rates for two-earner couple (two children) when the 'low wage' spouse is unemployed, first insured, then follow-on scheme, while the other works, 2000.**

| APW inc. | DK | FIN | S | NL | IT | ES | GB |
|---|---|---|---|---|---|---|---|
| 1.00 | 99/101 | 80/72 | 94/83 | 86/55 | 74/67 | 84/71 | 85/85 |
| 1.20 | 97/89 | 77/64 | 93/72 | 86/56 | 73/66 | 87/73 | 74/74 |
| 1.50 | 90/72 | 77/48 | 91/58 | 86/57 | 72/63 | 86/72 | 60/60 |
| 1.88 | 85/65 | 78/46 | 92/58 | 88/57 | 71/61 | 85/63 | 57/57 |
| 2.25 | 81/63 | 78/49 | 92/58 | 88/58 | 72/61 | 83/63 | 57/57 |

Source: '7 country study'.

For the two-earner couple the 'high wage' spouse moves from the insurance scheme to the follow-on scheme, while the 'low wage' spouse continues to work. Table 8 contains the results.

The replacement rates in front of the / are identical to those in table 4. Denmark, Great Britain and Sweden have high compensations at the two lowest income levels for the follow-on schemes. In this case Spain and Italy have higher replacement rates than the Netherlands, where the loss of the 'high wage' has a very severe impact at the middle to high income levels.

What happens when it is the 'low wage' spouse who moves from scheme to scheme while the 'high wage' spouse continues to work? The results are in table 9.

**Table 10. Net replacement rates for two-earner couple (2 children) when both spouses are unemployed, first insured, then follow–on scheme, 2000.**

| APW inc. | DK | FIN | S | NL | IT | ES | GB |
|----------|-------|-------|-------|-------|-------|-------|-------|
| 1.00 | 93/97 | 69/60 | 84/83 | 60/50 | 46/48 | 50/19 | 79/79 |
| 1.20 | 87/83 | 67/52 | 83/72 | 62/40 | 46/41 | 56/15 | 67/67 |
| 1.50 | 71/66 | 58/41 | 72/57 | 64/31 | 47/34 | 62/12 | 52/52 |
| 1.88 | 57/53 | 49/33 | 62/45 | 66/25 | 30/27 | 62/9  | 41/41 |
| 2.25 | 48/44 | 43/28 | 55/38 | 68/21 | 31/22 | 56/8  | 34/34 |

Source:'7 country study'.

The first set of replacement rates are well known, they are identical to those in table 4 behind the /. Denmark, Sweden and Great Britain again show potentially serious incentives problems in relation to work at the low income levels for the follow-on schemes Higher up in the income scale it is surprisingly how large the impact is from losing 1/3 of the gross wage of the family. Finland, Sweden and the Netherlands have replacement rates below 67 percent, which this simple gross wage calculation would suggest. There is no social assistance left, it is tapered away against the income of the working spouse, and no special supplements for housing and children, and the housing costs weigh relatively heavily for the family which is now effectively a one earner couple.

It is relatively rare that both spouses in a couple are unemployed at the same time, but it happens and in that case table 10 contains the results.

Denmark and Sweden have high replacement rates for both schemes at the two lowest income levels, Great Britain at the lowest. Denmark has the most generous follow-on scheme at all income levels of all seven countries. Danish replacement rates are twice those of Italy, which again are more than twice those of Spain. While the 'follow-on' scheme for the Netherlands was among the two most generous for families with one income at all income levels, it is much more modest for families with two income earners, where one or both spouses receive benefits from the 'follow-on' scheme.

The benefits from the follow-on scheme will be received, when the benefit period from the insurance scheme has expired, but is this sequential approach of any significance for the benefit level? It is in the case of Denmark, where social assistance will be lower when it follows the insurance benefits instead of employment at the income levels used here.

## Benefit Duration

All follow-on schemes, except for Spain, have no time limitations why potential incentives problems from these schemes are severe, because they can last for a very long time. This should be kept in mind when the results are summarized below.

## Main Results

The replacement rates are sometimes higher for the follow-on scheme than for the insurance scheme. For the single person only the Netherlands has serious incentives problems at the lowest income level in the follow-on scheme. For the single provider the Netherlands and Denmark have high replacement rates at the two lowest income levels. For the one-earner couple it is the Netherlands, Finland and Sweden who have serious incentives problems in the follow-on scheme at the lower to medium income levels. For Sweden the replacement rate is over 100, as it also can be for Denmark in special cases. For the two-earner couple Denmark, Sweden and Great Britain have high to very high replacement rates at the lower income levels whoever of the spouses are unemployed and receiving benefits from the follow-on scheme. If both spouses are unemployed at the same time Denmark and Sweden have incentives problems at the lower income levels in both schemes.

The change in compensation from the insurance scheme to the follow-on scheme is sometimes drastic, especially in Spain, but sometimes also in Italy and Finland.

## EARLY RETIREMENT SCHEMES

Early retirement from the labour market is very popular in several European countries. In some countries it is possible to retire early only from a situation of employment, this is the case in the Netherlands and Great Britain. In other countries it is also possible to retire early from a situation of unemployment. The schemes, public or private, used in this study are shortly described in the following.

## Denmark

*Main characteristics:* Long contribution record, access from employment as well as unemployment, no labour market obligations attached.

*Access conditions for benefits:* Access to the early retirement scheme requires a long contribution record both for the unemployment insurance scheme and the early retirement scheme, 25 years out of the last 30 with various transition arrangements. It is a condition for benefit eligibility that the early retiree is eligible for unemployment insurance benefits when early retirement benefits are claimed. This implies, that there is no access to the early retirement scheme for recipients of social assistance. Minimum age is 60 years.

*Entitlements:* When entering at the age of 60, or when the initial conditions are met after that age, the benefit is 91 percent of the actual or potential unemployment insurance benefits. If entering at the age of 62, or two years after the initial conditions are met, the benefits are identical to the actual or potential unemployment insurance benefits. Various premiums can be received by further deferral dependent on hours of work in the deferral period. Early retirement according to the rules described here has a maximum duration of 5 years.

*Recent developments*: The described structure is still valid.

## Finland

*Main characteristics:* Finland has several schemes for early retirement, the unemployment pension, early old-age pension and an individual disability pension. Only the early old-age pension will be described. No labour market obligations are attached to the scheme.

*Access conditions for benefits:* The access rules are the same as for ordinary old-age pension, which has a residence based component and an occupational component. The minimum age is 60 for drawing an early pension.

*Entitlements:* The pension is calculated as an old-age pension, where the maximum for the occupational component is 60 percent of the former income. The pension for the early retiree may be smaller because there are fewer years for accrual of the pension. An early drawn pension is furthermore reduced by 0.4 percent per month it is drawn before the age of 65, this is also the case for the residence based component. The maximum duration is 5 years, but the early drawn pension continues as old-age pension from the age of 65 years.

*Recent developments:* The unemployment pension and the individual disability scheme will be phased out. The minimum age will be 62 years from 2005.

## Sweden

*Main characteristics:* Sweden has no dedicated early retirement scheme but the flexible old-age pension scheme can be used for early retirement from the age of 61. No labour market obligations are attached to the scheme.

*Access conditions for benefits:* Swedes, and other nationalities, who meet the 'opening' criteria for public pensions, 3 years of residence for the basic pension and 3 years of work for the occupational pension, can draw a pension early from the age of 61.

*Entitlements:* A full pension requires 40 years of residence for the basic pension and 30 years of work for the occupational scheme. If the criterion is met for the occupational component, the residence requirement is reduced to 30 years for a full basic pension. If the requirements are not met, the pension is reduced accordingly, e.g. to 25/30 if the work record is 25 years. If the pensions are drawn early they are reduced by 0.5 percent per month they are drawn before the age of 65 years is reached. At the age of 61 the pension will be reduced by 24 percent for the rest of the life. It is possible to change decision, and return to work without receiving a pension, this will then be adjusted accordingly. The duration of early retirement in Sweden is 4 years as a maximum.

*Recent developments:* Sweden has implemented a new pension system, which gradually will replace the old one. It is also possible to draw some of the components in the new scheme early, but not the Guarantee Pension. The pension is then reduced directly by a demographic factor.

## The Netherlands

*Main Characteristics:* The early retirement schemes in the Netherlands are labour market agreed schemes called VUT. There is only access from employment. No labour market obligations are attached to the scheme.

*Access conditions for benefits:* The age range for access to the scheme is from 58 to 63 years, typically 60 years. The usual requirement is 10 years of employment within the same industrial sector immediately before the early retirement.

*Entitlements:* The compensation is usually 75 to 80 percent of the former wage, 80 percent have been used for the actual calculations. The benefits continue as old-age pension from the age of 65 in addition to the national pension.

*Recent developments:* The favourable VUT schemes are to an increasing extend being replaced by other 'pre-pension schemes', where early drawn pensions are reduced actuarially, also when received as old-age pensions.

## Italy

*Main characteristics:* Seniority Pension is possible in the 'old' income related pension scheme, which gradually will be replaced by the 'new' contribution based scheme. There are no labour market obligations attached to the scheme.

*Access conditions for benefits:* It is a requirement that there is a contribution record of at least 18 years up to and including 1995. Furthermore the requirement is a contribution record of at least 37 years disregarding age or 35 years with contributions and an age of at least 57 years. This is the relevant scheme for our case.

*Entitlements:* The benefits are calculated in the same way as income related old-age pension, the main difference being, that the total contribution record for early retirement usually is shorter than for ordinary old-age pension, where the maximum contribution record is 40 years. The accrual rate is 2 percent of an average of indexed earnings over the last 10 years, up to a relatively high income level, above which the accrual rate drops, but there is no cap on the income generating pension rights. The benefit period can be up to 10-12 years.

*Recent developments:* The Seniority Pension scheme will gradually be phased out, new workers entering the labour market from 1996 will follow a new contribution based pension scheme, where early retirement is also possible but at an actuarial reduction determined by the longer remaining expected life span of an early retiree compared with an old-age pensioner. The Seniority Pension has also been tightened up, a 5 year 'qualifying period' which allowed no contributions but counted as years with contributions, has been abolished and the minimum contribution record of 37 years will be prolonged to 40 years from 2008.

## Spain

*Main characteristics:* Early retirement in Spain takes place by using the flexible old-age pension scheme. Only workers belonging to the old-age pension scheme from before 1967 have this option. No labour market obligations are attached to the scheme.

*Access conditions for benefits:* The age range for access to the scheme is from 60 to 64 years, typically 60 years (assumed for the actual calculations). A long contribution record is also required.

*Entitlements:* The pension is calculated as an old age pension but is reduced by 8 percent per year the pension is drawn before the age of 65. If the work record has a length of 40 years the reduction is by 7 percent per year, it is the assumption used here. The benefit period is to the age of 65, after which the pension continues as old age pension.

*Recent developments:* The scheme is temporary in the sense that during the coming 5-10 years it will be closed for new entrants.

## Great Britain

*Main characteristics:* Great Britain has no dedicated public schemes for early retirement but private schemes (company schemes) and schemes for public sector employees contain early retirement options. These schemes can be accessed from employment only. Early retirees have no labour market obligations.

*Access conditions for benefits:* 50 years of age seems to be pivotal in Great Britain. Above that age an occupational pension will usually be received by early retirement. A long work record, 30 years or so, is usually required as well.

*Entitlements:* There are many schemes and a considerable variation for the outcome of an early drawn pension. A relatively poor outcome after 30 years of work would be a pension of 50 percent of the final earnings and reduced for actuarial reasons by 25 percent for the 60 years old and by 50 percent for the 55 years old. A relatively generous outcome could be a pension of 2/3 of final earnings with no actuarial reductions. The last mentioned option could be in case of compulsory retirement or in cases where the age plus the length of the working period exceeds the number 85, this is primarily for public sector employees. A pension of 40 percent of the final earnings has been used for the actual calculations.

*Recent developments:* The 'Minimum Income Guarantee' (MIG) introduced from 1999 for persons who are 60 or more and who have a low income might be considered as a kind of public early retirement scheme. The MIG was replaced by the 'Pension Credit' scheme from 2003, this scheme also includes a benefit component, which can be received from the age of 60.

## NET REPLACEMENT RATES AS INSURED UNEMPLOYED AND EARLY RETIREE

It is assumed that the route to early retirement is via unemployment. This is, however, not always possible but then unemployment and early retirement can often be considered as alternatives, at least for relevant age groups, and a comparison of the economic position in either situation becomes relevant. Table 11 contains the results for a single in the relevant age group moving from unemployment to early retirement or having the two schemes as alternatives (the Netherlands and Great Britain).

In Italy, the Netherlands, Finland and Great Britain the compensation is higher as an early retiree than as an unemployed, sometimes by a very substantial margin. At the lowest income level Italy and the Netherlands have very strong incentives to join the early retirement scheme. Denmark has a slightly lower compensation for early retirement than for unemployment. In Sweden, the low income earners only receive a reduced basic pension as early retirement benefits. It is lower than the unemployment insurance benefit. Higher up in the income range the early retiree in Sweden also receives a reduced occupational pension, but it is income related, and then the situation as early retiree is financially better than as unemployed.

**Table 11. Net replacement rates for a single as insured unemployed and as early retiree, 2000.**

| APW inc. | DK | FIN | S | NL | IT | ES | GB |
|---|---|---|---|---|---|---|---|
| 0.67 | 74/68 | 55/67 | 68/46 | 82/86 | 31/95 | 53/53 | 49/56 |
| 0.80 | 57/53 | 50/55 | 71/45 | 64/69 | 31/65 | 60/60 | 38/46 |
| 1.00 | 46/42 | 44/47 | 55/47 | 60/72 | 33/70 | 63/63 | 29/37 |
| 1.25 | 36/33 | 37/51 | 42/50 | 62/74 | 33/70 | 51/63 | 22/30 |
| 1.50 | 30/28 | 34/54 | 35/47 | 66/77 | 33/70 | 41/64 | 18/26 |

Source: '7 country study'.

When the replacement rate for early retirement is calculated, it should be remembered that the benefits are obtained after many years of income and/or payment of contributions at the specified APW income levels, a long stable work and income record at the specified income level is required and also assumed.

There is no case with a single provider as an early retiree, the next case is for the one-earner couple. The results for this family type are contained in table 12.

**Table 12. Net replacement rates for a one-earner couple when the breadwinner is unemployed and an early retiree, 2000.**

| APW inc. | DK | FIN | S | NL | IT | ES | GB |
|---|---|---|---|---|---|---|---|
| 0.67 | 78/73 | 96/87 | 68/46 | 99/95 | 45/109 | 50/51 | 73/72 |
| 0.80 | 62/58 | 95/75 | 71/45 | 92/84 | 44/69 | 55/55 | 62/61 |
| 1.00 | 50/47 | 95/60 | 55/47 | 74/77 | 45/75 | 61/61 | 46/48 |
| 1.25 | 39/37 | 78/53 | 42/50 | 67/79 | 42/72 | 50/65 | 35/38 |
| 1.50 | 34/32 | 65/54 | 35/47 | 70/78 | 41/71 | 41/66 | 28/33 |

Source: '7 country study'.

Italy and the Netherlands, now joined by Finland, have very high net replacement rates for early retirement at the lowest income level also for this family type, but, generally speaking, early retirement is not so favourable compared to unemployment as in the case for the single. However, if the non-working spouse in Sweden is 61 or more he or she is eligible for a reduced basic pension, and then the replacement rates would be 105, 91, 80, 75 and 68 respectively, much higher than for unemployment. If the non-working spouse in Denmark is willing to work, the corresponding replacement rates in early retirement would be 108, 86, 69, 55 and 47 respectively, and the replacement rates for unemployment would also be higher. More or less special situations for this family type in these two countries may result in very strong incentives to join the early retirement scheme.

**Table 13. Net replacement rates for two-earner couple when the 'high wage' spouse is unemployed and then (or) an early retiree while the other spouse works, 2000.**

| APW inc. | DK | FIN | S | NL | IT | ES | GB |
|---|---|---|---|---|---|---|---|
| 1.00 | 96/95 | 74/69 | 90/65 | 74/79 | 57/77 | 67/70 | 84/63 |
| 1.20 | 90/80 | 71/66 | 90/65 | 76/81 | 57/77 | 73/75 | 72/54 |
| 1.50 | 72/62 | 62/67 | 78/66 | 77/83 | 56/80 | 76/77 | 56/50 |
| 1.88 | 63/55 | 57/70 | 67/68 | 78/84 | 54/82 | 77/77 | 39/46 |
| 2.25 | 58/53 | 57/72 | 62/66 | 80/86 | 54/81 | 72/77 | 34/45 |

Source: '7 country study'.

The two-earner couple, this time without children, where first one spouse, then the other and finally both spouses follow the route over unemployment to early retirement or as alternatives are the next cases. The couple should be without children both as unemployed and in early retirement, but for unemployment it is the situation with children, which is contained in the following tables. The net replacement rates are then somewhat higher than they should be in case of unemployment. In table 13 it is the high income spouse, who becomes unemployed and/or an early retiree.

Replacement rates for early retirement are high at the lower income levels in Denmark, the Netherlands and Italy. A strict comparison with unemployment is not possible, but early retirement is better than unemployment in the Netherlands, Italy and Spain at all income levels and in Finland, Sweden and Great Britain at the higher income levels.

What happens when it is the 'low income' spouse, who becomes unemployed and/or an early retiree is contained in table 14.

**Table 14. Net replacement rates for two-earner couple when the 'low wage' spouse is unemployed and then (or) an early retiree while the other spouse works, 2000.**

| APW inc. | DK | FIN | S | NL | IT | ES | GB |
|---|---|---|---|---|---|---|---|
| 1.00 | 99/94 | 80/106 | 94/96 | 86/89 | 74/87 | 84/98 | 85/85 |
| 1.20 | 97/93 | 77/98 | 93/93 | 86/89 | 73/88 | 87/90 | 74/79 |
| 1.50 | 90/88 | 77/91 | 91/89 | 86/90 | 72/90 | 86/84 | 60/73 |
| 1.88 | 85/82 | 78/87 | 92/87 | 88/91 | 71/89 | 85/86 | 57/69 |
| 2.25 | 81/78 | 78/84 | 92/85 | 88/91 | 72/89 | 83/88 | 57/65 |

Source: '7 country study'.

There are strong financial incentives quite high up in the income range in all countries for the low wage spouse to join the early retirement scheme instead of working. The replacement rates for unemployment in this case are high for almost all countries at all income levels, cf. the comments for table 4, but those for early retirement are even higher in Finland, the Netherlands, Italy, Spain (except at one income level) and Great Britain. In Denmark and Sweden they are close. It should be remembered that the replacement rates for unemployment are for a family with children and then higher than for a family without children.

The last case is when both spouses are unemployed and then (or) early retirees, the results are contained in table 15.

**Table 15. Net replacement rates for two-earner couple when both spouses are unemployed and then (or) early retirees, 2000.**

| APW inc. | DK | FIN | S | NL | IT | ES | GB |
|---|---|---|---|---|---|---|---|
| 1.00 | 93/73 | 69/69 | 84/53 | 60/68 | 46/67 | 50/67 | 79/59 |
| 1.20 | 87/66 | 67/61 | 83/53 | 62/71 | 46/66 | 56/64 | 67/50 |
| 1.50 | 71/50 | 58/57 | 72/51 | 64/73 | 47/70 | 62/61 | 52/40 |
| 1.88 | 57/39 | 49/55 | 62/52 | 66/75 | 30/71 | 62/62 | 41/34 |
| 2.25 | 48/32 | 43/55 | 55/49 | 68/77 | 31/70 | 56/65 | 34/33 |

Source: '7 country study'.

There are no strong financial incentives for both spouses to join the early retirement scheme at the same time in any of the countries, but it is better for the couple to be early retirees than unemployed in the Netherlands, Italy, Spain (except at one income level) and in Finland (except at two income levels).

## Benefit Duration

Early retirement lasts up to ordinary old-age retirement age in all the countries. The years which can be spend in early retirement is 5 years in Denmark and Finland, 4 years in Sweden, 5 years or more in the Netherlands, 12 years or more in Italy, 5 years in Spain and 10 years or more in Great Britain. In all the countries, except the Netherlands and Great Britain, the early retirement period can be preceded by a period in unemployment and the benefit period for unemployment insurance benefits is often prolonged for this age group. In e.g. Denmark it is possible to have unemployment benefits for 4 years, then a prolonged benefit for 5 years and finally early retirement benefits for 5 years, in total a combined benefit period of 14 years from the age of 51 to the pension age of 65 years. In Italy this period can be even longer.

## Main Results

Early retirement is permanent in the sense that only few return to work, the majority stays in the scheme until old-age pension takes over. Early retirement schemes are popular in Europe. The results of this section show that there are strong incentives to join these schemes especially for the low wage spouse in almost all the countries at almost all income levels. The incentives to join the scheme for the 'high wage' spouse are concentrated at the lower income levels in three countries, Denmark, the Netherlands and Italy.

A 'pure' comparison with unemployment is not possible (benefits related to children are included in one situation but not in the other) but it is often so, that the compensation is higher in early retirement than in unemployment, implying financial incentives to select the more permanent scheme if possible and then almost exclude the possibility of returning to work.

## SICKNESS BENEFIT AND DISABILITY PENSION SCHEMES

Access to these schemes is different from the former ones described. Sickness and permanent health problems are access conditions, which have to be met. The risk of becoming ill is different from the risk of becoming unemployed, but sickness, especially long term, might lead to unemployment. There are, however, separate schemes for sickness and disability and it is relevant to study the financial incentives of returning to work. The debate about using the sickness benefit scheme as a short term 'leave' scheme is well known, e.g. in Sweden. The financial consequences of moving from sickness to disability are also important. If the disability benefits are attractive compared with sickness benefits there might be an incentive at least to try to move to the disability pension scheme.

The formal access to the disability pension scheme is from relatively long term sickness in most countries and then only after all attempts for rehabilitation have been exhausted. These 'tests' may, however, be performed more or less stringent.

### Sickness Benefit Schemes

These schemes are similar in most of the countries and will only be described very shortly. Labour market agreements will often provide full compensation at least for some time, but here it is the insurance schemes, which will be described.

### Denmark

*Access conditions for benefits:* The employer is obliged to pay sickness benefits for the first two weeks if the employee has a certain work record, a minimum number of hours within 8 weeks with the same employer. The obligation to pay benefits is passed on to the municipality after the first two weeks.

*Entitlements:* The benefits are based on an hourly rate, which is multiplied by the weekly working hours in order to derive the weekly benefits. The compensation is 100 percent of the lost income up to a relatively low cap, where the benefit reaches its maximum. The maximum benefit period is 52 weeks.

### Finland

*Access conditions for benefits:* A certain work record, 3 months, is required to be eligible for benefits.

*Entitlements:* The benefits are calculated on the basis of 95 percent of the gross wage. Compensation is approx. 70 percent up to APW income level, somewhat lower for income above that level. There is no cap and then no maximum for the benefit. There is a waiting period of 9 weekdays before benefits can be received. The maximum benefit period is 50 weeks.

## Sweden

*Access conditions for benefits:* All who work in Sweden have immediate access to sickness benefits, there is no qualifying period.

*Entitlements:* The employer is obliged to pay 80 percent of the lost income for the first two weeks, with no cap. There after the insurance takes over. The compensation is still 80 percent, but now with a cap. The benefits can be supplemented by 10 percent of the lost income in this period. There is one waiting day, before benefits can be received. There is no time limitation for the benefit period but after 1 year and 3 months, a disability pension will be allocated if the criteria for this scheme are met.

## The Netherlands

*Access conditions for benefits:* Dutch workers have immediate access to sickness benefits. The employers are responsible for the scheme and they finance it entirely.

*Entitlements:* The compensation percentage is 70 of the lost income up to a cap. There is a waiting period of 2 days. Labour market agreements often wave the waiting period and have a compensation percentage of 100. This is the situation used for calculation of Dutch sickness benefits in this study. The benefit period is 1 year as a maximum.

## Italy

*Access conditions for benefits:* Italian workers have immediate access to sickness benefits. Employers are obliged to pay, but they are reimbursed by the insurance scheme.

*Entitlements:* The compensation is 50 percent of the lost income for the first 20 days of illness, thereafter 66 percent. The benefit period is ½ year as a maximum.

## Spain

*Access conditions for benefits:* Spanish workers have access to sickness benefits (temporary incapacity benefits) after a qualifying period of 180 days with payment of contributions. The employer is obliged to pay for the first 15 days.

*Entitlements:* Compensation is 60 percent of the income basis for payment of social contributions for the first 20 days of illness, 75 percent thereafter. There are 3 waiting days in the scheme. The maximum benefit period is 12 months with a possibility of prolongation.

## Great Britain

*Access conditions for benefits:* The Statutory Sick Pay (SSP) scheme is immediately available for workers who earn more than the Lower Earnings Limit.

*Entitlements:* The SSP benefit is a flat rate benefit. Labour market agreements often supplement the SSP benefit to provide up to full compensation for the lost wage, this is the situation used for calculation of sickness benefits for Great Britain in this study. The SSP scheme has 3 waiting days and the maximum benefit period is 28 weeks. When the rights for SSP expire short term Incapacity Benefits may be received, if the requirements for this scheme are met, a certain amount of minimum contributions paid or allocated over the last 2 years.

## Disability Pension Schemes

In some of the countries these schemes are related to the old-age pension scheme, in other countries they are more like sickness or unemployment benefit schemes.

## Denmark

*Main characteristics:* Residence based scheme with flat rate benefits. The scheme is related to the old-age pension scheme.

*Access conditions for benefits:* The working capability must be reduced by at least 50 percent for eligibility and the reduction must be permanent. The scheme is residence based, a 'full' pension requires that 4/5 of the 'theoretical time' between the $15^{th}$ year and the time of the pension case is spent in Denmark. There are several degrees of disability in the scheme, the lowest being 50 percent.

*Entitlements:* The benefits are flat rates. The basic one and the pension supplement are shared with those in the old-age pension scheme. Other supplements depend on the degree of disability. The benefit period lasts until the old-age pension starts to be received at the age of 65 for some, 67 for others.

*Recent developments:* A new scheme was introduced in 2003. The rate structure was simplified and the emphasis was changed from degrees of disability to remaining capabilities. The scheme is no longer related to the old-age pension scheme.

## Finland

*Main characteristics:* The disability pension is basically calculated as an old-age pension based on 'anticipated years'.

*Access conditions for benefits:* The working capability must be reduced by at least 60 percent for a full pension, by 40 percent for a partial one. Access is for persons who also have access to the old-age pension, both to the basic component, which is residence based, and to the occupational component, which depends on earlier work and income. For the residence based component Finland applies a 4/5 rule similar to that of the Danish scheme, but from the $16^{th}$ year.

*Entitlements:* The disability pension is calculated as if it was an old-age pension at the age when the disability occurs. The years from this age until ordinary retirement, at 65, are 'anticipated'. The accrual rate for the last 15 years is, however, smaller than for ordinary old-age pension. Partial pension is 50 percent of a full one. The benefit period lasts until ordinary retirement age.

*Recent developments:* The described structure has not been changed in recent years.

## Sweden

*Main characteristics:* The disability pension is calculated in a similar way as the old age pension, with a difference for the rates of the basic pension and its supplement.

*Access conditions for benefits:* The claimant must have lost his or her working capability partly or completely. Access conditions are the same as for old-age pensions, the basic pension is residence based, the occupational component depends on the former work record. For the residence based component Sweden applies a 4/5 rule similar to that of the Danish scheme but from the 16th year. There are, as already mentioned, several degrees of disability in the scheme.

*Entitlements:* The pension is calculated as an old-age pension, but the basic pension component is smaller than for old-age pension, the supplement for the basic pension is, however, largest for the disability pension. This supplement is tapered against the occupational component, which is calculated just as for old-age pensions, the years until old-age retirement, at 65, being 'anticipated'. There is, however, an option where the occupational pension is only based on very recent income, and this is often an advantage for the claimant, who receives according to the most advantageous option. The pension can be drawn in shares of ¼, ½, ¾ and 1/1 according to the degree of disability. The benefit period lasts until the ordinary retirement age of 65.

*Recent developments:* The described scheme was replaced by two new schemes from 2003, one for younger persons and another one for older persons. The new schemes are not related to the old-age pension scheme, which was also reformed from 2003 for pensioners having reached the age of 65 years. The new disability pension schemes are more like labour market related schemes, sickness and unemployment.

## The Netherlands

*Main Characteristics:* The Dutch disability pension scheme is related to the sickness benefit and the unemployment benefit scheme rather than to the old-age pension scheme.

*Access conditions for benefits:* It is a requirement that at least 15 percent of the working capability has been lost to be eligible for benefits. A full pension requires the loss of at least 80 percent of the working capability. All employees meeting these criteria have access to the scheme, there is no qualifying period.

*Entitlements:* The benefit level depends on the degree of disability, the former income and the age of the claimant. A full pension is 70 percent of the former income up to the same cap as for unemployment insurance benefits. This benefit can be received for less than a year for persons below 38 years of age, for a person who is 59, the benefits can be received until ordinary retirement age, which is 65 in the Netherlands. For those who's rights for the benefit expire, there is a lower follow-on benefit for the rest of the benefit period, which lasts until the ordinary retirement age.

*Recent developments:* Persons who receive disability pension in the Netherlands have been controlled more vigorously in recent years for meeting the criteria also after allocation of the pension.

## Italy

*Main characteristics:* The Italian disability pension scheme is closely related to the old-age pension schemes.

*Access conditions for benefits:* Loss of 2/3 of the working capability to be eligible for the disability allowance, complete or almost complete loss of working capability for disability pension, the case to be described here. Access to the 'old' income related pension system requires 18 years of contributions before 1996. If this condition is met the disability pension is calculated just as an old-age pension, 'anticipated years' are used for the period from the pension case to the age of 60, maximum 40 years. This might result in lower pensions than a corresponding old-age pension where the pension age is 65 for men. If the 18 years are not met, but there are some years with contributions before 1996 the disability pension is calculated as a mix of the 'old' income related scheme and the 'new' contribution based scheme. With no contribution record before 1996 and at least 5 years after the pension is calculated according to the new scheme.

*Entitlements:* Basis for the income related pension is an average of indexed earnings over the last 10 years. This average is multiplied by the length of the contribution record, maximum 40 years, and by an accrual rate of maximum 2 percent, implying a pension of max. 80 percent of the average earnings. The accrual rate decreases with increasing income but there is no cap. Low pensions can be topped-up to a guaranteed minimum. In the new scheme the accrual rate is constant and the average life income, indexed differently, is basis for calculation of the pension. The benefit period is until the age of 60.

*Recent developments:* Italy is in the process of moving from one pension system to a new one. The new one is already in use for disability pensioners with less than 18 contribution years before 1996.

## Spain

*Main characteristics:* Spain has different types of disability pension schemes all dependent on former labour market activities. The type 'absolute permanent incapacity for any work' has been applied here.

*Access conditions for benefits:* The mentioned criterion for incapacity has to be met. The claimant must have worked for at least ½ the time between the age of 16 and 26 or ¼ of the time between the age of 20 and the year of the pension case if this happens at an age higher than 26.

*Entitlements:* The compensation is 100 Percent of the contribution base with a guaranteed minimum. Pension income from this scheme is non-taxable implying net replacement rates above 100 percent in all cases.

*Recent developments:* The described structure has not been changed in recent years.


## Great Britain

*Main characteristics:* The British Incapacity Benefit scheme (IB) is a follow-on scheme to the Statutory Sick Pay scheme or an alternative to it. The long term Incapacity Benefit constitutes the British disability pension.

*Access conditions for benefits:* The claimant has to pass a personal non-capability test to be eligible for long term Incapacity Benefits. You either get full benefits or none at all. Eligibility for IB also requires a certain contribution record. For those who could not meet the requirements for IB there was a non-contributory scheme, the 'Severe Disablement Allowance' with lower benefits.

*Entitlements:* Long term Incapacity Benefits is a flat rate benefit which can be supplemented if there is a dependent spouse (low income) and children. The scheme can also be topped up with Income Support (social assistance) to a guaranteed minimum.

*Recent developments:* The Severe Disablement Allowance was abolished in 2001, and replaced with versions of the IB scheme, implying that many who do not meet the requirements for contributions for the ordinary IB scheme receive Income Support as an alternative.


## NET REPLACEMENT RATES AS SICK AND DISABLED

The results for a single person of becoming sick and later disabled are contained in table 16. It is assumed that the person is completely disabled, and then not able to work. This is also the assumption for all other cases in this section.

**Table 16. Net replacement rates for a single becoming sick and then disabled, 2000.**

| APW inc. | DK | FIN | S | NL | IT | ES | GB |
|---|---|---|---|---|---|---|---|
| 0.67 | 74/142 | 80/87 | 68/111 | 100/82 | 66/107 | 64/115 | 100/65 |
| 0.80 | 57/110 | 80/80 | 71/92 | 100/64 | 68/78 | 70/121 | 100/55 |
| 1.00 | 46/88 | 79/72 | 73/77 | 100/60 | 73/83 | 71/126 | 100/41 |
| 1.25 | 36/69 | 75/71 | 73/80 | 100/62 | 73/81 | 71/129 | 100/31 |
| 1.50 | 30/58 | 72/71 | 61/80 | 100/66 | 73/82 | 72/132 | 100/25 |

Source: '7-country study.

Two countries, the Netherlands and Great Britain, always have replacement rates of 100 percent in case of sickness, this is clearly more than the basic insurance schemes, private or public, would usually provide. The compensation for disability is higher than for sickness in Denmark, Sweden, Italy and Spain, sometimes by a very substantial margin. In Finland the two situations are quite similar as far as compensation is concerned. One country, that is Spain, has increasing replacement rates when income increases. The reason is that disability pensions are non-taxable income while wage income is taxed according to a progressive tax schedule.

Corresponding results for the single provider are recorded in table 17.

**Table 17. Net replacement rates for a sole provider (two children) becoming sick and then disabled, 2000.**

| APW inc. | DK | FIN | S | NL | IT | ES | GB |
|---|---|---|---|---|---|---|---|
| 0.67 | 89/111 | 102/94 | 90/93 | 100/84 | 78/86 | 45/110 | 100/65 |
| 0.80 | 82/101 | 93/92 | 89/92 | 100/76 | 78/83 | 64/109 | 100/62 |
| 1.00 | 72/89 | 95/90 | 88/91 | 100/71 | 84/87 | 68/112 | 100/57 |
| 1.25 | 63/78 | 89/84 | 83/87 | 100/62 | 79/87 | 73/118 | 100/51 |
| 1.50 | 55/69 | 82/79 | 72/84 | 100/64 | 77/84 | 73/122 | 100/45 |

Source: '7-country study'.

It is still so that the compensation in Denmark, Sweden, Italy and Spain is higher for disability than for sickness but the margin is much smaller than for the single in almost all cases. For Sweden the main explanation is the increased access to housing benefits. In the case for the single only the disabled could receive housing benefits, but for the single provider housing benefits are also available in the situation when she works and when she is sick. This lowers the replacement rates for the disabled sole provider, especially at lower income levels, and increases the replacement rate for the sick sole provider compared with the case for the single person. The gap has narrowed.

The next case is for the one-earner couple when the breadwinner becomes sick and then disabled.

**Table 18. Net replacement rates for one-earner couple (no children) when the breadwinner becomes sick and then disabled, 2000.**

| APW inc. | DK | FIN | S | NL | IT | ES | GB |
|---|---|---|---|---|---|---|---|
| 0.67 | 78/113 | 90/98 | 68/125 | 100/99 | 73/81 | 61/110 | 100/77 |
| 0.80 | 62/90 | 90/98 | 71/109 | 100/92 | 72/80 | 64/111 | 100/70 |
| 1.00 | 49/72 | 89/98 | 73/94 | 100/74 | 76/83 | 69/116 | 100/63 |
| 1.25 | 39/57 | 80/97 | 73/86 | 100/67 | 74/82 | 70/121 | 100/48 |
| 1.50 | 33/49 | 74/88 | 61/80 | 100/70 | 74/82 | 71/125 | 100/39 |

Source: '7-country study'.

The countries, where the compensation for disability is higher than for sickness, Denmark, Sweden, Italy and Spain are joined by Finland in this case. The replacement rate for the one-earner couple receiving disability pension in Denmark is lower than for the single, the reason being that the pension rate for a married person is lower than for a single. The higher replacement rate in case of sickness for the Danish one-earner couple is due to taxation, where unused tax allowances can be transferred between spouses, in case to the breadwinner. This is also the case for disability, but here the lower pension rate dominates the result.

The next case is the two-earner couple with children when the 'high wage' spouse is sick and then disabled, while the other spouse continues to work, cf. table 19.

**Table 19. Net replacement rates for two-earner couple (2 children) when the 'high wage' spouse becomes sick and then disabled, while the other works, 2000.**

| APW inc. | DK | FIN | S | NL | IT | ES | GB |
|---|---|---|---|---|---|---|---|
| 1.00 | 96/118 | 95/97 | 90/106 | 100/74 | 86/92 | 74/107 | 100/90 |
| 1.20 | 90/100 | 93/94 | 90/102 | 100/76 | 83/89 | 79/111 | 100/85 |
| 1.50 | 72/79 | 88/87 | 85/88 | 100/77 | 83/89 | 82/115 | 100/67 |
| 1.88 | 63/68 | 85/83 | 84/88 | 100/78 | 83/88 | 82/117 | 100/54 |
| 2.25 | 58/61 | 83/83 | 77/88 | 100/80 | 84/89 | 82/120 | 100/46 |

Source: '7-country study'.

The loss of 2/3 of the family gross wage is in most countries compensated in such a way that less than 10 percent of the disposable income is lost at the two lowest income levels, and in no country is more than 21 percent lost in case of sickness at these income levels. For disability the compensation is in many cases more than 100 percent and Spain, Italy and Sweden have very high replacement rates in case of disability all over the income span, just a little more than 10 percent is the maximum loss at the highest income level in Italy and Sweden. Denmark and Great Britain have replacement rates declining to almost half the value from the bottom to the top of the income range.

What happens when it is the 'low wage' spouse who becomes sick and thereafter disabled is contained in table 20.

**Table 20. Net replacement rates for two earner couple (two children) when the 'low wage' spouse becomes sick and then disabled while the other works, 2000.**

| APW inc. | DK | FIN | S | NL | IT | ES | GB |
|---|---|---|---|---|---|---|---|
| 1.00 | 96/127 | 96/91 | 94/119 | 100/86 | 93/97 | 87/103 | 100/91 |
| 1.20 | 91/115 | 94/86 | 93/106 | 100/86 | 90/93 | 90/108 | 100/90 |
| 1.50 | 83/101 | 92/76 | 91/95 | 100/86 | 91/94 | 88/111 | 100/78 |
| 1.88 | 79/93 | 92/68 | 92/94 | 100/88 | 90/93 | 88/114 | 100/75 |
| 2.25 | 76/88 | 92/61 | 92/94 | 100/88 | 91/94 | 90/117 | 100/74 |

Source: '7-country study'.

For most countries the loss of 1/3 of the family gross wage due to sickness of the 'low wage' spouse does not result in a loss of more than 10 percent of the disposable income except in Spain where it is maximum 12 percent and in Denmark, where it reaches 24 percent at the highest income level.

The replacement rates for disability are higher than for sickness in Denmark, Sweden, Italy and Spain and at the lower income levels more than 100 percent in 3 of the countries, Italy is the exception. Finland has surprisingly small replacement rates for disability at the two highest income levels, cf. comments for table 21.

It may be a relatively rare event that both spouses are sick and then become disabled at the same time, but it happens. Table 21 contains the results.

**Table 21. Net replacement rates for two-earner couple (two children), when both spouses become sick and then disabled, 2000.**

| APW inc. | DK | FIN | S | NL | IT | ES | GB |
|---|---|---|---|---|---|---|---|
| 1.00 | 93/138 | 91/91 | 84/114 | 100/60 | 79/84 | 61/110 | 100/76 |
| 1.20 | 87/118 | 89/86 | 83/101 | 100/62 | 77/83 | 67/114 | 100/73 |
| 1.50 | 69/94 | 83/76 | 79/84 | 100/64 | 77/83 | 70/118 | 100/58 |
| 1.88 | 56/76 | 77/68 | 77/82 | 100/66 | 74/82 | 70/120 | 100/46 |
| 2.25 | 47/63 | 75/61 | 69/82 | 100/68 | 74/83 | 72/123 | 100/37 |

Source: '7-country study'.

The replacement rates for sickness are relatively high at all income levels for all the countries except for Denmark at the two highest income levels. Disability pensions are even better in Denmark, Sweden, Italy and Spain. Spain have replacement rates above 100 percent for disability in all cases at all income levels, cf. the description of the disability scheme for Spain. The replacement rates for Finland are exactly the same in disability for the case where the 'low wage' spouse is disabled and the case where both spouses are disabled. This can hardly be correct, the figures are probably for the case where both spouses are disabled.

## Benefit Euration

The benefit period for sickness benefits is 1 year in almost all the countries included in this study, in Finland it is a little shorter, in Italy only ½ year. These benefit periods can in several cases be prolonged if rehabilitation is promising, otherwise sickness benefits will be replaced by disability pensions. These will last until old-age pension replaces the disability pension typically in the age span 60-65 years. There might be checks during the disability period to confirm that the claimant still meets the access criteria.

## Main Results

The schemes for sickness and disability are different from those for unemployment and early retirement because they are health related. Compensation for sickness often results in high replacement rates, which could be an invitation to short term leaves. Disability pensions are consistently higher (combined with housing benefits) than sickness benefits in Denmark, Sweden Italy and Spain and net replacement rates are often over 100 percent, in Spain always over 100 percent. This might imply a strong incentive to move to the disability pension scheme. This is, however, not a free choice but schemes with such incentives require stringent controls, also repeatedly, to confirm that the access criteria always are met.

# REFERENCES

*"Remain in or withdraw from the Labour Market?":* A comparative study on incentives (referred to as: '7-country study'). Werkdocumenten no 286, the Dutch Ministry of Social Affairs and Employment, SZW. Also published by the European Commission in European Economy, Economic Papers Number 193, October 2003.

*"MISSOC 2003"*: Mutual Information System on Social Protection. Directorate-General for Employment and Social Affairs. European Communities, 2004.


## Related Literature

*"Taxing Wages":* Annual publication from the OECD

*"Benefit Systems and Work Incentives":* Annual publication from the OECD.

*"Unemployment Insurance in the Netherlands, Denmark and Sweden"*: DGSZ/FEBO Research Memorandum 93/1, the Dutch Ministry of Social Affairs and Employment, SZW.

*"Unemployment Benefits and Social Assistance in Seven European Countries"*: Werkdocumenten no. 10, the Dutch Ministry of Social Affairs and Employment, SZW. Also published in Chinese.

"Income Benefits for early exit from the Labour Market in Eight European Countries": Werkdocumenten no. 61, the Dutch Ministry of Social Affairs and Employment. Also published by the European Commission in European Economy no. 3 1998.

*"Transition from Unemployment to Social Assistance in Seven European OECD countries":* Empirical Economics, Volume 23 1998, Issue 1-2.

In: Economics of Unemployment
Editor: Mary I. Marshalle, pp. 187-216
ISBN: 1-60021-138-0

*Chapter 9*

# THE EFFECTS OF THE MINIMUM WAGE ON THE BRAZILIAN LABOR MARKET

## *Francisco Galrão Carneiro*
The World Bank
1818 H Street, N.W.
Washington, DC 20433
United States

## ABSTRACT

The debate about the impact of the introduction of a minimum wage into the economy, or even of changes in the level of the minimum wage on employment, wages, and poverty is the subject of a separate chapter in the literature on labor markets. In the case of Brazil, this debate dates back to the 1970s, when a controversy arose as to whether or not changes in the minimum wage could affect all wages in the economy [e.g., Souza and Baltar (1979)]. Now this debate has been revived, in terms not only of the possible impact of the minimum wage on other wages, but also of its effects on the levels of employment, informal labor, and poverty in this country. The debate becomes more relevant when discussions are held regarding possible future trends in the minimum wage policy in Brazil as a result of its impact on government accounts, and the feasibility of adopting a system that combines regional minimum wages with a national wage floor.

In this chapter, we review the literature on the impact of the minimum wage on the Brazilian labor market. First, we will examine the key results pertaining to the employment-effect of the minimum wage in Brazil, and contrast the results that were based on data at the family level and at the individual level. Similarly, we will analyze the main results with respect to the impact on other wages and on poverty levels. Since in Brazil there is a direct connection between the minimum wage and the benefits paid by the social security system, we will also present an analysis of the impact of changes in the minimum wage on the government accounts. Lastly, we undertake a critical analysis of some options for the minimum wage policy in Brazil.

As regards the impact of the minimum wage on the levels of formal and informal employment, all the studies reviewed point to negative effects on formal employment. On the other hand, some results suggest that increases in the minimum wage generate increments in informal employment, a situation compatible with the existence of dual labor markets in which the impact of the minimum wage on the unemployment rate is attenuated by the absorption of workers in the informal areas of the economy.

Considering the impact on the other wages in the economy, the hypothesis usually tested by the studies we reviewed was about the validity of the so-called light house effect. The debate on this point was initiated in Brazil in the 1970s, with Baltar and Souza (1979) presenting empirical evidence that suggested that changes in the minimum wage impact all the other wages in an economy in the same proportion. Those results were the opposite of those found by Macedo and Garcia (1978), who found elasticities lower than unity for a different period of time than that analyzed by Souza and Baltar (1979). More recent evidence based on time-series analyses prove that the minimum wage has some effect on the other wages, but there is no consensus in the literature on the existence of a unitary elasticity of the other wages in relation to the minimum wage.

In general, what has become clear is that there are certain costs associated with a poverty-reduction strategy that relies heavily on a minimum wage policy. Those costs may manifest themselves most directly in the short run via the impact of an increase in minimum wage on the government accounts and a rise in informality and/or unemployment. Furthermore, we have observed from the analysis of the literature on the effects of the minimum wage in Brazil that there are winners and losers, which leads to ambiguous results as to the redistributive effects of the minimum wage policy. Therefore, more specific analyses must be done in order to determine whether the expenditure associated with a minimum wage policy can effectively help, over the long term, to lift families out of poverty.

# I. INTRODUCTION

The debate about the impact of the introduction of a minimum wage into the economy, or even of changes in the level of the minimum wage on employment, wages, and poverty is the subject of a separate chapter in the literature on labor markets. In the case of Brazil, this debate dates back to the 1970s, when a controversy arose as to whether or not changes in the minimum wage could affect all wages in the economy [e.g., Souza and Baltar (1979)]. Now this debate has been revived, in terms not only of the possible impact of the minimum wage on other wages, but also of its effects on the levels of employment, informal labor, and poverty in this country. The debate becomes more relevant when discussions are held regarding possible future trends in the minimum wage policy in Brazil as a result of its impact on government accounts, and the feasibility of adopting a system that combines regional minimum wages with a national wage floor.

The theoretical debate suggests that the effects of the minimum wage on the labor market depend on the structure of that market. In competitive markets with a homogenous labor force, the minimum wage tends to create unemployment if it is set above the equilibrium wage as determined by the market. Under imperfect competition, in the presence of monopsonies, the introduction of a minimum wage may help raise workers' wages without having deleterious effects on employment. In segmented labor markets, the minimum wage tends to generate informality and a certain amount of unemployment.

In general, there are two clearly dichotomic views as to the normative impact of a minimum wage policy for developing countries. On the one hand, there are those who argue that the minimum wage fosters a better distribution of resources in the economy, so as to improve the population's general welfare by helping reduce poverty, increase productivity, and stimulate economic growth. On the other hand, we hear holders of the distortionist view argue that the minimum wage produces an inefficient allocation of labor and encourages rent-seeking behaviors, thus negatively affecting investments and contributing to a reduction in the rate of economic growth [Freeman (1996)].

In this chapter, we review the literature on the impact of the minimum wage on the Brazilian labor market. First, we will examine the key results pertaining to the employment-effect of the minimum wage in Brazil, and contrast the results that were based on data at the family level and at the individual level. Similarly, we will analyze the main results with respect to the impact on other wages and on poverty levels. Since in Brazil there is a direct connection between the minimum wage and the benefits paid by the social security system, we will also present an analysis of the impact of changes in the minimum wage on the government accounts. Lastly, we undertake a critical analysis of some options for the minimum wage policy in Brazil. The next Chapter, by Wendy Cunningham assesses the international experience.

The chapter is structured in the following manner: after this Introduction, we will discuss briefly the history of the minimum wage policy in Brazil (Section 2), the current minimum wage policy (Section 3), and the profile of the workers who earn a minimum wage (Section 4). Then, in Section 5, we present the review of the results relative to the impact of the minimum wage on employment and wages. The results relative to the effects on poverty are reviewed in Section 6. Section 7 analyzes the effect on the government accounts, in particular the impact of the minimum wage on payroll at the three levels of government (federal, state, and local). Section 8 discusses policy alternatives for the future of the minimum wage in Brazil. Lastly, Section 9 summarizes the results and draws some conclusions.

## II. HISTORICAL BACKGROUND OF THE MINIMUM WAGE

Until the 1930s, there was no specific legislation on labor relations in Brazil. Unions were not recognized by the Government, and wage negotiations depended on each social group's bargaining power. The main demands in that era were higher wages and a reduction in the number of hours worked. It was not until 1930 that the Brazilian Government began to institutionalize these demands. The Ministry of Labor, Industry and Commerce was established in 1931, and both employee and employer organizations were recognized at that time.

The first official minimum wage began to take shape in 1936, when Law 185 (of January 14, 1936) was passed. Article 1 of that law provided that "every worker shall have the right, in payment for the service rendered, to a minimum wage capable of meeting, in a given region of the country and in a given time period, his normal needs for food, housing, clothing, and transportation." Initially, the legislation ordered that the value of the minimum wage, to be set by a Wage Commission, should be sufficient to provide remuneration to an adult worker for a normal working day. Not until 1946 was the law changed to recognize that the minimum wage should be high enough to satisfy the needs of both the worker and his family.

Although the law that established the lowest wage to be paid to an active worker was enacted in 1936, the first such wage was not established until 1940, when it was initially set at Cr$ 0.24 (in nominal terms), to remain in effect for three years (until 1943). In 1943, a nominal increase of 25 percent occurred in July, followed by another 26 percent in December. After that, the minimum wage remained frozen until 1952. As a result, there was a substantial decline in its value. In 1962, an attempt was made to reconcile its value with the objectives set forth in the

Constitution, when President Goulart created the "family wage," a kind of bonus equivalent to 5 percent of the minimum wage for every child age 14 or under.

A period of successive changes in wage policy legislation began in 1979. Between 1979 and 1985, the Government modified wage policy seven times, sparking a series of debates about the impact of the wage increases on the inflation rate. The changes adopted altered the percentage of inflation that could be passed along to wages, and the frequency of the adjustments (which were now occurring every six months). The formula used to calculate the wage increases that could be applied to all the policies in effect during the 1979-85 period was:

$$W_{i(t)} = \{1 + (A_i + B_i / \theta_i)R_s\}\theta_i S_{(0)} \tag{1}$$

where:

$\theta_i = W_{i(0)}/S_{(0)}$
$W_{i(t)}$ = nominal wage of the i[th] wage bracket at the beginning of the six-month period;
$R_s$ = change in prices during the six-month period, measured by the INPC [Consumer Price Index];
$S_{(0)}$ = the highest minimum wage in effect during the month of the adjustment;
$A_i$ and $B_i$ = correction coefficient per wage bracket, furnished by the wage policy.

As we can see, this formula shows that the minimum wage played a key role in the determination of the size of the wage readjustments. It should also be noted that any real increase in the minimum wage would have repercussions for the entire structure of wages that were governed by the wage policy, since it would change the composition of the wage brackets and hence the magnitude of inflation that each wage would receive in the form of an adjustment.

With respect to the minimum wage in particular, the most significant change occurred in 1984, when its value was standardized nationwide. The minimum wage for all regions was raised to the level in effect in southern and southeastern Brazil. Prior to that change, there was a wide variety of regional minimum wages. When the minimum wage was originally created, there were 14 different regional minimum wages, but by 1963, there were 39 of these. There were at least two in effect immediately prior to the unification.

## III. CURRENT MINIMUM WAGE POLICY

The current minimum wage policy was defined by the new Constitution of 1988, which stipulated that the minimum wage should be the same nationwide and sufficient to meet the basic needs of a worker, as well as those of his family, in terms of housing, education, health, recreation, clothing, hygiene, transportation, and social security. The wage is to be adjusted periodically to preserve its purchasing power, and there is an explicit prohibition against its use as an indexing tool.

Several aspects related to the treatment of the minimum wage in the new Constitution are worth mentioning:

- the new Constitution increased the list of needs to be met by the minimum wage, by adding health, recreation, and social security to the existing needs;
- the nationwide standardization of the minimum wage was introduced into the body of the Constitution;
- periodic adjustments of its value were made mandatory, in order to preserve its purchasing power;
- the 1988 Constitution ratified the prohibition against using the minimum wage as an indexing tool in the economy;
- the normal work week was cut from 48 to 44 hours, which meant an increase of about 10 percent in the hourly value of the minimum wage.

The most important change introduced by the 1988 Constitution was the determination that social security benefits could not be lower than the equivalent to one minimum wage. As Foguel, Ramos, and Carneiro (2000) point out, this rule ultimately proved to be the main stumbling block for policies that sought to raise the real value of the minimum wage, since the new benefits had a heavy and significant impact on the government accounts.

## IV. PROFILE OF WORKERS WHO EARN MINIMUM WAGE

The profile of the workers who earn the minimum wage was examined in Foguel, Ramos, and Carneiro (2001) using data from the 1998 National Household Sample Survey (PNAD). Knowledge of the characteristics of the labor force that is directly affected by the minimum wage is important in determining the scope and effectiveness of a minimum wage policy. The data presented in Table 7.1 cover the economically-active population (EAP), equivalent to 40.2 million workers. Of this total, about 22.5 million workers, 55 percent of the total EAP, are in the formal sector. The number of workers receiving up to one minimum wage is 2.4 million, which is equivalent to 6 percent of the EAP.

The characteristics of the workers who earn the minimum wage are summarized in Table 7.2. About 42 percent of such workers are female, 52 percent are 10-29 years of age, and 40.6 percent are heads of households. Comparing those figures with the composition of the total EAP, we see that those who earn only one minimum wage have less education than the average and are young, female, and predominantely non-white. Also with respect to the total EAP, workers between the ages of 30 and 49 and heads of households are under-represented.

Table 7.2 enables us to study the profile of minimum wage earners in terms of the kind of jobs they hold. In regional terms, there is a clear distinction between the state of São Paulo and the Northeast. For example, while São Paulo is home to about 30 percent of the total EAP and the formal sector, only 8.2 percent of those who earn a minimum wage are found in that state. In the Northeast, on the other hand, the local work force does not represent even 20 percent of the EAP, but about 40 percent of the workers who earn a minimum wage are found in this region.

Similarly, the São Paulo labor market is much more formalized than the labor market in the Northeast, which may indicate that the imposition of an official minimum wage is becoming less restrictive in more dynamic labor markets. Thus the adoption of a national minimum wage may have different effects in each region, to the extent that the nature and composition of their labor markets are not homogenous. In principle, therefore, one could argue that the adoption of regional minimum wages could be part of a more effective strategy, since it may potentially permit a better "marriage" between the level of the minimum wage and the characteristics of each labor market.

### Table 7.1. Profile of Workers who Earn Minimum Wage in Brazil Urban Sector– 1998 (%)

|  | EAP | Formal Sector | Workers who Earn MW |
|---|---|---|---|
| **Sex** | | | |
| Male | 66.5 | 61.0 | 58.3 |
| Female | 33.5 | 39.0 | 41.7 |
| **Age** | | | |
| 10-19 | 9.6 | 6.7 | 18.1 |
| 20-29 | 28.8 | 32.3 | 34.9 |
| 30-39 | 27.7 | 30.3 | 21.4 |
| 40-49 | 20.5 | 20.9 | 15.1 |
| 50-64 | 11.7 | 9.1 | 9.5 |
| 65+ | 1.8 | 0.7 | 1.0 |
| **Education** | | | |
| Illiterate | 7.4 | 4.5 | 12.8 |
| Elementary | 25.9 | 19.4 | 31.5 |
| Middle School | 27.4 | 25.6 | 32.2 |
| High School | 27.3 | 33.8 | 22.3 |
| University | 12.0 | 16.7 | 1.2 |
| **Position in the Family** | | | |
| Head | 53.9 | 51.9 | 40.6 |
| Non-Head | 46.1 | 48.1 | 59.4 |
| **Race** | | | |
| White | 58.8 | 62.4 | 41.1 |
| Non-White | 41.2 | 37.6 | 58.9 |
| **No. of Workers (Millions)** | **40.2** | **22.5** | **2.4** |

Source: Foguel, Ramos, and Carneiro (2001), p. 7.

## V. IMPACT ON THE LABOR MARKET

Government intervention in the labor market via minimum wage policy has been the subject of intense debate in many countries [OECD (1998)]. Many recent studies have been devoted to investigating the impact of the minimum wage on the labor market in different countries. For the United Kingdom, for example, Bell and Wright (1996) analyzed the impact of the so-called Wage Boards and Councils and found that the minimum wage had not raised the wages of workers in the formal sector above the level of the wages paid in the informal sector. Thus their work suggested that there existed only minor effects on the levels of wages and employment in the economy. Machin and Manning (1994) concluded that the decline in the level of the minimum wage relative to the average wage in the economy contributed significantly to broadening wage dispersion during the 1980s in the United Kingdom. Furthermore, Machin and Manning (1994) emphasized the fact that the abolition of the Wage Boards and Councils in the United Kingdom resulted in a reduction in new jobs and did not generate any gains in terms of wages (p. 672).

**Table 7.2. Profile of Workers who Earn Minimum Wage Characteristics of Jobs Held - 1998 – (%)**

|  | EAP | Formal Sector | Workers Who Earn MW |
|---|---|---|---|
| **Region** | | | |
| South | 16.2 | 17.4 | 11.7 |
| São Paulo | 27.6 | 30.3 | 8.2 |
| Southeast | 22.3 | 23.7 | 27.1 |
| Northeast | 20.8 | 17.1 | 38.1 |
| Other | 13.1 | 11.6 | 14.8 |
| **Area** | | | |
| Metropolitan | 37.7 | 41.9 | 25.2 |
| Non-Metropolitan | 62.3 | 58.1 | 74.8 |
| **Business Sector** | | | |
| Manufacturing | 15.6 | 20.2 | 19.1 |
| Construction | 9.5 | 4.4 | 6.7 |
| Commerce | 17.0 | 13.8 | 17.6 |
| Services | 27.6 | 22.5 | 24.2 |
| Other | 30.3 | 39.1 | 32.4 |
| **No. of Workers (Million)** | **40.2** | **22.5** | **2.4** |

Source: Foguel, Ramos, and Carneiro (2001), p. 8.

Studies also exist that associate increases in the minimum wage with the number of small business bankruptcies. Waltman *et al.* (1998) and Fischer (1997), for example, examined whether increases in the minimum wage were responsible for the departure of small companies from the market.[1] The conclusion reached in these studies was that in the case of the United States, increases in the minimum wage did not cause small businesses to go bankrupt at a higher rate than observed in periods when the minimum wage was not rising.

In the case of developing countries, there are conflicting results regarding the impact of the minimum wage on the labor market. Bell (1997), for example, found significant negative effects on employment in the case of Colombia, and insignificant effects on the labor market in Mexico. Maloney (2000) presents a summary of the literature on minimum wage in Latin America that indicates that while the minimum wage has a positive effect on other wages in Latin American economies, the effect on employment and poverty is unclear. In other words, while it has been

---

[1] The argument underlying this point is that since small companies presumably employ their resources at the point of maximum efficiency, increases in labor costs must somehow be absorbed. Since demand may be inelastic for certain industries and the replacement of labor with capital may require expensive investments, some firms might indeed be forced out of the market.

observed that increases in the minimum wage tend to contribute to a reduction in poverty, negative effects on employment have also been noted. Furthermore, Maloney (2000) states that the minimum wage is also an important determinant of employment and wages in the informal sector in most Latin American economies.

In the case of Brazil, Carneiro and Faria (1997) and Carneiro and Henley (1998) concluded that the minimum wage was an important determinant of the average level of other wages during the 1980s, but that this importance gradually declined during the 1990s. Lemos (1997) showed that the minimum wage has a positive effect on other wages in the economy for a period of five quarters, after an initial shock. Emphasizing the bicausality, the author also shows that the average wage positively affects the minimum wage for a period of three trimesters after the shock. Lemos (2002) estimates that increases in the minimum wage tend to compress the distribution of wages and have moderately adverse effects on the level of employment. Finally, Carneiro (2004) finds a robust and negative impact of changes in the minimum wage in the employment levels of formal sector workers in the long run, with the reverse taking place in the case of informal employment.

The classic textbook description indicates that under perfect competition, setting a minimum wage above the equilibrium level of the market will reduce the demand for labor and cause unemployment. More commonly, however, the negative effects of the minimum wage will depend on a series of factors, among which are the level at which it is fixed (its absolute value relative to worker productivity), the elasticity of the demand for labor (the more elastic the demand, the greater the negative effect), the elasticity of the supply of labor (the more inelastic, the greater the negative effect), and the responses in terms of investments by firms and individuals (the smaller the investment, the greater the negative effect). The greater the elasticity of the substitution between skilled and less-skilled workers, the greater the negative effect tends to be for the less-skilled. The size and indication of the effect of the minimum wage on employment may therefore differ among firms, individuals, and geographical areas, and depending on its value.

However, some alternative models suggest that the introduction of a minimum wage in an economy will not significantly affect the level of employment, and may even have a slightly positive impact on the demand for labor [Card and Krueger (1995)]. The simplest model that reached this conclusion is the one that examined the labor market under the assumption of a monopsonistic employer. In this model, workers have little or no bargaining power since they cannot easily find jobs with other employers. This enables an employer to set the wage level below the marginal product of the labor. In general, imposing a minimum wage above the level that would be determined by an employer in a monopsonistic market may, therefore, raise the level of employment.

Other models that predict that the minimum wage will have a positive effect on the level of employment are the models associated with the theory of the efficiency wage, the theory of human capital, and the theoretical framework of job search. In efficiency wage models, it is assumed that employers will set the wages of their employees above the market equilibrium level in order to increase their productivity, reduce production softness, and cut the costs associated with labor turnover. In that context, the minimum wage can result in an increase in employment. The evidence presented by Rebitzer and Taylor (1995), however, shows that in a context of efficiency wages, the positive effect of the minimum wage on employment may dissipate over the long term, depending on the position of the firms along their profit curves and on subsequent changes in the price of the products and the number of firms operating in the market.

Models based on the theory of endogenous growth and elements of the theory of human capital also generate forecasts that the minimum wage will have a positive effect on employment. The principal hypothesis here is that the minimum wage creates incentives for workers whose productivity is low to invest in more training or education in order to boost their productivity and, therefore, their paychecks. The resulting increment in human capital will have a positive impact on economic growth and, consequently, on employment. In this respect, Cahuc and Michel (1996) show that a reduction in the minimum wage may bring about a reduction in economic growth. Cubit and Hargreaves-Heap (1996) argue that the net loss of employment expected with the introduction of the minimum wage may be zero for a given interval of minimum wage values, since its introduction will raise the investment in physical capital by firms and in human capital by the workers. Similarly, Acemoglu and Pischke (1998) also argue that the minimum wage may increase the amount of training that firms offer their less-skilled workers.

## Estimates of the Employment-Effect of the Minimum Wage

There is little empirical evidence available in literature regarding the impact of changes in the value of the minimum wage on the level of employment in the case of Brazil. Some contributions on this point are found in Foguel (1997, 1998), Corseuil and Morgado (2000), Foguel, Ramos, and Carneiro (2000, 2001), Lemos (2002), Carneiro (2000), Carneiro and Corseuil (2001), and Carneiro (2004).

Foguel (1998) used data from the Brazilian Institute of Geography and Statistics (IBGE) Monthly Employment Survey (PME) to conduct a natural experiment considering the period of convergence of minimum wage values in Brazil and its impact on the labor market. The idea of a natural experiment is borrowed from such fields as the biological, physical, chemical, and medical sciences and consists of testing the effectiveness of a certain medication in fighting a specific disease. Randomly selected patients are therefore divided, also randomly, into two groups: (a) the treatment group, which is given the medicine; and (b) the control group, which does not get the medicine. Since both groups are selected randomly, there is no reason to believe that, were they not to be given the medicine, the average behavior of the people in the treatment group would be different from the average behavior of the control group. The effects of the medicine can therefore be evaluated when the evolution of the state of health of the two groups is compared. The control group ends up serving as a counterfactual for the treatment group, which makes it possible to assess the nature and extent of the effect of the medication.[2]

Therefore, in order to apply the natural experiment methodology for purposes of analysis of the impact of the unification of the minimum wage on the labor market, it was necessary to select one date associated with the period of convergence of the values of the minimum wage and a second date corresponding to the post-convergence period. Since the regional values of the minimum wage were unified in May 1984, Foguel (1998) selected a pre-convergence period prior to this date, and a post-convergence period after 1984. The pre-convergence period

---

[2] See Foguel (1988) for further details concerning this explanation.

corresponded to the 24 months preceding the unification of the minimum (May 1982 to April 1984). The post-convergence period covered the 24 months between May 1985 and April 1987. Note that the period between May 1984 and April 1985 was excluded from the study in order allow for an interval of market adjustment to the convergence of the minimum before evaluating the effect of the unified minimum wage.

The author also selected two groups of metropolitan regions for which the values of the minimum wage were convergent during the pre-convergence period: (a) Recife and Salvador, and (b) Belo Horizonte, Rio de Janeiro, São Paulo, and Porto Alegre. The results of the exercise in comparison between the pre- and post-convergence periods permitted analysis of the impact of the unification of the minimum wage for a set of labor market indicators that included the activity rate and the percentage of employed and unemployed, the unemployment rate, the degree of informality, and the sectoral structure of employment. Since the author worked with the level of those indicators and the logarithm of the minimum wage, the estimates obtained should be interpreted as semi-elasticities of the minimum wage with respect to those indicators.

The results estimated by Foguel (1998) indicate that convergence of the regional values of the minimum wage led to a decline in the percentage of employed. It also led to increases in the proportion of both the unemployed and the inactive, a higher rate of open unemployment, an increase in the presence of workers whose jobs are registered on their employment record cards among the total employed, and a decline in the percentage of employed persons in industry and commerce, with a corresponding increase in their participation in the services sector and other activities. With regard to the unemployment rate in particular, Foguel (1998) suggests that an increase of about 10 percent in the minimum wage could raise the open unemployment rate by 0.5 percentage points.

The analysis by Foguel (1998) made an important methodological contribution to the discussion of the question of the impact of the minimum wage on the Brazilian labor market. The idea of treating the process of unification of minimum wage values as a natural experiment was a creative alternative adopted to attempt to explain how, in fact, the minimum wage impacts key labor market indicators. The responses generated, however, were limited to a specific period when the concern for achieving economic stabilization and cutting the inflation rate was still quite intense. We can speculate whether the results found might not have been contaminated by the high inflation rates observed in the Brazilian economy during the period considered. We would therefore need to evaluate the extent to which those results hold up in a different economic environment, even if later studies use different methodologies.

Lemos (2002) also used the Monthly Employment Survey to evaluate the impact of the minimum wage on levels of employment in Brazil. Using monthly data for the period 1982-2000, the author estimated wage equations by following the traditional time-series analysis methodology. Four different specifications were tested: group against group; first differences of the ordinary least squares (OLS); the twelfth differences; and the first difference of the twelfth difference (to obtain the rate of variation of the annual variation in the value of the minimum wage).

In all the specifications, lags of the dependent variable were introduced into the model, since changes in the minimum wage may not have immediate contemporaneous effects on employment, but rather future effects [Brown (1982); Neumark and Washer (1992)]. Other explanatory variables included were lags of the inflation rate, dummy variables for different periods, as well as the percentages of workers who are young, female, students, retired persons, civil servants, people whose jobs are not registered on their employment record card, and those employed in the construction sector and in manufacturing.

According to the estimated coefficients, the elasticities of employment with respect to changes in the minimum wage ranged between −0.006 and 0.005, but in many cases were not statistically different from zero. The author also used alternative methodologies to analyze in greater depth the impact of changes in the minimum wage on employment. One of these alternatives was to use instrumental variables to verify whether the results obtained were being affected by problems of endogenicity of the explanatory variables. The instrumental variables were values that lagged by 12 months, a proxy for the election cycle, and a proxy variable for capacity for political intervention. On this point, the author attempts to capture the importance of the election cycle in the process of determination of employment, together with the impact of changes in the minimum wage, by introducing into the model a variable that incorporates the percentage of politicians considered as being "leftist," the political cycle, and the minimum wage multiplicatively. The justification for this is that the incentives for politicians on the left to seek increases in the minimum wage are greater not only during election years, but also when the value of the minimum wage is low.

The estimation procedure was the least squares method, in three stages. The elasticities obtained this time ranged from −0.020 to 0.035. The results obtained earlier suggested that a 10 percent increase in the minimum wage would tend to curb employment by about 0.06 percent, while the estimates obtained by the instrumental variables method could generate a decline in employment of about 0.20 percent. Once again, we must be careful in reading these results, which may be spurious owing to the possible existence of unit roots in the time series used for the study.

Furthermore, the introduction of variables such as the percentage of "leftist" politicians, the election cycle, and the capacity for political intervention really needs additional detail and justification; absence of this casts doubt as to their actual explanatory capacity. In general, however, Lemos (2002) presents a creative way of analyzing the impact of the minimum wage on the labor market and offers additional evidence that this impact can be adverse in aggregate terms.

Other estimates of the employment-effect of the minimum wage that took into consideration the problem arising from the possibility that the variables in the estimated model are not stationary were presented by Carneiro (2000), Foguel, Ramos, and Carneiro (2000), Foguel, Ramos, and Carneiro (2001), Carneiro and Corseuil (2001), and Carneiro (2004). In general, the empirical modeling strategy present in these articles adopts the more general idea with respect to the existence of a relationship of long-term equilibrium between the level of employment, the product, and the minimum wage.

The long-term elasticities of employment with regard to changes in the minimum wage found in these studies are situated in the interval between −0.001 and −0.020 for workers in the formal sector, and between 0.0004 and 0.003 for workers in the informal sector. Although these elasticities are low in absolute values, they suggest important long-term trends in the adjustment process of employment for both sectors of the labor market. In the formal sector, changes in the minimum wage tend to affect employment negatively, while in the informal sector such changes tend to affect employment positively. One explanation for this might be that the informal sector ends up serving as a temporary refuge for workers who lose their jobs in the formal sector.

Another interesting result of these studies is related to the way in which the level of employment in both sectors behaves throughout the economic cycle. In the formal sector, employment tends to react pro-cyclically to changes in economic activity, while employment in the informal sector reacts anti-cyclically to fluctuations in the product. The perception underlying this process is simple, and suggests that economic growth tends to create more jobs, to stimulate the emergence of formal occupations and, therefore, to discourage informality.

With regard to short-term dynamics, the more general pattern encountered for the long term remains the same. Changes in the minimum wage tend to have a negative effect on formal employment and a positive effect on informal employment. Similarly, note the pro-cyclical behavior of formal employment in the short term, and observe that the opposite occurs in the informal sector. Meanwhile, the adjustment speed of the models stood at 5 percent to 9 percent per month, suggesting that deviations from the long-term trajectory of equilibrium among employment, product, and minimum wage are fully corrected within a period of approximately one year. This seems to be consistent with a slow adjustment by employment.

One limitation of these studies is that, although they allow us to separate the long-term and short-term effects of the minimum wage on the level of employment, they cannot tell us precisely who loses and who wins when the minimum wage changes. The analysis is carried out with aggregate data and furnishes only an indication of the net effect on the labor market caused by a change in the value of the minimum wage. In general, time-series studies assume that the impact of the minimum wage on the labor market tend to be concentrated among young, inexperienced workers whose income is close to the minimum. The only fact that one can glean from those studies, however, is that the minimum wage does tend to generate a certain amount of unemployment.

Hoping to fill this gap and trying to answer the question as to which workers end up losing their jobs when the minimum wage is raised, Corseuil and Morgado (2001) and Carneiro and Corseuil (2001) used an alternative methodology based on the idea of natural experiments and the differences-in-differences method [Angrist and Krueger (1999)]. The treatment group consisted of workers whose employment was affected by the minimum wage, and the control group was comprised of workers whose employment was not affected by the minimum wage, but by other factors that had also affected the employment of the first group. The difference in the change in employment of the treatment group in relation to the change in employment of the control group can be seen as an estimate of the change in employment of the treatment group that would occur had this group been affected solely by a change in the minimum wage.

In order to identify the treatment and control groups, the authors used as a tool the results of an analysis of the impact of changes in the minimum wage on wage distribution that will be discussed later in this chapter. Since changes in the minimum wage tend to have a more obvious effect on the incomes closest to the minimum wage, i.e., the wages that are on the left tail of the wage distribution, the treatment group chosen was composed of workers who were earning the equivalent to one minimum wage between April and May. The control group chosen consisted of workers who had incomes equivalent to a value that lay between one minimum wage at the April level and twice the minimum wage at the May level, on the assumption that the characteristics of those workers are the same as those in the treatment group, but that their jobs were affected primarily by factors other than the change in minimum wage.

After the treatment and control groups were defined, implementation of the differences-in-differences method requires the use of the following equation:

$$Y = (\Delta E^t/E^t) - (\Delta E^c/E^c) \tag{2}$$

where $E^t$ and $E^c$ denote the levels of employment of the treatment and control groups, respectively, and $\Delta$ denotes the change in each variable before (April) and after (May) the increase in minimum wage.

The results obtained using this methodology showed that increases in the minimum wage cause reductions in the level of employment. The elasticities reported in Carneiro and Corseuil (2001) indicate that a 10 percent increase in the minimum wage contributed to a 3 percent decline in employment among the treatment group in 1995 and a drop of about 13 percent in 1999. In the case of the informal sector, the elasticities indicate that a 10 percent increase in the minimum wage were responsible for a 2.2 percent growth in informal employment in 1995, and about 15 percent in 1999.

The authors offer no explanation for the difference in the magnitude of the impact of changes in the minimum wage between 1995 and 1999, but we can speculate that the greater sensitivity observed in 1999 is associated with an economic context of lower inflation rates and greater competitiveness in the market for products. Therefore, the effects of any variations in cost would be much more marked in 1999 than in 1995. When relative prices are aligned, it is much more difficult to pass along cost increases than it is in situations of high inflation, where the price system loses much of its signaling ability.

Fajnzylber (2001), assessing the effect of the minimum on the wage distribution, also found that the minimum wage has a negative impact on employment in the formal sector. His estimates were lower for the formal sector (elasticity of –0.10) than for the informal sector (elasticities between –0.25 and –0.35). According to the author, his results are consistent with a movement of informal workers into the formal sector after a rise in the minimum wage, or even their departure from the labor market because of (i) low prospects for employment or (ii) increases in family income brought about by rises in income experienced by other members of the family.

Note, therefore, that the results obtained using different methodologies, for different periods and contexts, appear to converge toward a more traditional view of the impact of the minimum wage on the labor market. Consequently, after the minimum wage is raised, one can expect some reduction in aggregate employment, with a greater impact on workers who earn incomes at levels close to the minimum wage, as well as growth in informal occupations. While the aggregate results suggest that the net effect is small, the disaggregated analysis seems to suggest that the people most affected by job loss, after an increase in the minimum wage, are the lower-income workers.

## The Impact of the Minimum Wage on Other Wages

The debate as to whether the minimum wage impacts other wages in Brazil began in the 1970s. Macedo and Garcia (1978) were the first to argue that changes in the value of the minimum wage had only a limited impact on the current wage rate. Their argument was based on estimates of an elasticity less than unity between the minimum wage and the wage rate during the period 1964-74. Souza and Baltar (1979), on the other hand, considered a longer sampling period and offered a rather different interpretation of the data. Those authors argued that minimum wage policy was an important determinant of other wages in Brazil. Their argument was based on the fact that changes in the real value of the minimum wage were followed closely by the real wages of workers in the state of São Paulo between 1961 and 1976, which they concluded was consistent with unitary elasticity. This finding gave rise to the term "light house effect," inasmuch as it suggested that changes in the minimum wage would induce increases in all wages, even among less-skilled workers in the informal sector.

The debate as to whether or not the light house effect is valid persisted throughout the 1980s. Countless studies were done on the question of whether the wage policy in Brazil was effective. Since the wage policy expressed all wages as multiples of the minimum wage for purposes of indexation, the way to test its effectiveness was to make a comparison between an institutional wage index constructed by strictly applying the wage policy principles, and an average market wage. If the institutional wage were to remain below the market wage for a long time, the conclusion would be that the wage policy was ineffective and, consequently, the theory of the light house effect would lose credibility [Carneiro (1995)].

Velloso (1990) considered an additional explanatory variable and introduced the business cycle as a new explanatory variable in the wages equation. He estimated the impact of changes in the real value of the minimum wage and changes in the business cycle (measured by the rate of open unemployment) on the real value of the wages in the formal and informal sectors throughout the 1976-86 period. For workers in the formal sector, a 10 percent increase in the real value of the minimum wage would mean increases of between 3.6 percent and 6.3 percent in real wages of workers whose hold an employment record card. For workers in the informal sector, a 10 percent increase in the minimum wage would raise their earnings by 4.3 percent to 6 percent. The proximity between the elasticities found would suggest that wages and earnings by both formal and informal workers responded in a fairly similar manner to changes in the minimum wage. The effect of changes in the business cycle, however, was more pronounced for the informal workers. A 10 percent increase in open unemployment is thought to have caused a negative impact of about 0.4 percent on wages in the formal sector, while it negatively impacted earnings in the informal sector by approximately 0.8 percent.

However, all the literature of the 1980s was later considered to have been contaminated by the problem of spurious regression, since the time series used in the estimated regressions invariably possessed a unit root and did not receive appropriate statistical treatment. So once again, an avenue opens for testing the robustness of the earlier results as to the validity or invalidity of the light house effect and the effectiveness of the minimum wage as an important determinant of the other wages in the economy.

A methodology of analysis different from those used prior to the early 1990s was implemented by Carneiro and Faria (1997), Lemos (1997), and Soares (1998). Instead of calculating elasticities, these authors investigated the temporal precedence between the minimum wage and the other wages in the economy. Using aggregate monthly data on the trend in the average industrial wage, considered as a proxy for the market wage, and data on the minimum wage for the period 1980-93, Carneiro and Faria (1997) identified the temporal precedence of changes in the official minimum wage over changes in the average market wage between 1980 and 1985. For the subsequent period, 1986-93, however, the authors found that the two wages were determined simultaneously. The results for the first sub-period corroborated the so-called "beacon theory," under which the minimum wage is believed to be an important determinant of the other wages [Souza and Baltar (1979)]. For the second sub-period, the simultaneous determination of the minimum wage and the market wage was interpreted as an indicator of (i) the minimum wage's loss of effectiveness and (ii) the increased bargaining power of unions beginning in the second half of the 1980s [Carneiro and Henley (1998)].

Adopting a similar methodology, Lemos (1997) showed that the minimum wage has a positive effect on the other wages in the economy for five quarters, after an initial shock. Emphasizing the simultaneity between the minimum wage and the other wages, the author also showed that the average wage positively affects the minimum wage for a period of three quarters after the shock. Soares (1998), using the same methodology, concluded that the minimum wage behaved reactively toward the labor market during the 1990s.

A limitation of this methodology is that because it does not supply elasticities, it is hard to quantify the extent to which a change in the minimum wage impacts the other wages in the economy. Furthermore, the fact that there is temporal precedence does not mean that there is a cause-and-effect relationship; therefore, there also exists a limitation in terms of the causal relationship between the minimum wage and the other wages. Compensating for this methodological limitation, Foguel, Ramos, and Carneiro (2000) present econometric results based on the methodology known as co-integration analysis of time series in order to investigate the impact of changes in minimum wage on the other wages in the Brazilian economy during the period 1983-99. The equation estimated by the authors takes the following general form:

$$W = f(m, q - l, u, h, \pi) \tag{3}$$

where all the variables are expressed in their logarithmic form, $W$ is the average nominal wage, $m$ is the minimum wage, $q - l$ represents the productivity of labor, $u$ is unemployment, $h$ is a proxy for labor costs, and $\pi$ is the rate of inflation.[3] Just as in the case of the examination of the employment-effect of the minimum wage, it was possible here to obtain short- and long-term estimates for the wage-elasticity of the minimum wage. Over the long term, the model presented a unitary elasticity of wages with respect to the minimum wage and positive coefficients for labor productivity, cost of labor and inflation, with the unemployment rate attracting the expected negative signal.

Furthermore, the same behavioral pattern was observed for the formal and informal sectors, indicating that the two sectors adapt to demand shocks in a fairly similar manner. For workers whose jobs are registered on their employment record cards, a 10 percent increase in labor productivity would lead to a 4 percent increase in their nominal wages, but a 10 percent increase in unemployment would provoke a decline of about 6 percent in their wages. The price-elasticity of the nominal wages for the workers in the formal sector varied between 0.3 and 0.5, indicating that those workers are no longer able to recover all their inflation-related wage losses. For workers in the informal sector, the impact of changes in the unemployment rate on their income was much more pronounced than in the formal sector, since the unemployment-elasticity of the informal earnings ranged from –0.38 to –0.89. On the other hand, the workers in the informal sector appear to be able to adjust their earnings more effectively with respect to inflation, since the price-elasticity for that sector was higher than unity. In both sectors, increases in labor

---

[3] In the authors' formulation, "$q$" represents aggregate industrial product, $l$ the total employed, and the ratio between them a measure of labor productivity. Then labor costs are measured by the ratio between the real wage from the standpoint of the producer and the real wage received by the worker; the numerator incorporates the taxes paid when a formal worker is hired and the denominator deducts the income tax on worker wages [see Layard *et al.* (1993) for further details].

productivity result in wage increases, suggesting that in both the formal and informal sectors, workers are able to convert positive demand shocks into wage gains.

With regard to the finding of a short-term dynamic, the authors note that the minimum wage has only a limited power to influence the other wages. The minimum wage-elasticity declines considerably over the short term and does not exceed 0.10 for the formal sector and 0.24 for the informal sector. This result seems to indicate that changes in the minimum wage have a more pronounced impact on the earnings of informal workers. In addition, earnings by informal workers are also more sensitive to short-term fluctuations in economic activity. The employment-elasticity of nominal wages for informal workers was –0.12, while it was only –0.09 for formal workers.

Despite presenting elasticities that enables one to measure the impact of changes in the minimum wage on the other wages in the economy, this methodology of analysis does not allow one to identify which wages would be most directly affected by changes in the minimum wage. To accomplish this, one would need to study the behavior of the wage distribution in the economy in the presence of changes in the minimum wage. On this point, the work of Lemos (2002), Corseuil and Morgado (2000), Carneiro and Corseuil (2001), and Fajnzylber (2001) presents empirical evidence of the impact of changes in the minimum wage on the wage distribution.

Lemos (2002), Corseuil and Morgado (2000), Carneiro and Corseuil (2001), and Maloney (2000) present evidence that suggests that the wages most affected by changes in the minimum wage are precisely those that are close to the minimum. Indeed, Corseuil and Morgado (2000) and Carneiro and Corseuil (2001) show that the wage distribution changes little after a change in the minimum wage for wages above the equivalent of two minimum wages. This behavior pattern remained practically the same throughout the 1990s, according to the authors.

The study by Fajnzylber (2001), however, deviates from this rule by presenting evidence that the wages farthest from the minimum are also influenced by changes in the minimum wage, thus corroborating the so-called "light house effect." The author argues that this result can be observed via the wage distribution if we acknowledge that the use of the minimum wage as a unit of measure is a widespread practice in the labor market. Furthermore, the author postulates that in an environment of perfect competition, one should expect that employers would respond to increases in the minimum wage by replacing workers whose productivity is deemed to be lower than the minimum wage with workers whose initial earnings and productivity are above the minimum.

In contrast to earlier works, Fajnzylber (2001) does not limit his analysis to those workers who earn one minimum wage or less than that, or to those workers who are paid multiples of the minimum wage. Instead, the author estimates the impact of changes in the minimum wage on different points in the wage distribution, calculating both the contemporaneous effects and the lagged effects of the minimum wage. The analysis is developed using data from the Monthly Employment Survey for the period 1982 to 1999. Simply put, the procedure followed involves estimating the impact of changes in the real minimum wage on real monthly earnings, thus permitting the occurrence of differentiated effects throughout the wage distribution, as well as lagged effects. Furthermore, they are controlled for individual characteristics (race and years of schooling), as well as for the survey month (May and September) and interactions between the metropolitan area and some years for which there were significant interventions in the economy (in order to see whether different regions respond differently to political intervention).

The results obtained by Fajnzylber (2001) suggest that the impact of changes in the minimum wage is not restricted to those workers who earn up to one minimum wage in the formal sector. Instead, the author finds that the minimum wage has a significant impact on the entire wage distribution in the formal sector, as well as the earnings of workers in the informal sector, thus corroborating the so-called "light house effect". Moreover, the author reports results that indicate that the income of adult male workers and of heads of households are the ones most affected by the changes in the minimum wage, *vis a vis* the income of women, young people, and workers who are not heads of households.

Possible extensions of that study and the agenda for research on the impact of the minimum wage on employment would cover an analysis of the behavior of hours worked and the hourly wage in the presence of increases in the minimum wage. Those points have not yet been explored in the Brazilian literature and would certainly add relevant information to the debate on the behavior of the labor market after a change in the value of the minimum wage.

In the next section, we will discuss the principal results available in the literature relating to the impact of the minimum wage on poverty, inasmuch as the primary objective of a minimum wage policy is directly associated with protection of the income of the lowest-income workers, the ones closest to the poverty line.

## VI. IMPACT OF THE MINIMUM WAGE ON POVERTY

In principle, considering the main objective of a minimum wage policy, we would say that real increases in that wage tend to reduce poverty. However, this cause-and-effect relationship is not always that clear. Considering a change from the traditional Harris and Todaro model, for example, one might argue that when the economy includes a large informal sector, an increase in the minimum wage in the formal sector can lead to an increase in informal employment and a reduction in formal employment. Given the surplus of labor in the informal sector, the earnings sof the low-income workers who find work in that sector will tend to fall, and this can actually generate an increase in poverty [Lustig and McLeod (1996)].

Alternatively, one might argue that the effects of the minimum wage on poverty will depend on the elasticities in the formal and informal sectors. If, for example, demand for formal labor is inelastic, wages in both sectors will rise if the wages in the formal sector rise. Consequently, if the elasticity of the other wages with respect to the minimum wage is positive and close to unity, any increase in the minimum wage will be transmitted to the other wages in the economy, and the ultimate effect will be to reduce poverty levels, because of the inelasticity of the employment in the formal sector [Hamermesh (1993)].

One can also argue that in small open economies, increases in the wages of the formal sector always lead to an increase the wages in the formal and informal sectors, while at the same time reducing the rate of return on capital. This is because an increase in the minimum wage cannot be passed along to prices, hence profits decline and we see a migration of capital, instead of labor, in the formal sector. Capital would therefore move to the informal sector, boosting both the earnings and employment of the informal workers [Carruth and Oswald (1981) and Leamer (1985)].

Furthermore, there are some factors that would constrain an increase in the income of poor families following an increase in the minimum wage. First, the increase in the income of poor families resulting from the increase in the minimum wage must exceed the decline in family income that occurs as a result of the loss of earnings of the low-income workers in the family who become unemployed after the minimum wage is raised. Second, it is important to know the direction and magnitude of the effect of the minimum wage on the supply of labor by the other members of the family. And, lastly, since changes in the minimum wage affect family income—for example, through the loss of earnings by some members who become unemployed—it is also important to consider what types of monetary compensation are received through mechanisms such as government transfers, as in the case of the unemployment insurance program.

In general, there is a certain bias in the literature in crediting increases in the minimum wage with reducing poverty in developing countries. [Lustig and McLeod (1996)]. Some studies have attempted to research this matter specifically for the case of Brazil. Barros *et al.* (2000), and Neri *et al.* (2000), are recent examples. In the study by Barros *et al.* (2000), the poverty gap for six metropolitan regions of the country is broken down so as to isolate the impact of the minimum wage on poverty throughout the period 1995 to 1998. More specifically, this breakdown attempts to capture the effects of the minimum wage on the incomes of workers who would probably be affected by the minimum wage in the formal and informal sectors, i.e., those who had an income situated between the old minimum wage and the new one.

It is important to note that the methodology captures only the impact on the earnings of those workers who did not lose their jobs after the increase in the minimum wage. This way, the results should be viewed as an upper limit of the impact of the minimum wage on poverty, since they do not consider the possible negative effect on employment of an increase in the minimum wage. The results by Barros *et al.* (2000) show that the impact of increases in the minimum wage on poverty during the period considered was positive: the elasticity of the poverty gap with respect to the minimum wage found by the authors was 0.4, which means that a 10 percent increase in the minimum wage would reduce poverty by 4 percent. The authors also concluded that about two-thirds of the reduction in poverty associated with the minimum wage is attributable to increases in the income of workers in the informal sector.

The study by Neri *et al.* (2000) used a different methodology. Instead of breaking down the effects of the minimum wage on poverty, the authors simulated the effect of real adjustments in the minimum wage on the incomes of individuals from different segments of the labor market for which the minimum wage policy is effective. The analysis was based on data from the 1996 National Household Sample Survey. The simulations, however, do not take into account the effects of the minimum wage on employment, since the authors assume that the wage-employment elasticity is zero (p. 6)[4]. Simulating a real 43 percent adjustment in the minimum wage, the authors found that there would be a 6 percent reduction in the proportion of poor people.

In general, the study concluded that there is a direct relationship between increases in the minimum wage and poverty reduction. However, the results indicate that the bigger the adjustments in the value of the minimum wage, the smaller its effects on poverty. That relationship persists even when one considers the change in the poverty that is associated with changes both in earnings and in jobs linked to the minimum. The authors further found that the

---

[4] Using the 43 percent increase in the minimum wage approved in May 1995, Neri (1997) demonstrated that the probabilities that groups of formal employees affected by the minimum wage would become unemployed or informal workers are greater than for unaffected groups. Amadeo and Neri (1998), however, present evidence that the month of May 1995 represents an inflection in the poverty series in Brazil.

reduction in poverty related to the increment in earnings associated with the minimum is more significant for informal earnings.

In the study by the Institute for Applied Economic Research (IPEA, 2000), it is argued that there are three ways to measure the impact of the minimum wage on poverty. In the first, one measures the direct effect of the increase in the level of the minimum wage on poverty, without considering the impact that such increase will have on the level of employment and the cost of living. In the second, one takes into account the fact that raising the minimum wage should have negative effects on the demand for labor, thus reducing the level of employment. And, lastly, a third way would be to consider a computable general equilibrium model in which it is possible to examine indirect effects on poverty, such as changes in the degree of informality of the labor market and increases in social security benefits.

The IPEA study presents some simulations with respect to the impact of the minimum wage on poverty, based on indexation scenarios and the ability of the minimum wage to impact the other wages in the formal and informal sectors. The simulations were developed according to the following expressions:

$$W_n = (1 + \alpha)W_a \qquad\qquad \text{if } W_a \leq M$$

and

$$W_n = \{1 + \alpha \exp[-\lambda (W_a - M)/M]\}W_a \text{ if } W_a > M \qquad\qquad (4)$$

where $M$ is the old level of the minimum wage, $W_n$ represents the new wages and $W_a$ the old wage. The parameter $\alpha$ indicates the percentage by which the minimum wage is raised and the parameter $\lambda$ its ability to impact the other wages. The larger this parameter, the more rapidly will the impact of the minimum wage increase on higher wages decrease. Therefore, when $\lambda = 2$, for example, a 15 percent increase in the minimum wage would lead to a 2.0 percent increase for someone who earns 2 minimum wages. When $\lambda = 1$, a 15 percent increase in the minimum wage would lead to a 5.5 percent increase for someone who earns 2 minimum wages.

Looking at a case in which only those workers whose wages are below the new minimum wage benefit from an increase in the minimum wage, the effect of an increase in the latter on poverty would be rather limited. Under this scenario, IPEA estimates that a 15 percent increase in the minimum wage would reduce poverty by less than one percentage point, even considering that the minimum wage impacts employees without employment record cards and the self-employed. Considering a scenario under which changes in the minimum wage tend to affect not only wages below that level but also the higher wages, a 15 percent increase in the minimum wage could reduce poverty by about 3.3 percentage points.

However, these simulations still do not take into account the possible negative impact of the minimum wage on the level of employment. Taking this aspect into consideration, the effect of increases in the minimum wage on poverty would depend, additionally, on the price-elasticity of the demand for unskilled labor in the formal sector. Based on estimates calculated by Ramos and Reis (1995), the IPEA study simulated several different scenarios for the impact of the minimum wage on poverty, taking into account the effect of the minimum wage on employment. In general, the impact on poverty does not seem to be very significant when the employment-effect of the minimum wage is considered. Leaving aside the so-called "light house effect," for example, a hypothetical increase of 25 percent in the minimum wage would result in a reduction of 1.4 percentage points in the proportion of poor people, adopting the hypothesis that the demand for unskilled labor is inelastic. For the case in which the demand for labor is unitary, the effect of a 25 percent increase in the minimum wage would result in a reduction of less than 1 percentage point in the proportion of poor people.

Lastly, the IPEA study estimates the effect of increases in the minimum wage on the poverty level in Brazil, taking into account its various effects on the economy, in addition to wage changes, based on a general equilibrium model developed by Cury, Barros, and Corseuil (1999). The model makes it possible to estimate what the level of poverty would be if the minimum wage were the only parameter to be changed in the economy. The exercise consists of allowing wage changes for workers whose wages are tied to the minimum. For purposes of illustration only, we will cite the results of one of the simulations. Assuming a 20 percent increase in the minimum wage and recognizing that all the wages in the economy are affected by this increase, an increase of 0.1 percentage point in the proportion of poor people was registered. Several alternatives were considered, and in all of them, the impact of increases in the minimum wage on poverty was quite insignificant. Therefore, the study concluded that minimum wage policy appears to be irrelevant in combating poverty in Brazil

Clearly, the debate about the effects of the minimum wage on poverty in Brazil is far from reaching a consensus. Some studies found results that indicated that increases in the minimum wage reduce the percentage of poor people, but the strongest criticism of those results is that they do not take into consideration the possible negative effects of the minimum wage on employment. When those effects are taken into account, the effectiveness of minimum wage policy in relieving poverty is substantially reduced. As shown in the next chapter, the international evidence seems to be similarly ambiguous. Studies that use the family, rather than the individual, as a unit of analysis tend to obtain results that indicate that the minimum wage has a fairly modest impact on the poverty level.

In the next section, we will review the main results about the impact of increases in the minimum wage on the government accounts in Brazil. Our assessment of this issue is relevant, since it can indicate whether the mechanisms for combating poverty, such as minimum wage policy, compromise the country's fiscal situation.

## VII. THE FISCAL IMPACT OF THE MINIMUM WAGE POLICY

In this section, we examine the impact of changes in the minimum wage on two important components of the fiscal deficit in Brazil: (i) the payroll at all three levels of government (federal, state, and local), and (ii) the social security system budget. Foguel, Ramos, and Carneiro (2001) are credited with developing the evidence in this respect, which is based on simulations of the impact that the minimum wage would have on the government accounts when that wage assumes certain arbitrary values.

## Impact on Payroll

Increases in the minimum wage can have a direct impact on the payroll at the three levels of government, since the salaries of those civil servants who earn the equivalent of a minimum wage must be automatically adjusted when the minimum wage rises.[5] Identifying which of the three levels of government suffers the heaviest impact due to changes in the minimum wage can make an important contribution to the future of minimum wage policy in Brazil.

The analysis by Foguel, Ramos, and Carneiro (2001) was done using data from the Annual Social Information Report (RAIS) compiled by the Ministry of Labor and Employment for 1997.[6] This database contains information on the number of workers in the formal sector and their wages and salaries as of December of that year. The sample was constructed using only civil servants who were assigned to units of the "direct" government administration. More specifically, only civil servants who were employed in the executive, legislative, and judiciary branches of the federal, state, and local government were considered, including those who were working in semi-autonomous government agencies, the armed forces, and the police. It is important to observe that workers whose employment contracts are governed by both the Single Legal Regime (RJU) and the Consolidated Labor Laws (CLT) were represented in the sample, and that the sample did not include employees of state-owned companies.

The methodology was based on simulations in which certain arbitrary values were assigned to the minimum wage and used to calculate the change in the payroll at each level. The base value of the minimum wage used for the calculations was R$136, the level in effect in April 2000. The figures used in the simulations were R$151 (the value established in May 2000), R$163 (equivalent to a 20 percent increase), R$177 (a 30 percent increase), and R$204 (a 50 percent increase).

**Table 7.3. Impact of the Minimum Wage on the Payroll, in R$ Million**
**Federal, State, and Local Governments – Annual Figures**

| Minimum Wage | Federal | State | Local | Total |
|---|---|---|---|---|
| 151 | 3.1 | 129.6 | 197.7 | 330.4 |
| 163 | 4.9 | 211.0 | 359.2 | 575.0 |
| 176 | 9.1 | 324.2 | 553.6 | 886.9 |
| 204 | 23.6 | 562.0 | 1017.2 | 1602.7 |
| Relative Impact (%) | | | | |
| 151 | 0.02 | 0.52 | 1.41 | 0.64 |
| 163 | 0.04 | 0.84 | 2.55 | 1.11 |
| 176 | 0.07 | 1.29 | 3.94 | 1.71 |
| 204 | 0.19 | 2.24 | 7.23 | 3.09 |

Source: Foguel, Ramos, and Carneiro (2001), p. 18.

The results of the simulations by Foguel, Ramos, and Carneiro (2001) appear in Table 7.3. The figures are on an annual basis, including the year-end bonus (the "13th salary"). The results indicate that changes in the minimum wage do not seem to have an important impact on the

---

[5] According to the 1988 Constitution, no public wage or benefit can be less than the minimum wage.

[6] The 1997 RAIS is the most recent available at present.

federal government payroll, since only 0.2 percent of federal government workers have earnings equivalent to one minimum wage or less. The impact on the payroll of state governments is much more pronounced, since about 1.9 percent of state government employees receive the equivalent to one minimum wage. Local governments experience the biggest impact on payroll, since about 13 percent of civil servants at that level have earnings equivalent to the value of up to one minimum wage. In relative terms, the elasticities of the payroll at the three levels of government with respect to changes in the minimum wage are placed at 0.003, 0.045, and 0.134, respectively. This means that a 10 percent increase in the minimum wage would increase the payrolls at the three levels of government by 0.03 percent, 0.45 percent, and 1.34 percent, respectively.

## Impact on the Social Security System Budget

With the promulgation of the 1988 Constitution, the minimum wage became the floor for social security benefits. This means that every adjustment in the minimum wage is passed along to the pensions and other benefits paid by the social security system. Foguel, Ramos, and Carneiro (2000) present estimates of the effect of the minimum wage on the social security budget, obtained through an exercise similar to the one they performed with the government payroll—by assuming different values for the minimum wage, ranging from R$151 to R$177.

The authors investigated the impact of changes in the wage on both the revenues and expenses of the social security system. The data used were obtained from the Brazilian Institute of Geography and Statistics (IBGE) National Household Sample Survey, and from the Statistical Bulletin and Statistical Yearbook published by the social security system, for 1996, 1997, and 1998. The impact on the social security budget was calculated by subtracting the aggregate increase in revenues from the aggregate increase in expenditures, and the results appear in Table 7.4. The figures indicate that the increase in the expenditures that is derived from the increases in the minimum wage is approximately 13 times greater than the increase in revenues. In general, each R$1.00 increase in the minimum wage generates an additional deficit of about R$160 million in the social security budget. This finding demonstrates how vulnerable the government's fiscal situation is to the minimum wage policy.

**Table 7.4. Impact of the Minimum Wage on the Social Security Deficit**
**Annual Figures in R$ Million**

| Minimum Wage | Impact on Revenue | Impact on Expenditure | Net Impact |
|---|---|---|---|
| 151 | 171 | 2.340 | 2.169 |
| 160 | 290 | 3.820 | 3.530 |
| 165 | 360 | 4.660 | 4.300 |
| 170 | 432 | 5.520 | 5.088 |
| 177 | 537 | 6.740 | 6.203 |

Source: Foguel. Ramos, and Carneiro (2001). p. 18.

# VIII. ALTERNATIVES FOR THE MINIMUM WAGE POLICY[7]

In this section, we discuss policy options that may contribute constructively to the debate on the future of the minimum wage policy in Brazil. The intention here is not to offer a preferred alternative, but rather to identify the features of each policy option, along with its advantages, disadvantages, and prospects for the Brazilian situation. We discuss in general terms the issue of regionalization *vis a vis* the maintenance of a national minimum wage, the sectoral approach to the minimum wage, differentiated coverage, criteria for adjustment, and alternatives for managing the minimum wage policy. All the options discussed here are summarized in Table 7.5.

## National vs. Regional Minimum Wages

In general, there are four possible types of minimum wage: national, regional, occupational, or by industry, which are not necessarily mutually exclusive. The first two have already been used in Brazil. From 1940, when the minimum wage was first introduced, until 1984, the minimum wage was differentiated by region. From 1984 to 2000, the minimum wage was standardized at a single nationwide value. More recently, the country has adopted a combination of a national minimum wage defined as the "floor" and regional minimum wages set by the local governments.

One of the main advantages of the national minimum wage is that it is easy to implement and monitor. Additionally, if we consider that wage differentials are a potential source of migration, the establishment of a single level of a minimum wage for the entire country would tend not to encourage migration by rural workers to densely-populated urban areas.

The main disadvantage of this system, however, is that it presupposes both the existence of a homogenous labor market and the presence of few regional economic disparities. When those conditions do not exist, the fixing of a single wage floor for an entire country can produce significant negative effects. If labor productivity is significantly differentiated among the various regions of the country, it is to be expected that regions with lower average labor productivity will tend not to respect the official minimum wage. We might then see a growth in informality in the labor market, or even a rise in open unemployment in the less developed regions. Furthermore, in the case of Brazil, the national minimum wage system tends to impact significantly the government deficit because of its relationship with the pensions and other benefits paid by the social security system.

With regard to the option for a regional minimum wage, there are two alternative configurations. In the first, there is a differentiated minimum wage for each unit in the federation, as it was the case in Brazil until 1984. In the second, a system can be adopted that is a combination of the national and regional systems, with the Federal Government defining a minimum floor to be observed throughout the country, and the local governments establishing minimum wages above that floor, depending on their ability to pay and the nature of their particular labor markets.

---

[7] This section closely follows the discussion of minimum wage policy options presented in Foguel, Ramos, and Carneiro (2001).

The main advantage of having minimum wages that are differentiated by region is that this system can reduce the negative effects in terms of informality and unemployment in the less developed regions, situations observed in the case of the national system. Furthermore, establishing regional wages may be more appropriate since the minimum wage of each region would necessarily reflect more accurately the differences in terms of cost of living and configuration of the different labor markets. The principal disadvantage, however, is the potential encouragement of migratory flows to more dynamic and more densely populated regions. Since the flow of low-skilled workers increases the labor supply in regions that have a higher average labor productivity, the expected result would be an increase in informality and under-employment.

Moreover, minimum wages differentiated by region can encourage the migration of the more highly-qualified workers from the less developed regions to areas where labor productivity is higher. Therefore, the average productivity in the less developed regions would tend to decline, reducing per capita income in the less developed regions, thus delaying their development even further.

For this reason, implementation of a combination of national and/or regional minimum wage systems demands a careful review of the economic conditions and the degree of heterogeneity among the various regions of the country. In the implementation of that combination of polices, the functions of labor supply and demand, distributions of productivity, degree of worker aversion to risk, and the ability of state and local government to pay, as well as political factors, must be evaluated.

## Occupational or Sectoral Minimum Wage

There is yet another alternative, one that does not necessarily substitute for the options of a regional minimum wage and/or nationally-unified minimum wage. It is the system that differentiates the official minimum remuneration by industry sector or a certain occupation. In most of the countries where this system has been applied (Germany, Austria, Sweden, and Denmark), the value of the minimum wage is determined by collective agreements at the industry level. The occupational minimum wage is defined in a similar way and is based on fairly specific occupations. It has been applied in countries like Costa Rica, Colombia, Spain, Luxembourg, and some African and East European countries.

The chief advantage of the industrial system is related to the heterogeneity observed among industrial sectors. To the extent that different sectors present different productivity levels, it seems reasonable to differentiate the wage floor for each of them. In the case of occupation-based minimum wages, the primary objective is to protect groups of less well-organized workers, who do not have enough bargaining power to negotiate their own minimum wage rates.

The disadvantage of the industrial or occupational-based systems has to do with the complexity of implementing them and monitoring compliance, which requires a major coordination effort. In order to function properly, the system also presupposes a decentralized wage bargaining structure, to prevent better-organized groups from setting higher wage floors. In the case of Brazil, the prevailing intermediate bargaining structure, along with the high geographical concentration of industry and the heterogeneity of the labor market, tend to make this alternative unfeasible.

## Differentiated Coverage

Under the differentiated-coverage system, there is a choice of two alternative strategies. The first would be to allow certain types of industrial establishments, employing small numbers of workers, to be exempt from paying the official minimum wage. Under the second, wages lower than the minimum can be adopted for young people and trainees. The main argument to justify these procedures has to do with small business' limited ability to pay. It is harder for them to get credit, and they have fewer means of surviving periods of lower economic activity. In the case of young people and trainees, the argument is that their productivity is lower than that of adult workers.

In weighing the advantages and disadvantages, one might argue that lower wages for young workers tend to encourage them to remain in school longer, thus improving their future prospects and the allocative efficiency of the labor market. On the other hand, in a country with a large informal sector, the lower the minimum wage is for young people, the greater will be the incentive for small businesses to hire young workers.

Thus the incentive to staying in school will be stronger in the more developed regions, but the opportunity cost of doing so may perhaps be too high in the less developed regions, which have a large informal sector and higher poverty rates. We would therefore have to know precisely the extent of the demand for young workers and its function in the labor supply before thinking about implementing the alternative of minimum wages differentiated by age.

## Criteria for Adjustment and Management of the Minimum Wage Policy

With regard to the determination of the criteria for adjusting the minimum wage, there are independent or combined criteria involving: (a) basic needs of workers; (b) their impact on employment and wages; and (c) macroeconomic factors. A strategy that combines all three criteria would seem to be better than one that takes into account only one or the other.

However, combining the three criteria would involve a certain amount of coordination among the interests of workers, companies, and the Government. Certainly such a policy would be more easily implemented in countries that have centralized collective bargaining structures. Its viability presupposes the existence of tripartite negotiating committees that would meet periodically to study and decide on changes in the minimum wage.

In Brazil, where the bargaining structure is intermediate, there is no single entity that can be considered capable of representing the interests of the working class as occurs in countries where the bargaining structure is centralized. Furthermore, fiscal difficulties would always tend to force the Government to depart from the initial objectives of the minimum wage policy. Therefore, this is not seen as a viable alternative for the Brazilian situation.

# Table 7.5. Matrix of Options for Minimum Wage Policy in Brazil

| | GENERAL CHARACTERISTIC | ADVANTAGES | DISADVANTAGES | PROSPECT FOR THE BRAZILIAN SITUATION |
|---|---|---|---|---|
| **National Minimum Wage** | Single minimum wage for the whole country. | Simple to apply and monitor; reduction in rural-urban migration. | Assumes economic and labor market homogeneity; significant fiscal impact; unemployment and informality in less developed regions. | Sub-optimal option in light of fiscal vulnerability, major economic disparities, and heterogeneous labor markets. Can be combined with a policy of minimum wages differentiated by region or level of government. |
| **Regional Minimum Wage** | Different values for different regions. | Reflects regional differences in terms of cost of living and productivity. | Incentive to migration; unemployment/informality; decline in productivity in less-developed areas. | Since April 2000, has been implemented in this country, using a mix of a national floor and regional minimum wages. |
| **Sector or Occupation-based Minimum Wage** | Different values for certain industry sectors or specific occupations. | Reflects heterogeneity of economic sectors and productivity; protects the less well-organized worker groups. | Complicated application and monitoring. Assumes decentralized bargaining so as to avoid favoring better-organized groups. | Intermediate bargaining existing in this country makes this alternative impracticable. Highly concentrated industrial sector and heterogeneous labor market would make it difficult to apply here. |
| **Differentiated Coverage** | Some companies with a certain number of employees may be exempt from paying minimum wage; minimum wage differentiated by age bracket. | Takes into account company ability to pay. Can be an incentive for young people to stay in school. Increases the allocative efficiency in the economy.. | Difficulty in defining the exempt groups or those entitled to differentiated minimum wage. | Existence of a significant informal sector in the economy reduces effective scope of this alternative. |
| **Adjustment Criteria** | Independent or combined criteria, involving: (a) basic needs; (b) impact on employment and wages; (c) macroeconomic factors. | (a) Meets workers' nutritional needs; (b) considers possible impact on the labor market; (c) takes into account impact on inflation, the government deficit, and economic growth. | Political factors may divert the minimum wage policy from its initial objectives. Links social security benefits to the minimum wage, and its impact on the public sector deficit. | Efficient allocative criteria for adjusting the minimum wage will be possible only if the link with social security pensions and other benefits is broken. |
| **Centralized Management** | Definition of the scope, coverage, and rules for adjusting the minimum wage are established by Government. | Can facilitate macroeconomic coordination and monitoring. Can be used for regional or sectoral - occupational minimum wages. | Fiscal problems may dictate the rules of minimum wage policy, resulting in inefficient allocation of resources. | Difficulty in management in light of the heterogeneity of the labor market and sharp regional disparities. |
| **Tripartite Commissions** | Government, employers, and employees decide jointly on the rules of minimum wage policy. | Democratic system. In economies with centralized bargaining, facilitates macroeconomic coordination. Government can represent the interests of the outsiders (the unemployed). | In economies that have an intermediate bargaining structure, may favor the better-organized groups, which has deleterious consequences for the economy and worsens income distribution. | Not feasible because of the presence of an intermediary bargaining structure. |

# IX. CONCLUSION

This chapter has presented a comprehensive review of the literature on the impact of the minimum wage on the Brazilian economy. The aspects examined involve the impact of the minimum wage on the level of employment--both formal and informal--on the other wages, on the percentage of the population that is poor, and on the government accounts. Also briefly reviewed were the first minimum wage policies implemented in this country, and the profile of the workers whose earnings are close to the minimum. A summary table (Table 7.6) presenting the main results reviewed in the text appears in the Appendix.

As regards the impact of the minimum wage on the levels of formal and informal employment, all the studies reviewed point to negative effects on formal employment. On the other hand, some results suggest that increases in the minimum wage generate increments in informal employment, a situation compatible with the existence of dual labor markets in which the impact of the minimum wage on the unemployment rate is attenuated by the absorption of workers in the informal areas of the economy.

Considering the impact on the other wages in the economy, the hypothesis usually tested by the studies we reviewed was about the validity of the so-called light house effect. The debate on this point was initiated in Brazil in the 1970s, with Baltar and Souza (1979) presenting empirical evidence that suggested that changes in the minimum wage impact all the other wages in an economy in the same proportion. Those results were the opposite of those found by Macedo and Garcia (1978), who found elasticities lower than unity for a different period of time than that analyzed by Souza and Baltar (1979). More recent evidence based on time-series analyses prove that the minimum wage has some effect on the other wages, but there is no consensus in the literature on the existence of a unitary elasticity of the other wages in relation to the minimum wage.

Some methodological advances were introduced into the debate by studies that examined the effects of the minimum wage, not on an average of other wages in the economy, but on the distribution of wages. This made it possible to examine which wage bracket is most affected by changes in the minimum wage. Here too, the evidence does not help us reach a consensus, since there are studies that conclude that the minimum wage tends to affect only those wages that are closest to it [see Corseuil and Morgado (2001), Carneiro and Corseuil (2001), and Lemos (2002)], and findings that suggest that the entire distribution of wages in the economy is affected by changes in the minimum wage [see Fajnzylber (2001)].

One point on which there existed a certain amount of consensus in the literature is related to the impact of the minimum wage on the percentage of poor people in the country. In general, all the studies reviewed seem to suggest that increases in the minimum wage have a fairly limited impact on poverty levels. That finding comes as an unpleasant surprise, to some extent. Because of the specific objectives of the minimum wage policy, one would expect to find a direct relationship between increases in the minimum wage and a reduction in the number of poor people. Indeed, such a correlation does exist for Brazil, but what the studies reviewed here show is that the increases in the minimum wage in real terms would have to be fairly significant before we could observe significant reductions in poverty levels.

The frustration with the success of wage policy in negatively affecting poverty intensifies when we consider its effects on the government accounts. The results presented in this chapter show that, although a different impact was observed for each level of government (federal, state and local), the biggest and most significant impact is on the social security accounts. In general, each R$1.00 increase in the minimum wage adds about R$160 million to the deficit in the social security budget. This situation demonstrates the vulnerability of the Government's fiscal situation in terms of the minimum wage policy and makes clear the limitation in the Government's ability to use the minimum wage policy as a meaningful tool in a more aggressive poverty-reduction strategy.

Lastly, we presented a critical discussion concerning several possible alternatives for the future of the minimum wage policy in this country. We looked at options for regionalization versus unification of the minimum wage, sectoral and occupation-based minimum wages, differentiated coverage, and alternatives for managing the minimum wage policy. Instead of pointing to one political option as being the best among all those presented, what we showed was that isolated positions tend to have serious limitations.

In general, what has become clear is that there are certain costs associated with a poverty-reduction strategy that relies heavily on a minimum wage policy. Those costs may manifest themselves most directly in the short run via the impact of an increase in minimum wage on the government accounts and a rise in informality and/or unemployment. Furthermore, we have observed from the analysis of the literature on the effects of the minimum wage in Brazil that there are winners and losers, which leads to ambiguous results as to the redistributive effects of the minimum wage policy. Therefore, more specific analyses must be done in order to determine whether the expenditure associated with a minimum wage policy can effectively help, over the long term, to lift families out of poverty.

# REFERENCES

Acemoglu, D. and Pischke, J. (1998), The Structure of Wages and Investment in General Training, National Bureau of Economic Research, Working Paper, 6357, Boston, Massachusetts.

Amadeo, E. and Neri, M. (1998), Politica Macroeconomica y Pobreza en Brasil, in: Ganuza, E. e Taylor, L. (org.), *Política Macroeconomica y Pobreza en America Latina y el Caribe*. Mexico: Fondo de Cultura.

Angrist, A. and Krueger, A. (1999) Empirical Strategies in Labor Economics, in Ashenfelter, O. and D. Card (org.) *Handbook of Labor Economics*, Vol. 3, Elsevier.

Barros, R.P., C.H. Corseuil, M.N. Foguel, and P.G. Leite (2000) Uma Avaliação dos Impactos do Salário Mínimo sobre o Nível de Pobreza Metropolitana no Brasil, IPEA, mimeo.

Bell, D.N.F. and Wright, R.W. (1996), The impact of minimum wages on the wages of the low paid: evidence from the Wage Boards and Councils, *Economic Journal* 106, 650-656.

Bell, L.A. (1997), The Impact of Minimum Wages in Mexico and Colombia, *Journal of Labour Economics* 15, S102-S135.

Brown, C., Gilroy, C. and Kohen, A. (1982), The Effect of the Minum Wage on Employment and Unemployment, *Journal of Economic Literature*, 20: 487-528.

Cahuc, P. and Michel, P. (1996), Minimum Wage Unemployment and Growth, *European Economic Review*, August: 1463-1482.

Card, D. and Krueger, A. (1995), *Myth and Measurement: The New Economics of the Minimum Wage*, Princeton University Press, New Jersey.

Carneiro, F.G. (1995), Government Intervention, Institutional Factors and Market: An Analysis of the Wage Barganining in Brazil, *Análise Econômica*, 23-24:19-36.

Carneiro, F.G. (2000), Time Series Evidence on the Employment Effects of Minimum Wages in Brazil, Texto para Discussão No. 18, Mestrado em Economia de Empresas, Universidade Católica de Brasilia.

Carneiro, F.G. (2004), Are Minimum Wages to Blame for Informality in the Labour Market?, *Empirica*, 31:295-306.

Carneiro, F.G. and Corseuil, C.H. (2001), The Impact of Minimum Wage Changes on Employment and Wages in Brazil: Evidence from Time Series and Longitudinal Data, *Proceedings of the III International Colloquium*, pp. 163-189, Brasília-DF.

Carneiro, F. G. and Henley, A. (1998), Wage Determination in Brazil: The Growth of Inside Power and Informal Employment, *Journal of Development Studies*, 34, 117-138.

Carneiro, F.G. and Faria, J. R. (1997), Causality between the Minimum Wage and Other Wages, *Applied Economics Letters*, 4, 507-510.

Carruth, A. and Oswald, A.J. (1981), The Determination of Union and Non-Union Wage Rates, *European Economic Review*, 16, 285-302.

Corseuil, C.H. and W. Morgado (2001), Salário Mínimo, Distribuição de Salários e Emprego no Brasil, Série de Seminários Acadêmicos, Departamento de Estudos Sociais - Instituto de Pesquisa Econômica Aplicada, Rio de Janeiro, IPEA, mimeo.

Cubitt, R.P. and S.P. Hargreaves-HEAP (1996), Minimum Wage Legislation, Investment and Human Capital, Economics Research Centre, University of East Anglia, mimeo.

Cury, S., Barros, R.P. and Corseuil, C.H. (1999), Modelo Aplicado de Equilíbrio Geral para Simulação de Impacto sobre Pobreza e Desigualdade: Simulações Comparativas de Mudanças no Comércio Exterior e no Fluxo Externo entre 95 e 98, Anais do Seminário Desigualdade e Pobreza, IPEA, Rio de Janeiro.

Fajnzylber, P. (2001), Minimum Wage Effects Throughout the Wage Distribution: Evidence from Brazil's Formal and Informal Sectors, Departamento de Economia e CEDPLAR, Universidade Federal de Minas Gerais, mimeo.

Fischer, C.C. (1997), A Note on In Defense of the Minimum Wage, *Journal of Economic Issues* 31, 261-263.

Foguel, M. (1997), Uma Análise dos Efeitos do Salário Mínimo sobre o Mercado de Trabalho no Brasil, Dissertação de Mestrado, Departamento de Economia, Pontifícia Universidade Católica do Rio de Janeiro, Rio de Janeiro, pp.179.

Foguel, M. (1998), Uma Avaliação dos Efeitos do Salário Mínimo sobre o Mercado de Trabalho no Brasil, Texto para Discussão No. 564, Instituto de Pesquisa Econômica Aplicada, Rio de Janeiro.

Foguel, M., Ramos, L. and Carneiro, F.G. (2000), The Economic Impact of Minimum Wages, XXVIII Encontro Anual de Economia - ANPEC, Campinas.

Foguel, M., Ramos, L. and Carneiro, F.G. (2001), The Impacts of the Minimum Wage on the Labor Market, Poverty and Fiscal Budget in Brazil, Texto para Discussão - *forthcoming*, Instituto de Pesquisa Econômica Aplicada, Rio de Janeiro.

Freeman, R.B. (1996), The Minimum Wage as a Redistributive Rool, Economic Journal 106, 639-649.

Hamermesh, D. (1993), *Labor Demand*, Princeton University Press.

IPEA (2000), O Nível do Salário Mínimo no Brasil, Instituto de Pesquisa Econômica Aplicada, Diretoria de Estudos Sociais, Rio de Janeiro, mimeo.

Layard, P., Nickell, S., and Jackman, R. (1993), *Unemployment: Macroeconomic Performance and the Labor Market*, Oxford University Press.

Leamer, E. (1995), The Heckscher-Ohlin Model in Theory and Practice, Princeton Studies in International Finance No. 77, Princeton University.

Lemos, S. (1997), O Efeito da Política de Salário Mínimo na Determinação do Nível de Salário Médio no Brasil no Período de 1970 a 1994, Tese de Mestrado, UFPE/PIMES.

Lemos, S. (2002), Robust Quantifications of Minimum Wage Effects on Wages and Employment Using a New Data Set: A Menu of Minimum Wage Variables, University College London, mimeo.

Lustig, N. and McLeod, D. (1996), Minimum Wages and Poverty in Developing Countries: Some Empirical Evidence, Brookings Discussion Papers, 125, The Brookings Institute, Washington.

Macedo, R. and Garcia, M. (1978), Observações sobre a Política Brasileira de Salário Mínimo, Trabalho para Discussão, 27, Instituto de Pesquisa Econômica, Universidade de São Paulo, São Paulo.

Machin, S. and Manning, A. (1994), The Effects of Minimum Wages on Wage Dispersion and Employment: Evidence from the U.K. Wages Councils, *Industrial and Labour Relations Review* 47, 319-329.

Maloney, W. (2000), A Note on Minimum Wages in Latin America, The World Bank, Washington, mimeo.

Neri, M. (1997), O Reajuste do Salário Mínimo de Maio de 1995, *Anais da Sociedade Brasileira de Econometria*, Recife.

Neri, M., Gonzaga, G. and Camargo, J. (2000), Efeitos Informais do Salário Mínimo e Pobreza, Texto para Discussão No. 724, Instituto de Pesquisa Econômica Aplicada, Rio de Janeiro.

Newmark, D., Schweitzer and Wascher, W. (2000), The Effects of Minimum Wages Throughout the Wage Distribtuion, Working Paper No. 7519, National Bureau of Economic Research, Cambridge, Massachussets.

OECD (1998), Making the Most of the Minimum: Statutory Minimum Wages, Employment and Poverty, *Employment Outlook*, June, Paris.

Ramos, L. and Reis, J.G. (1995), Salário Mínimo, Distribuição de Renda e Pobreza no Brasil, *Pesquisa e Planejamento Econômico*, Vol. 25, No. 1.

Rebitzer, J. and Taylor, L. (1995), The Consequences of Minimum Wage Laws: Some New Theoretical Ideas, *Journal of Public Economics*, 56: 245-255.

Soares, F.V. (1998), A Existência e a Direção de Causalidade entre o Rendimento dos Trabalhadores Não-Qualificados por Posição na Ocupação e o Salário Mínimo entre 1982 e 1995 - Uma Análise Empírica, *Anais do XXVI Econtro Nacional de Economia*, pp. 1149-68.

Souza, P. and Baltar, P. (1979), Salário Mínimo e a Taxa de Salário no Brasil, *Pesquisa e Planejamento Econômico*, 9: 629-660.

Velloso, R.C. (1990), Salário Mínimo e Taxa de Salários no Brasil, *Pesquisa e Planejamento Econômico*, 20(3).

Waltman, J.; McBride, A. and Camhout, N. (1998), Minimum Wage Increases and the Business Failure Rate, *Journal of Economic Issues* 32, 219-223.

## Table 7.6. Summary of the Results of Studies on the Impact of the Minimum Wage in Brazil

| Source | Methodology | Type of Data | Sample Period | Effects On | | Poverty |
|---|---|---|---|---|---|---|
| | | | | Employment | Wages | |
| Macedo and Garcia (1978) | Time-series analysis | Aggregate time series | 1964-74 | | Limited Impact $\Sigma < 1$ | |
| Souza and Baltar (1979) | Time-series analysis | Aggregate time series | 1961-76 | | Validates the lighthouse effect $\Sigma = 1$ | |
| Velloso (1990) | Time-series analysis | Aggregate time series | 1976-86 | | Limited Impact Formal Sector: $0.36 < \Sigma < 0.63$ Informal Sector: $0.43 < \Sigma < 0.60$ | |
| Carneiro and Faria (1997) Lemos (1997) Soares (1998) | Causality analysis | Aggregate time series | 1980-97 | | Granger Minimum wage Causes other wages | |
| Foguel, Ramos and Carneiro (2000) | Time-series analysis Co-integration and exogenicity | Aggregate time series | 1980-99 | | Validates the lighthouse effect in long term $\Sigma = 1$ Limited impact in the short term $\Sigma < 1$ | |
| Foguel (1998) | Differences-in-differences Natural experiment | Aggregate time series | 1980-87 | Negative informality | | |
| Lemos (2002) | Time-series analysis Impact on wage distribution | Aggregate time series | 1982-98 | Negative $-0.020 < \Sigma < 0.006$ | Positive impact on wages close to the minimum | |
| Carneiro (2000) | Time-series analysis Co-integration and exogenicity | Aggregate time series | 1982-99 | Negative formal sector $-0.020 < \Sigma < 0.001$ Positive informal sector $0.0004 < \Sigma < 0.003$ | | |

# Table 7.6. (Continued)

| Source | Methodology | Type of Data | Sample Period | Effects On | | Poverty |
|---|---|---|---|---|---|---|
| | | | | Employment | Wages | |
| Carneiro and Corseuil (2001) Corseuil and Morgado (2001) | Kernel functions Time-series analysis Differences-in-differences | Aggregate time series and longitudinal data | 1982-99 | Negative formal sector $\Sigma = -0.3$ Positive informal sector $\Sigma = 0.22$ | Positive impact on wages close to the minimum | |
| Fajnzylber (2001) | Impact on Wage Distribution (see Neumark, 2000) | Time series based on longitudinal data (small businesses) | 1982-99 | Negative formal sector $\Sigma = -0.10$ Negative informal sector $\Sigma = -0.25$ | Positive impact on all wages | |
| Corseuil et al. (2000) | Breakdown of effects of increases in the minimum wage | Cross-section of families (PNAD) | | | | Limited impact $\Sigma = 0.4$ |
| Neri et al. (2000) | Simulation of impact of increases in the minimum wage | Cross-section of families (PNAD) | 1996 | | | Insignificant impact |
| Barros et al. (2000) | Breakdown of effects of increases in the minimum wage | Longitudinal data on small business | 1995-98 | | | Decreasing impact |
| IPEA (2000) | Various methodologies Simulations | | | | | Insignificant impact |

# INDEX

## C

## F

# M

## N

## O

## P

**Q**

**R**

## T

## U